Charles Chaplin's
The Freak

The Story of an Unfinished Film

David Robinson

Edited by Cecilia Cenciarelli

Sticking Place Books
New York

Contents

The Freak, or In Zero Gravity by Cecilia Cenciarelli   ix

1. The Next Film   1

2. The Script   41

3. The Lure of The Winged Humanoid   165

4. Evolution of a Script   187

5. A Story Finally Told:
   A Conversation with Victoria Chaplin and Gerald Larn   227

6. Ready to Go   249

The Last Chaplin by Gian Luca Farinelli   261

Chronology 1953—1977   265

Dedication

This book could only be dedicated to Sarapha, the first of an innumerable lineage of other-worldly beings created by Victoria Chaplin in the half century since *The Freak*.

Victoria's father declared that she had inherited the gift of comedy, and with it his gift for instant self-transformation (in his case, perhaps into a porcupine, an automaton or a plump oven-destined chicken).

In 1970 *The Freak* was abandoned, while Le Cirque Bonjour was created by Victoria and her husband Jean-Baptiste Thierrée. Over the years the circus has changed its name a couple of times, but not its disposition. Jean-Baptiste clowns divinely, while Victoria pursues her life-time of transformations. On stage she battles or caresses floating silks or umbrellas or ropes or anonymous bits of furniture which somehow serve to transform her into mythical beasts, sea creatures, geometrical equations, prancing horses, irrational machines. She can grow to fill the stage or vanish into a plant pot. Hung about with resonant receptacles out of Cinderella's kitchen, she is transformed into a human music box.

In time their children Aurelia and James graduated from the Cirque to follow their own artistic paths — Aurelia through her performances and James through the shows he creates — each giving Victoria the chance to imagine and design new generations of mythical creatures.

But Sarapha, though she exists only in fragmentary snatches of film, photographs, drawings and a pair of wings frozen in a museum, is the first of the enchanted throng, and therefore the dedicatee of this account of *The Freak*.

Preface
The Freak, or In Zero Gravity
Cecilia Cenciarelli

And then finally, at the sudden spark of that long-awaited idea, a surge of
energy would run through his strong, supple body, lifting him up.
And believe it or not, dear reader—defying even the conclusions of
Isaac Newton—in those moments I truly saw with my own eyes
Charlie Chaplin moving forward without touching the ground.

Monta Bell

The unmade films that haunt the history of cinema are often likened to restless ghosts—faded images that never came to life, or half-dreamed dreams. Some are closer to genies trapped in a lamp, locked away in drawers and archives, waiting for that unfinished artistic impulse to be freed at last, so it may tell its story. *The Freak* by Charlie Chaplin belongs to this second category.

The idea of dedicating a book to this film first emerged almost twenty years ago, when the Cineteca di Bologna and the Chaplin family forged a pact of trust and foresight with the aim of fully preserving—through digitization and cataloguing—the work of one of the greatest masters of the twentieth century. The Chaplin Project, which from the outset took shape as a pioneering challenge, began its first steps on the rails. From the Gare du Nord, the overnight Intercity train carried us back to Bologna, loaded with documents, files, envelopes: thousands of papers, images, and photographs as valuable as a cache of diamonds.

On returning from one of these archival expeditions, we came across several boxes crammed with pencil notes and scripts bearing a mysterious title, one that even David Robinson's biography, the sacred text for any archivist or film historian, failed to clarify. *The Freak* would remain an enigma for quite some time, because first we had to familiarize ourselves with the geography of the Chaplin archive, to navigate more than a hundred thousand pages back and forth until we knew them intimately.

It is a slow process, one that allows for detours but no shortcuts, and which only grows clearer when those deep connective threads of meaning linking the papers begin to reveal themselves. In 2015, Kate Guyonvarch—the true guardian spirit of the archive, and thus of our project—announced that the Chaplin Office had acquired some of Jerry Epstein's personal and professional archive. Epstein's career had intersected significantly with Chaplin's from the 1950s onwards. This documentation included about a thousand items relating to the production of *The Freak*, an essential keystone that provided the final impetus for the publication of this volume.

These previously unseen materials revealed that *The Freak* was not merely an unfinished project but a film that came within a hair's breadth of being shot. The synchronic study of the scripts—on one side—and the financial projections, minutes of technical meetings, production schedules, and scene breakdowns—on the other—finally enabled us to establish a complete chronology and to identify the film's final script, which we publish here for the first time.

With his customary generosity and insatiable curiosity for detective stories, David Robinson agreed to shed light on this tale for us, and in doing so returned to the depths of that creative laboratory he had first explored, tracing possible sources of inspiration for the story and analyzing its many variants. Unlike what happens with a film "in the flesh," here the discarded pages enrich and give depth to the spare writing of the screenplay, which is, after all, a narrative meant to break free from the page and become an experience.

In *The Freak*, the various layers of character development, for instance, help us to know and understand the figures more fully, supporting the reader in the complex exercise of imagining the film. At first glance, *The Freak* shows no obvious points of contact with the body of work Chaplin had begun more than half a century earlier. His children clearly remember the opening of the story, mingled with other enchanted, terrifying fairy tales Chaplin would tell them as children. Victorian-flavored fables, magical and pagan tales steeped in that same late-nineteenth-century culture of theatrical transformations, phantasmagorias, and traveling circuses, each with its own sideshow attraction.

And yet Chaplin's winged heroine recalls Rousseau's noble savage far more than the Fish-Woman or Bird-Girl of fin-de-siècle freak shows: innocent, she regards the world without morality, guided only by primal instincts. The untamed wilderness of Chile, where she is born, does not hinder her flight: she is alone, yet free. In these opening pages, *The Freak* takes shape as a philosophical meditation, a story entirely suspended, outside of time. One does not sense the presence of Chaplin or of his cinema—always so deeply rooted in, and at the very center of, the twentieth century, from which he left us, like few others, with a lucid and modern synthesis.

It is the girl's abduction, and the shift of the action from the remote Chilean cliffs to the British capital, that gives the story a change of register. In the "civilized" West, governed by consumerism, Sarapha—like Charlot—is ontologically out of place. Without understanding why, she is, like him, perpetually pursued, hounded, and on the run.

In the hands of two unscrupulous men who dream of turning her into a global business, she is passed off as a redeeming angel and thrown before a desperate crowd in search of faith. In the various drafts of the treatment, Chaplin found himself at an ambitious crossroads: whether to make of this unconscious creature the symbol of a new spirituality capable of changing the fate of the world. Into this kind of utopia, he wove attempts to stage the anti-nuclear protests, the fight against Apartheid, and the demonstrations against the Vietnam War—those same movements that flooded London's streets and squares at the close of a turbulent, unrepeatable decade, and which Chaplin must have witnessed while working on *The Freak* during his frequent visits to the British capital.

In the end, he chose not to develop fully the spiritual or Christological dimension that runs like an undercurrent through his entire body of work, resurfacing abundantly in his archive: from the discarded endings of *A Woman of Paris* and *Modern Times*, both set in a convent, to *Christianity*, the surreal and brilliant story idea of Christ's Passion staged in a nightclub, which so scandalized Rachmaninov and Stravinsky. Already in the 1920s, when he declared his intention to bring to the screen Giovanni Papini's *Storia di Cristo* (1921), it was clear that Chaplin's interest was secular in nature. His most serious attempt to grapple with the question of religion in a dramatic film was his adaptation of *Shadow and Substance* (1937), a four-act play by the Irish dramatist Paul Vincent Carroll, on which he worked with great vigor—though not continuously—for nearly ten years, beginning in 1942.

An echo of *Shadow and Substance* can be heard in the preparatory versions of *The Freak*, but in the screenplay the focus returns squarely to the essence of the human condition. "There is nothing in the world that interests me more than exploring the human soul," Chaplin repeated up to his final interview, "nothing more inexhaustible than the human equation." The urgency of clarifying Sarapha's identity—bird, angel, freak of nature—runs through the script as a leitmotif: what, in the end, defines a human being? Who can truly decide?

Of course, Chaplin is less interested in answering these questions than in posing them, in exposing hostility and suspicion toward the foreigner, fear of the Other. It is an individual fear, but, as he reminds us—and we think of Verdoux's "relativity of evil"—it is legitimized by politics. The matter in fact reaches the British Parliament, where the issue is debated with urgency for fear that the bird-woman might spread an avian pandemic. The creature must be examined and quarantined and, unless proof of her British citizenship is provided, immediately expelled from the country.

It is impossible not to catch an autobiographical resonance in this scene, or not to recall Hannah Arendt's clear-eyed analysis: "In the eyes of society, Chaplin is always, by definition, a suspect. Long before the suspect turned into the figure of the stateless person, Chaplin had embodied the age-old Jewish fear before the policeman, in whom a hostile environment takes shape."

The years he spent in neutral Switzerland, withdrawn from the world, are often called his "years of exile." But they were also the years of correspondence and encounters with Jean Cocteau, Jean Renoir, Graham Greene, James Agee; of neighborly exchanges with Simenon and Noël Coward; of lunches with Truman Capote and Clara Haskil; of many travels through Europe. And of course, of life with the children he had with Oona, born over the span of eighteen years, who allowed Chaplin to remain, for a very long time, in touch with the innocence and beauty of childhood.

The Freak is perhaps also this: a song to the radiance of youth, and to its absence of gravity.

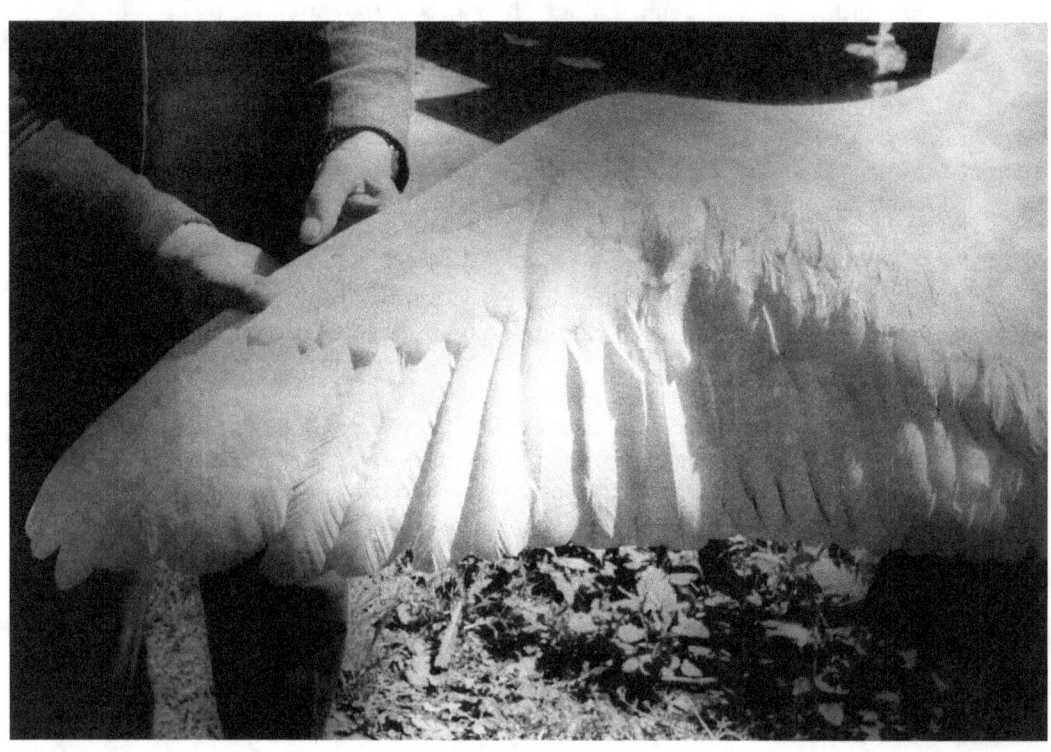

The Wings of Sarapha.

1
The Next Film

Who can foretell what one is going to do in this life?
I have no intention of giving up anything
until I give up my last breath.

—Charles Chaplin, 1968

History has unwittingly misrepresented the story of Charles Chaplin's *The Freak*. It has come down to us as a script on which he laboured dedicatedly and persistently for the last decade of his life and which only time and age finally prevented from being realised.

It was not quite like this.

Recognising that time was not on his side, he began considering his next project immediately after the release of *A Countess from Hong Kong* in January 1967. By September that year he had decided it would be "the bird-woman story." The earliest mention of the definitive title *The Freak* so far traced is from May 1969.

In November 1968, he announced that the project would go into production in "six or seven months," and by early 1969, Jerry Epstein, Chaplin's close friend and collaborator, was working hard to be ready to start shooting in September or October. Later the date was postponed to January 1, 1970, with the firm intention of releasing the film at Christmas. In fact, this project would never see the light of day.

The Freak, therefore, should not be considered an unrealised screenplay, but rather an unfinished film.

A Countess from Hong Kong, which was to prove Chaplin's last completed film, was the first of his films to be produced by a major company, Universal, his first in colour and Cinema-Scope and no doubt (if direct comparison were possible) his most costly. The story updated a script titled *Stowaway*, written three decades before to star Paulette Goddard. The production was fraught with difficulties he had not previously faced. Two major international stars— Marlon Brando and Sophia Loren—were engaged, and arrived accompanied by a game of ruthless competition for top billing. Chaplin worked very happily with Loren, but Brando's initial enthusiasm to work with him soon faded: as a disciple of Stella Adler and her interpretation of the Stanislavski "Method," he was disconcerted by Chaplin's style of direction. Chaplin had his own distinct vision of every character he created (no doubt he would have preferred to play each one of them himself) and sought to mould each actor's performance in his own image. Relations between director and actor became increasingly problematic, and often Jerry Epstein, who sincerely loved both men, had to act as an intermediary on set, conveying messages from one to the other.

Charles Chaplin with Marlon Brando, Sophia Loren, Jerry Epstein (the film's producer),
and Sydney Chaplin on the set of *A Countess from Hong Kong*, 1966.

Shooting began on January 25, 1966 and was completed in twelve weeks. Despite the interruption of a broken ankle—the first crippling injury of Chaplin's life—post-production was finalised in time for a British premiere on January 2, 1967. The press show was catastrophic. An inexperienced projectionist had neglected to fit the correct lens, so that the colour was washed out and the projector repeatedly crackled to a halt. The resulting reviews were generally couched more in sorrow than in anger: a gentle romantic comedy was an incomprehensible anachronism in the year of *The Dirty Dozen*, *The Graduate* and *Bonnie and Clyde*.

Yet despite the critics, London audiences responded positively to the film, inspiring Universal to take the unusual step of giving no press preview for the New York opening. Instead the critics were invited to see the film at the public premiere—which happened to take place on a forbiddingly snowy night. Bosley Crowther, the influential and arrogant critic of *The New York Times*, was outraged not to be accorded a private preview, and countered with two long and destructive reviews. (Crowther's equally hostile treatment of *Bonnie and Clyde* a few months later was a factor in his being replaced as the *Times* critic, after twenty-seven years in the job—but the damage to *Countess* had already been done.) No other reviews were quite so vitriolic as Crowther's, but *Time*'s review echoed a widely shared attitude: "*Countess* is bad enough to make a new generation of moviegoers wonder what the Chaplin cult was all about."

Charles Chaplin and Marlon Brando on the set of *A Countess from Hong Kong*, 1966.

The cover of *Noir et Blanc*, January 19–25, 1967.
The French premiere of *A Countess from Hong Kong* at the Paris Opera received a warm welcome.

Chaplin was handsomely vindicated by the French and Italian critics, who previewed the film in more favourable conditions and delightedly derided what they perceived as the myopia or prejudice of their Anglo-Saxon counterparts. Chaplin was more succinct, dismissing his critics as "bloody idiots."[*] He was all the same deeply and permanently wounded. At 78, most artists in this demanding profession would have decided the moment had come to call it a day. But his unalterable habit of life was work, and as he often said, "ideas keep popping into my head." In 1972 he told the American journalist Richard Meryman, "I know when I work, I'm happy. It's not the thing of putting on a great, beautiful thing or anything like that, it's because in work I'm very happy."[†] The only panacea for a setback like *A Countess from Hong Kong*, it seemed, was the next project. Early in the new year, he was juggling with several ideas. Although he was notoriously severe and critical when directing his son Sydney, he clearly valued him as an actor, and thought of a leading role for him as a wrongly convicted but incorrigibly well-intentioned prisoner, who while waiting to go to the electric chair, thoughtfully cleans and tidies his cell. He considered a story set in Ancient Rome, in which he himself would play the dual role of a Caligula-style emperor and the emperor's slave and double.

His family were more excited by the idea of a film about early Hollywood, in which his teenage daughters Josephine and Victoria (who'd had walk-ons in *A Countess from Hong Kong*) would play the sisters Lilian and Dorothy Gish. With this he progressed far enough to write a treatment for the dramatic opening sequence, which looked back to the "Patents War" which had riven the nascent American film industry several years before Chaplin set foot in the United States.

In 1908 Thomas Edison, having acquired a monopolistic portfolio of patents relating to film cameras and projectors, established the Motion Picture Patents Company, which required anyone profiting from the making of motion pictures to pay dues to Edison. Many of the major producers went along with the Trust, but the stand-out "Independents" constituted an obstinate resistance. The Edison interests set out to intimidate them by sending strong-arm gangs to smash up their units and cameras. One significant outcome was that the Independents were driven to flee the East Coast and the vicinity of Edison's New Jersey headquarters. Many gravitated to the recently incorporated municipality of Hollywood, sixteen kilometres west of Los Angeles, which provided year-round sunshine and exotic locations in easy reach. Chaplin's scene sets out to show that the Trust's gangs were still ready to pursue Independents across the continent.

The scene has an exceptional historical interest, in that the producer and star of the Independent unit shown under attack is a Native American whom Chaplin names Chief Eagle Feather. At the time of the Patents War, there was indeed a Native American producer, director and actor—the first and for a long time the only one. This was James Young Deer, who came from the Nanticoke people of Delaware. Following service in the navy in the Spanish-American War, he went on to be an actor and from 1909 a prolific director of one-reel films with Native American stories. Chaplin does not mention him in any of his memoirs, but he was certainly aware of his reputation. In 1910 Young Deer was engaged by Pathé and sent to take over direction of their west-coast studio in Glendale, not far from where Keystone's Edendale studio would be established two years later. More or less coincident with Chaplin's

---

[*] David Robinson, *Chaplin: His Life and Art*, rev. 2nd ed. (London: Penguin, 2001), p. 673.
[†] Original transcript of Richard Meryman's interview, published in part in "Love Feast for Charlie," *Life*, April 21, 1972.

Rome   1

Roman Warriors are returning ~~to Rome~~.   It is a
victory parade, ~~a glorious carnival~~, crowds ~~and~~ garlands
of flowers, etc.   Beautiful girls ~~in carts~~, slaves driven
through the populus - the spoils of war.
Emperor Nero, his right arm full of gout, appears on the
Palace balcony ~~before the tumultuous enthusiastic crowd~~. *to welcome the returning here*
The scene changes - typical Roman banqueting hall.
The EMPEROR makes an after-dinner speech of welcome to
MAXIMILIUS, conqueror of Britain.

            EMPEROR
    You have done credit to the Roman Empire. *our culture*
    ~~You have instilled into~~ the dark *recesses* of
    the outer world, ~~Roman culture, the beauty of its art~~
    ~~the Roman language~~. Through your ~~genius~~, even *the*
    ~~the~~ British heathen has ~~been conquered to the~~ *adopted*
    ~~Roman~~ way of life, ~~to the Roman way~~ of speech.
    Well done !   Hail (sic) Maximilius!

(As Maximilius rises, flowers are thrown at him and he
is pelted with garlands)
(The Emperor knocks ~~on the table~~ for quiet).

            MAXIMILIUS
    ~~I did my best, Sir~~.

            EMPEROR
    Where did you get that ~~cockney~~ accent ?

            MAXIMILIUS
    In ~~Great Britain, Sir~~.   It took ~~em~~ a long time
    to ~~say~~ 'em - ~~well you know, to have to our way~~
    ~~spoke~~.   ~~But~~ Latin *bloody* 'ard for 'em.

Project for a film set in ancient Rome. Typescript page with Chaplin's corrections, 1967.

arrival at Keystone in 1914, Young Deer relocated temporarily in London to evade a sex scandal involving a 15-year-old girl. It is tempting to think that the young Chaplin may have been in time to encounter him personally, but even if Young Deer had already departed Glendale when Chaplin arrived, he must still have been a lively topic of conversation around the studios.

The scene is short (and the surviving typescripts much edited, in barely legible manuscript), but it is precious evidence of Chaplin's links and fascination with the beginnings of Hollywood:

There was something intense and pleasant about the magnificence of the transcontinental trail, a feeling of pleasant frustration about the vastness of it. Three Indians were suspiciously and guiltily digging at the base of a sign post which read "Danger Indians."

When the digging was complete, one Indian loosened the post from its base, then lassoed it, mounted his mustang and galloped away, dragging the post after him.

Close by, Indians, some on horseback, others on foot, stood statuesque, peering into the distance. They took no notice of the three Indians who had ridden in trailing their post. The Chief Eagle Feather pointed with characteristic calmness to a small speck of dust in the distance, then turned to the rest and said calmly: "They're coming." Then turned his horse and exited behind a huge boulder. Others loaded their guns and disappeared into a small canyon. Soon the scene looked bare and innocent without a semblance of life. On a closer view, the speck of dust became life and personality. It was the Western Mail Coach coming at a rustling gait along the transcontinental trail.

The passengers were nondescript, save for two pretty young women dressed in 1860 costumes. Out of the noise of harness and tumbling wheels came a sudden crack!—A shot! Then from nowhere, Indians poured down from the rocks and surrounded the mail carriage. The women screamed, and the driver fell from his seat, shot dead. The horses took fright and galloped frantically. Very soon they were caught and surrounded by the Indians who dragged the screaming women off the driver's seat. As they struggled with the Indians, a man dressed in modern clothes entered the picture. "All right, cut," he said, and the actors stopped acting and the women stopped screaming and looked enquiringly at the Director. "All right—a new set up."

While they were thus occupied, an automobile drove up behind the camera and three men got out. One smashed the camera, and the others attacked the cameraman. In the melee, the Director and the actors ensued [sic] in the fighting, including the two ladies, until the attackers were forced to escape in their car.

The camera was broken and lay in a heap. Chief Eagle Feather pulled some of the tangled film out. "Look," he said, "a whole day's work ruined." Chief Eagle Feather, manager of the company, looked after the speeding car. "Did anyone take the license number?" "I guess not," said the cameraman dejectedly wiping blood from his nose.

Chaplin's notes for a film about the beginnings of Hollywood, 1967.

"Well," said the director, "that's what you get for coming to Hollywood. You wanted sunshine and you just got it." "I guess we'll call it a day and start early in the morning," said Chief Eagle Feather. "Where are you going to get a camera?" said the director. "I guess we can borrow one from Williamson." "All right," said the director, "We'll call it a day! Everybody at the studio, made up, eight o'clock tomorrow morning!"

Chaplin added an explanatory note about the Patents War, concluding: "The independents became the main producing companies of the West."

Now the monopolists were competing with merit, and gradually they faded into oblivion. Chief Eagle Feather, a small squat Indian, was one of the patent [mistyped in original as "pattern"] violators. He was relatively prosperous in those days, making one-reel cowboy pictures. His locations were authentic, for he invariably used the Indian Reservations of California for background, and although his stories were fictional, they had a certain realism which appealed to the public. Very soon, the Imp, Keystones, Universal, Bison, and many other film companies came to Hollywood.[*]

JEAN RENOIR

7, Avenue Frochot
PARIS IXe

Paris, March 21st 1968

Dear Charlie, dear Oona,

I must tell you the great joy I had seeing you again. This evening in your company was for me like a holiday. The time was flying away with an unbelievable speed.

I hope very soon I will see on the screen the characters you invented for your next picture. As a matter of fact they don't look invented but real.

Thank you for this wonderful evening.

With all my best wishes

Jean

JEAN RENOIR

P.S.- Mrs Doynel my assistant joins her thanks to mine.

Letter from Jean Renoir to Charles and Oona Chaplin, March 21, 1968.

---

[*] Typewritten treatment. Chaplin Archive, Ch00047.

Chaplin directing the first rehearsal of *Rain* (W. Somerset Maugham), one of the Circle Theatre's greatest successes, 1948. Behind him is Jerry Epstein; Sydney is on the far right.

Photographs of James Young Deer suggest that the unflattering description of Chief Eagle Feather as "small" and "squat" might not have been totally inappropriate to him: his military records give his height, in his twenties, as 5 feet 3½ inches, and he had clearly grown very muscular in later life. Chaplin's assessment of his films is very just.

By mid-September of 1967, rather to the disappointment of the family, Chaplin had abandoned the Hollywood idea—which would have been difficult to film on British locations—and was concentrating on his "bird woman" story. Early drafts of the story are untitled: the first certain mention of the title *The Freak* appears to be in May 1969. From the start there was no doubt that the role of Sarapha, the winged creature, was designed for Victoria, and that of Margaret, the wife of Edward Latham, the scientist on whose remote cliff house on the Chilean coast Sarapha first lands, for Josephine. Oona discreetly watched over him as he worked for two or three hours every morning, anxiously monitoring if he seemed tired or in low spirits: she told her daughters how one day when she was particularly worried about his rather haggard looks, he confessed that he had been going over the script until 2 a.m.

The many hundreds of often unsorted pages of typescript and manuscript that have been preserved (some no doubt reverentially rescued from Chapin's waste-paper basket) still leave us guessing at precisely what was his method of writing. Many pages are in manuscript, in Chaplin's erratic hand-writing and carefree spelling (if in doubt he simply spelt words as they sounded). Some, scribbled in a barely legible hand, are apparently personal aides-mémoire: for instance, a line of dialogue may be tried in several slightly variant forms. Others, written with

The Circle Theatre, 804 N. El Centro Ave., Hollywood.

a little more care and legibility, were presumably intended for conversion to typescript by the secretary, Monica de Montet, who otherwise worked from live or tape-recorded dictation. Pierre Smolik learned from her that "At times Chaplin acts the role he is creating, above all to analyse matters of rhythm. He speaks slowly, making sure that all his words are properly understood." Chaplin would then revise and edit each finished and typed page or version, which had then to be typed again. Pagination could become confused or corrected in this process. Madame de Montet appears to have been at the house most days, and when the unfortunate woman was twice afflicted with 'flu, her absence was regarded with indignation rather than sympathy, not just by Chaplin, but also by Oona, who was left to do the typing (at which she seems to have been perfectly skilled). However Madame de Montet liked her employer and remembered that they would laugh a lot. "If one does things according to his wishes, everything is fine [...] when he gets something into his head, he thinks about it all the time, even at night."*

While the story was still in progress, Chaplin evidently enjoyed talking about it with trusted friends. Jean Renoir visited the Manoir in March 1968, and afterwards wrote, "I hope very soon I will see on the screen the characters you invented for your next picture. As a matter of fact they don't look invented but real."†

---

* Interview with Monica de Montet, October 10, 1988. Pierre Smolik, *The Freak: Chaplin's Last Film*, trans. Philip B. Freyder (Vevey and Geneva: Call Me Edouard Éditeurs, 2016), p. 259.
† Letter from Jean Renoir to Charles Chaplin, March 21, 1968. Chaplin Archive, Ch06082.

Jerry Epstein, second left, and Sydney Chaplin, second right, during the Circle Theatre years.

In November 1968, Chaplin and Oona seem respectively to have informed Jerry Epstein that Chaplin believed he would be ready to start shooting in six or seven months. This was rather startling news, given the tough prospect of raising financing and contriving the elaborate technical effects demanded, but Epstein did not see these as insurmountable obstacles. He was a man of enormous energy and enthusiasm, with a gift for friendship which embraced a vast range of gifted people from politicians and playwrights to the young, pre-*Rocky* Sylvester Stallone. Jerry knew everyone and everyone knew Jerry. In 1946, with Chaplin's son Sydney, he had established the Circle Theatre in Hollywood. Their first shows were given in friends' drawing rooms, but they soon found and constantly enhanced their own premises. Chaplin regularly visited the theatre, which encouraged other Hollywood notables to patronise the Circle, and often take part in productions. Clearly excited to be involved with live theatre again, Chaplin took a hand in the direction of several shows, amazing the young actors with his command of stage mise-en-scène. His old friend Constance Collier, already a *grande dame* of the British stage when Chaplin was still a boy, worked alongside them, often sparring with Chaplin over points of interpretation ("But Charlie, you haven't even read the play!"). Epstein became a friend of the family, and Chaplin promised that he would engage him on his next production. He was as good as his word, and Epstein became his invaluable assistant on *Limelight* (1952).

After Chaplin's exodus to Europe, Epstein, equally relieved to escape McCarthy-era America, relocated in London, and so was available as producer for Chaplin's two British films, *A King in New York* (1957) and *A Countess from Hong Kong* (1967). This launched his own career as producer, writer and director: his first film *The Adding Machine*, from the 1923 Elmer Rice play which had been the Circle Theatre's first production, had a disappointing critical and commercial reception when it was released in September 1969, at a time when Jerry was already up to his ears in preparations for production of *The Freak*.

Epstein spent Christmas 1968 with the Chaplins at Vevey, and on December 27 was asked to read the script aloud to Chaplin, Oona, Victoria and the French actress Nöelle Adam, Sydney Chaplin's wife. The reading was a gratifying success. Victoria herself was touched to recognise the script as a gift of love, and remembers her mother's words, "He's been heroic... he is heroic."

Jerry was now clearly hooked—and he too was to be heroic. At that moment he and Sean Connery were planning a production partnership, and Connery was impatient to start work. Jerry had to choose whether to go ahead with him or embark on work with Chaplin and *The Freak*. He honoured his older loyalty and lost a prospective partner. By May he was working full-time, and for the next eight months laboured like a team of six. He had to establish a budget. He had to raise finance. He had to find artists, production designers and special effects wizards to realise the airborne protagonist. He had to book studios and technicians, and look ahead to publicity.

Charles Chaplin and Jerry Epstein on the set of *A Countess from Hong Kong*, 1966.

FOR MR. CHARLES CHAPLIN'S VISIT - SUNDAY, 30TH APRIL, 1969.

1. MERTON PARK STUDIOS - LIBerty 4291.   *Founder Commerce 2033.*

   Wally Vivers - makes wings and operates them.

2. Walt Disney film 'THE ABSENT MINDED PROFESSOR' - how they flew car (Company/equipment and details) can be obtained by calling MR. EASTWOOD, TRA 8010 tomorrow, Tuesday, 25th March, 1969.

3. Eugene Flying Wire Co.   Supply braces and wires to make people fly.

   Mr. Eric Dunning (try 688 5312)

   (To ring back Mr. Bill Hill at Pinewood on 'MARY STEWARD' Ext. 556 to find out location of this company.)

4. Mr. Charlie Staffle at Pinewood.

5. B.F.I. cannot help in connection with picture about half girl - half bird with wings. Comes down from heaven. They don't know how to cope with her. Try to get her to eat caviar but she will only eat eggs - has difficulty in sitting down, etc.

   Philip Jenkinson suggested 'BLUE BIRD' but said he would phone back to confirm. (SHE 8000 and home LEE 4156)

   Special Effects.
   FORBIDDEN PLANET
   Back ground.
   Pinewood *now*

Outline to be submitted to Chaplin containing films with flight scenes and companies specializing in flight techniques, April 30, 1969.

NOTES

MEETING BETWEEN MR. EPSTEIN, MR. RUDKIN
AND MAURICE CARTER AT SHEPPERTON ON MONDAY &
TUESDAY 29TH & 30TH SEPTEMBER, 1969.

****

GENERAL POINTS DISCUSSED.

1.   Will Vicky be wearing the same dress throughout the film?

2.   How will her hair be dressed?   If it is loose and flowing,
      how do we get round the problem of the wires becoming entangled?

3.   Will waiting for the tests (November) delay the schedule?

4.   The adobe house on cliff top.   Location - Maurice Carter
      suggested Portugal, because the house is on the cliff edge,
      and the sea must break over rugged rocks.   Mr. Rudkin suggested
      West Scotland, but warned of weather problems.   Cornwall was
      also mentioned.

5.   Regarding the wings Maurice Carter feels that really intensive
      tests are required.   It is essential to see that wings are g oing
      to stand up to the heavy treatment required of them.   He feels
      that three more sets of the feather wings are required and possibly
      five sets of a synthetic, plastic type that will be more durable.
      Maurice Carter estimates that a full test of trick work, Vicky
      jumping up onto the window cill, coming through window, flying
      out through adobe (this problem may be got round by having a
      wider window, angled, not made obvious to audience).   Top of
      windows will have to be open to enable wires through, matte to
      be made of top of window.(afterthought on this point was to have
      her jump onto window ledge, cut to a reaction and return to her
      poised, ready for take-off.   Mr. Carter also wants a test done
      of Vicky flying, with the Camera panning with her, taking off
      from verious points, e.g. from branch of tree, from street level
      necessary for Brook Street scene) and from window cill.

      To get these tests underway, Maurice Carter will require a staff.
      A detailed list to be made of things to be done in tests.

      Sketch artist also to be made available to him.

6.   Use of helicopter.   Maurice Carter feels that to be really
      sensational, a helicopter is essential for the coastline scene.
      To save expense later on he said that perhaps plates could be
      obtained from a company that has stock photos of all of London.
      Negative would have to be blown up and transition made for night
      shot.   This would be quite expensive and time absorbing but can
      be done.   Also we would be restricted because of the xxxxx height
      ruling for flying over London. (3,000 ft. over Thames).

      Both Maurice Carter and Ruddy said it is impossible to get a good
      plate using long focus camera.... too much juddering.

Notes from a meeting between Jerry Epstein and the Shepperton special effects department,
September 29–30, 1969.

```
CONFIDENTIAL.                                         10.7.69.


                      ' T H E     F R E A K '


                         CASTING.


           Robert Vaughn.

           James Fox

           Richard Chamberlain
```

Notes on the possible cast, 10 July 1969

Victoria and Josephine's roles were definite, and Geraldine sometimes said she would be in the film (the only role for her would have been that of the grand hostess, Lady Pentagon). For the leading male role of the English Professor Edward Latham, the names of the Americans Robert Vaughn and Richard Chamberlain and the English James Fox were discussed. Their ages at this time would have been 37, 35 and 30 respectively. Sydney and Michael Chaplin were also mentioned,* though with the exception of Latham, the featured male characters in the script are in various degrees deplorable, with no evident roles for the incorrigibly charming half-brothers. (The odious Jackson has some physical mitigation perhaps. The script describes Jackson and Ryman as "typical race track types… Jackson's eyes are perhaps too close together: otherwise he is handsome.")

There were about ten acting parts left to be cast, but there is no trace in the papers of any action taken in this direction, and casting decisions were evidently postponed. Shooting could certainly have gone ahead. There were enough scenes involving only Sarapha (Victoria) and Margaret (Josephine), alone together in interior sets, to occupy the studios without committing large sums to actors' contracts.

Inevitably, as we know from her correspondence with Jerry, Oona, like Jerry himself, was anxious about Chaplin's physical ability to withstand the effort of four months' shooting, knowing how he would drive himself when working. At the same time she sincerely loved the script and could only defend Chaplin's determination to make the film, if it was to be his last. She passed on to Jerry that Chaplin had told her, "I must make this before I go…" and

---

* At that time Michael had left home and was living a carefree hippie life in London. He had further distanced himself from his father by publishing a ghostwritten autobiography, *I Couldn't Smoke Grass on My Father's Lawn* (1966). Jerry, who was living in London, had—as usual—kept a watchful eye on Michael's well-being, discreetly smoothing relations with his mother. From this document one gathers Jerry's hope that *The Freak* might provide Michael with the chance to return to the fold. But that was a premature expectation. Michael and his father would reconcile years later.

The possible cast: Richard Chamberlain, Robert Vaughn, James Fox,
and Geraldine Chaplin for the role of Lady Pentagon.

3.

'THE   FREAK'

PRELIMINARY BUDGET - cont'd.   16th September, '69.

REQUIREMENTS FOR PLATE BACKGROUNDS AND EYELINES - PRELIMINARY COSTING OF THESE ITEMS
                                                                    - cont'd.

18. Interneg cost, Matte Room work, etc. ..   ..   ..   £ 2,000
     Camera crew and possible lights 1 night   ..   ..   £

19. Camera and lighting crews, Super Zoom Lens. 1 night   ..   £

20. Camera crew and camera car.   1 night ..   ..   ..   £

21. Camera crew and camera car.   1 night ..   ..   ..   £

22. Large model of house. Matching location and surrounding area
     Photo aerial survey required   ..   ..   ..   £   300
     Shot under existing gantry   ..   ..   ..   £ 3,800

23. All as above including aerial photographs location   .. £ 4,500

24. All as above   ..   ..   ..   £ 5,000

25. Included in Chilian coast shooting.

26. Medium stage for building and shooting plates   ..   ..   £
     Prefabing models off stage in sections   ..   .. £
     Calculating two weeks set up and shoot each   .. £21,600
     (It might be much more economical to put it out to Bowie Films
     at Bray Studios)

27. Painted and activated matte plate of audience below her   .. £ 1,200

28. Plate from model of Savoy Hotel and Embankment area   ..   £ 4,500

29. Plate from painted area or model of roof of Earls Court   .. £ 2,000
                                                                ─────────

                              TOTAL PLATE MAKING   £65,200

First detailed version of the budget, 16 September 1969.

when she asked, "Where are you going?" he laughed and replied "Italy!" She was heartened, too, when Jerry explored the possibilities of filming at Ardmore Studios in Ireland, which they agreed would to an extent recreate the pattern of Chaplin's own studio in Hollywood. *The Freak* would be the sole film shooting there, and Chaplin could take his time. Moreover they would be saved the two-hour drive in the rush hour every morning and evening that was the hazard of the English studios. But finally Ardmore proved impracticable. On September 5 1969, Oona wrote to Peggy Lloyd, wife of actor Norman Lloyd, who played the stage director Bodalink in *Limelight*: "No starting date for the film, but it can't be long now."

Chaplin had once been the world's biggest box-office star, but now Epstein was having difficulty seeking finance for *The Freak*, though British Lion offered a favourable distribution arrangement, while EMI seemed prepared to invest money for selected territories. Tirelessly but unsuccessfully he tried ABPC, Columbia, Warners, Joe Levine, ABC, Walter Reade, National General and Lew Wasserman of Universal. The most dispiriting blow came when *The Freak* was turned down by United Artists, the company which Chaplin—with Douglas Fairbanks, Mary Pickford and D. W. Griffith—had created exactly half a century before. Two executives and their wives were graciously hosted by the Chaplins at the Manoir de Ban, and after lunch Jerry read them the screenplay. They left, taking with them a copy of the script.

Several weeks later, when Epstein reminded them they still had it, the script was returned with an unsigned compliments slip and no thanks for lunch. The fact that United Artists was going through a period of extreme financial difficulties at that moment hardly excused the discourtesy. Victoria was outraged, but Chaplin told her the film would be made regardless. The budget had been brought down to a million dollars, and Chaplin proposed if necessary to finance it himself—a prospect which Epstein vigorously opposed.

With his usual diligence, Epstein investigated the facilities and costs of all the studios— Boreham Wood, Shepperton, Pinewood, Elstree—in the London area. The production would require three large stages, one of which, to be used for special effects, could be silent. Shooting would take approximately sixteen weeks, to begin in September or October. In May Epstein confirmed a booking with Shepperton. Adrian Worker, the studio's production head, subsequently suggested the date might be pushed back, as seven films would already be shooting in September. Everyone seemed a little relieved by the postponement. Besides the studio work, there would be seven days of location shooting and twenty-eight weeks of post-production.

At the end of March 1969 the Chaplins were in London, enthusiastically investigating ways of realising the flying scenes. Epstein consulted companies who created flying effects for the stage—the Eugene and Kirby Flying Ballets—as well as film special effects experts. The veteran production manager Leonard Rudkin had worked on James Bond films and on Epstein's *The Adding Machine*; the famous special effects wizard Wally Veevers as a teenager had worked on the 1936 film of H. G. Wells' *Things to Come*, and in recent years, *Dr Strangelove* and *The Battle of Britain*. Chaplin himself demonstrated a very precise concept of the individual technical challenges that each flying scene would present.

On March 31 Chaplin approached directly the Shepperton Special Effects Department, headed by Ted Samuels, where he worked with Gerald Larn, an easel painter who would do the technical drawings for the wings and backdrop paintings, and Peter Harman, the cameraman.

In addition to Larn's 150 drawings, John Rose, who had been technical illustrator on Stanley Kubrick's *2001: A Space Odyssey*, was engaged for two weeks in June to produce a series of fine designs for the proposed effects. They have left us a rich impression of the visual aspirations of *The Freak*.

INFORMATION RE: FLYING FOR MR. CHARLES CHAPLIN'S VISIT -
SUNDAY, 30TH MARCH, 1969.

1. EUGENE FLYING BALLET CO.   *FUL 8172)   GER 3108
    makes them fly   *TUL 7493)   Mr. Derek Botell.

    Contacted two numbers above marked **. The Fulham number
    had no reply; and, on ringing the second got referred to
    answering service on GER 3108. Mr. Eric Dunning was not
    known, but I left message for Mr. Derek Botell to ring you,
    who should be able to give you the whereabouts of
    ~~MR. ERIC DUNNING.~~

    (Eugene Flying Company supply braces and wings to make
    people fly)

                                                Tel No.
                                                Eugene.

2. **WALLY VIVERS**: Home tel. no. FARNHAM COMMON (369) 2033. *6.30 pm Tuesday*

    I have left a message for him at the following places to
    telephone you:

    (a) Merton Park Studios LIBerty 4291.
    (b) His home 369.2033.
    (c) Pinewood Studios Switchboard and with Tom, Commissionaire
                                    in main hall.

    (Makes wings and operates them?)

3. MR. CHARLIE STAFFLE at Pinewood. - Frenchman's name, etc.
    Ringing back in two days with information.

4. KIRBY FLYING WIRE COMPANY: Tel: HOVE 737133.

    10, Berriedale Avenue, HOVE, Sussex.

5. MR. LEONARD RUDKIN: Shepperton: ML5.2611. 'TAKE A GIRL LIKE
    The name of American specialist in Flying: YOU'.
    Dick Parker. Mr. Rudkin will let you know how to contact him.

6.

7. Please ring Jack Shampan   Shepperton 'TAKE A GIRL LIKE YOU'
                               ML5.2611.

    MR BOTELL,

    TED SAMUELS - Shepperton Wings
    Jerry Jarne - Sketch Artist
    Mr Gibb. 886 9663.
            (886)

Notes by Jerry Epstein for a meeting with Chaplin, March 30, 1969.

SHEPPERTON, MIDDLESEX. TELEPHONE: CHERTSEY 2611. TELEGRAMS: SHEPFILMS, MIDDLESEX

SHEPPERTON STUDIOS LTD

Jerome Epstein, Esq.,
14, Vincent Square,
LONDON S.W.1.

10th September, 1969

Dear Jerry,

I am sorry I missed you when you called in on Monday, but I have since seen Ted Samuels and would like to mention a few things in defence of Ted, and his department.

The wings which Ted has designed, and which are so nearly perfect for Mr. Chaplin's requirements, should have been designed by an aero-dynamics engineer like Barnes-Wallis.

This is the first time that a piece of machinery of this type has been made, and you may, or may not know that there are 120 mechanical working pieces in the wings, and the fact that we have so nearly got everything right is, I think, a wonderful achievement on Ted's part.

It was unfortunate that the feather suppliers went on holiday, but this was something which was not within our control. When I first heard of your predicament on Friday last, I instructed Ted, whatever the consequences, to try to find additional sources of supply for feathers, even if it meant phoning France or South Africa which is where, I believe, these come from in the first place.

Ted tells me that he has promised you that if his latest idea works, he will have the wings ready on Friday of this week, but if it does not work, he will have to think again, and this is quite understandable with such a complicated piece of mechanism.

I would like to reiterate what I think has already been pointed out, and that is that one pair of wings will not be sufficient for the making of the film. Mr. Chaplin may wish the wings to give many different expressions, and if any more mechanical movements have to be built in, then we are afraid that they will become too heavy for the artiste to wear. It may well be that you have to have different wings for different expressions and different actions, in which case I think we shall have to order feathers by the million, and they will almost certainly have to come from abroad.

Continued...

Directors: Sidney Gilliat (Chairman), Adrian D. Worker (Managing Director), John Boulting (Alternate Roy Boulting), Wilfred Moeller, M.B.E., F.C.A., Sir Max Rayne, William H. Rule

Letter from Adrian Worker (manager of Shepperton) to Epstein, September 10, 1969.

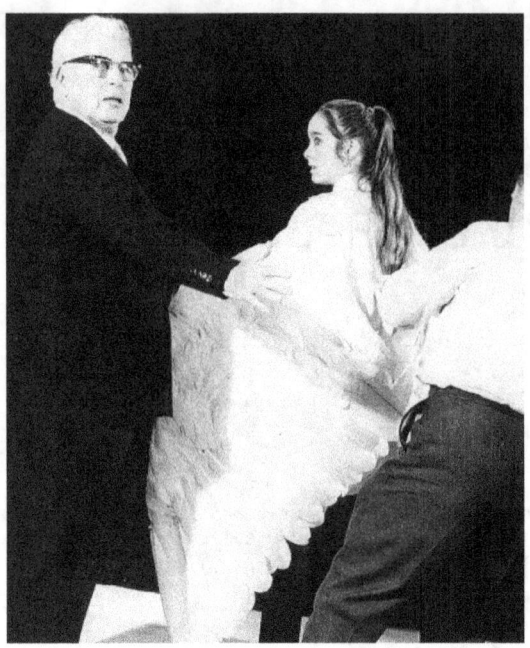

Chaplin helping his daughter Victoria
put on wings, Shepperton Studios, 1969.

The creation of the wings was to take months of continuing debate and experiment. The overall plan was that the wings would be operated by Victoria's arms, hidden in the structure, which would require a pair of false arms and hands for scenes where the wings were in action. When Sarapha was grounded, in domestic or social situations, the wings could be folded and deactivated, so that her own arms and hands were free. A precise specification was prepared:

Preparation of Wings
1) Size—to be on level with head, and proportioned as on model doll, with three joints based on bones of birds.
2) Probably to be made in special light aluminium.
3) Artist [Victoria] will need lots of practice with manipulating arms.
4) For actual flying will probably be necessary to use a harness with another set of wings attached.
5) Colour—definitely light—off white.
6) Will require the artist's arm measurements to prepare wings. Also photos of artist against 3 foot rule with arms extended etc.

In the event the wings were made of fibreglass, for lightness, covered with swans' feathers. Victoria also required the proposed special reinforced corset that would take the suspension wires needed for flying scenes. Victoria recalls that her father wanted Sarapha's wings and flight to be realistic, and that this is why it was decided that instead of having false wings attached to the back she would have false arms in front. The real arms were incorporated into the inside of the wings, which gave them a natural mobility. A mechanism allowed the wings to be spread out horizontally, combining them with the vertical or rotating arm movements.

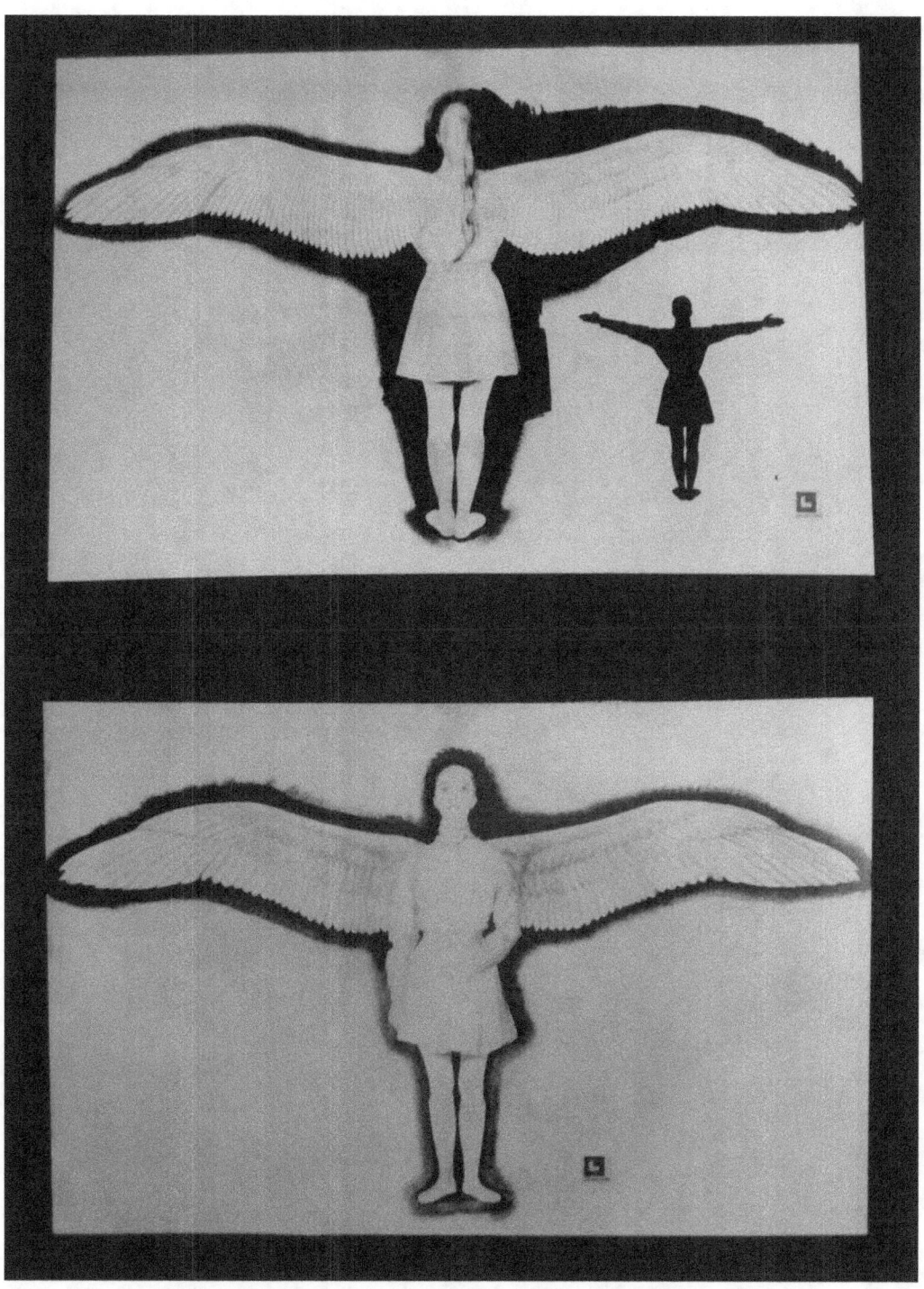

Technical drawings for the character of Sarapha made by Gerald Larn.

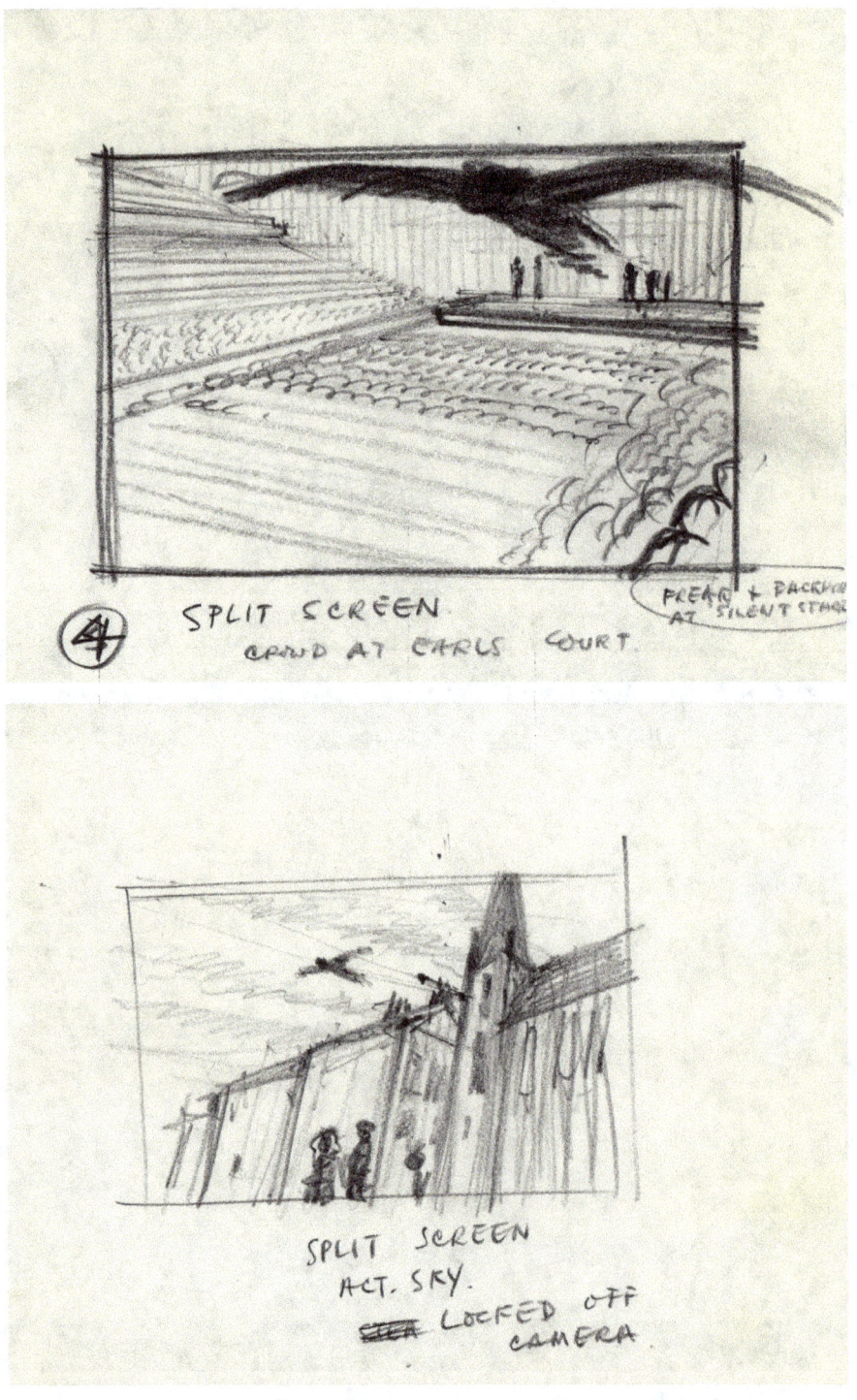

Storyboards by Larn featuring split-screens designed for the flight sequences.

```
PRINTS OF FILMS OBTAINED FOR MR. CHARLES CHAPLIN'S VISIT
10.7.69.
```
```
'MARY POPPINS'
'WATER BIRDS'
'BARBARELLA'
'THE ABSENT MINDED PROFESSOR'
'ISADORA'
"SWEET CHARITY"


M.C.A. Theatre Booked for following times:


Friday, 11th July, 1969:    7.30 p.m. onwards.
Saturday 12th  "       "    8.00  "        "
Sunday 13th    "       "    2.00 p.m.      "
```

Epstein books a cinema in London where Chaplin can watch some films
with flying scenes, July 10, 1969.

Plans to make two sets of wings were set in motion, but only one pair has survived, and was possibly the only one completed — commissioned by Epstein on June 4, 1969 at an estimated cost of £1,150. A second pair would have raised the challenge of tracing a sufficient supply of swan feathers, with South Africa the most promising source.

A visit to the exquisite Musée Baud, with its collection of mechanical musical instruments and automata, opened in L'Auberson in 1955, gave Chaplin the idea to commission an automated miniature model of Victoria, which could be used for distant flying shots. He had this installed in the Manoir for study.

In July the Chaplins were back on one of their now frequent trips to London, with Victoria, to inspect and test the prototype wings. Chaplin was very enthusiastic and inspired to new ideas, though he indignantly quashed Jerry's suggestion of having Victoria demonstrate them to prospective backers at Shepperton. On this trip also they spent Friday and Saturday evenings and Sunday afternoon viewing films to check out recent special effects work. The films that were booked were *Mary Poppins*, *Water Birds*, *Barbarella*, *The Absent-Minded Professor* and *Sweet Charity*.

Chaplin himself was sometimes impatient with the complication of modern (though pre-CGI) special effects work. Jerry recalled:

In Vevey, Charlie drew diagrams showing how the flying for *The Freak* could be achieved more simply. He would say, "They're making too much out of this flying business. We used these tricks years ago. It's all done with mirrors; the wires won't show." Then he would go over to his medicine cabinet with a pencil in his hand (to represent the girl). Holding the pencil horizontally in front of the cabinet door mirror, he'd shift the door from left to right. As you looked into the moving mirror, the pencil seemed to move.[*]

Already in June Chaplin was thinking about the music, and was excited to have found his theme tune. His musical arranger, Eric James, recalled that he was invited to the wedding of Chaplin's daughter Josephine that month. When Chaplin spotted James, having just flown in from London, in the receiving line, he instantly left his place beside Oona, ran across the room, and, "without even a formal word of greeting, said, 'Eric, I have a most marvellous idea for the theme music of our next film, *The Freak*,' and he at once began to go into rapturous details."[†] James recalled that he gently rebuked Chaplin for abandoning the wedding celebrations to talk about music and films. The theme was eventually to find its place in the score for *The Kid*, on which James worked with Chaplin in 1971.

By September 16, Epstein had meticulously worked out the production plan and established a budget in collaboration with the accountant Arno Rudolph. A fortnight later, he pared down his schedules to bring the cost down to a million dollars—probably after the disappointment of United Artists' rejection. These pages read almost like a documentary description of the actual day-to-day shooting of the film that was never to be. The detailed plans for the film do not altogether indicate how the film would have looked. In 1970 it would have been a quixotic venture to try to distribute a black-and-white film, so it seems most likely that the film would have followed *A Countess from Hong Kong* in using colour and widescreen. Larn's designs and storyboards, with their sophisticated use of colour, certainly reinforce this.

---

[*] Jerry Epstein, *Remembering Charlie: A Pictorial Biography*, Doubleday, 1989, p. 202
[†] Eric James, *Making Music with Charlie Chaplin: An Autobiography*, The Scarecrow Press, Inc., Lanham, MD, 2000, p. 108.

Left and above: Chaplin, with Epstein and Jay Kanter, signing the Universal contract for
A Countess from Hong Kong at his home, the Manoir de Ban, 1965.

At some point it had become apparent that not everything could be ready for the planned September-October start, and the date was put back to February-March 1970. This would probably have meant a change of studio—probably to Elstree—but in the end it was not to be.

When Jerry arrived in Vevey to celebrate Christmas 1969, he was met in the hall by Oona, who said, as he remembered, "There's no picture. I have to make the decision. He'll never survive this picture. If *The Freak* was an easy film, I would let it go ahead… But this picture would kill him."[*]

Only weeks earlier, she had appeared positive and even enthusiastic about the forthcoming production. It is not clear what had so abruptly reversed her view, but the most likely reason was some new anxiety about the 80-year-old Chaplin's health. Oona and Rachel Ford, Chaplin's business manager, succeeded throughout the years in maintaining total privacy about Chaplin's health. The medical issues of celebrities generally provide rich fodder for the press, but this was never the case for Chaplin in his Swiss years. His broken ankle on *A Countess from Hong Kong* and an operation to his back for a spinal fracture, probably resulting from the same fall, went virtually unreported. Even the children seem not to have been well informed about his medical affairs. Chaplin's later physical state, however, makes it certain that he did suffer strokes from the turn of the 1970s. It can only be speculative that some such problem may have influenced Oona's change of heart about going ahead with *The Freak*. There is no evidence of any reaction or concern on Chaplin's part at the sudden halt of work on the film, which might suggest that illness was at that moment distracting him.

---

[*] *Remembering Charlie*, op. cit., p. 203.

Chaplin's notes for the musical theme of *The Freak*, 1967–1968.

Josephine Chaplin, early 1970s.

Back in London, Jerry wrote to all the people who had been in one way and another engaged for the production, thanking them for their collaboration and informing them that

> right after Christmas the decision was made by us not to proceed with *The Freak*. It had nothing to do with cost—we managed to get the budget down to about 1 million dollars and Chaplin was willing to finance most of it. It was due entirely to personal reasons, which I cannot go into in this letter.[*]

The Freak was not to be. The only person who was not informed that the production was definitively abandoned was Chaplin himself.

In the weeks and years that followed Chaplin was still apparently going over his script with Madame de Montet, though none of the surviving pages of script drafts appear to post-date or to alter the "final" script. When Josephine and Victoria were available he would rehearse them. Whether in Vevey or on trips to London, he was always anxious to talk to Jerry about plans for the film, telling him, "I want to get it started," and Epstein played along.

At the Manoir de Ban for Christmas 1970, Epstein encouraged Chaplin to work on the *Freak* script with the girls, but the family may have been uncomfortable about this kindly intentioned deception. Josephine told Epstein that it was a mistake to encourage him to work, not least because Victoria was tired and having to care for her sick baby daughter, Aurélia.

---

[*] Chaplin Archive, Ch23764.

Victoria Chaplin as a child in shots from an album belonging to Jerry Epstein.

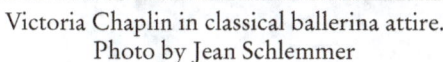

Victoria Chaplin in classical ballerina attire.
Photo by Jean Schlemmer

Le Cirque Invisible: Victoria Chaplin
and Jean-Baptiste Thierrée, c. 1970

Victoria of course was now keenly aware that the film was not to happen. During the frenzy of setting up the production, her principal task had seemed to be to model the wings through their challenging evolution. This rather side-stepped the fundamental circumstance that Victoria's persona, her aura and her genius were the first inspiration for the story and that throughout the process of Chaplin's creation of *The Freak*, Victoria was for him Sarapha. Chaplin very early declared that Victoria was the one who had inherited the gift of comedy, and the gift of being able to transform herself into any form of living creature or inanimate object. She has subsequently more than justified his confidence with the unique and inimitable creations of her independent stage/circus career.

But this trust by her father was a heavy liability in terms of *The Freak*. Victoria was born on May 19, 1951, so was sixteen and just going to a new school when Chaplin embarked on *The Freak*. In the succeeding years he wanted her close, so that she was always ready to try out scenes, and generally safe from distraction. Meanwhile, however, Oona and Miss Ford were eager to get her to London for some stage training and experience; but though Chaplin, too, wanted her to take her acting seriously (he warned the girls not to behave like "rich girl dilettantes"), he was always very suspicious of any talk of trips to London. Victoria could not wander far.

When the film was definitively called off in December 1969, however, Victoria was eighteen, and had officially reached her majority, as Oona reminded Chaplin. She now felt free to leave home to marry Jean-Baptiste Thierrée and to embark with him on their unique

Stills from the outtakes of *I clowns* (Federico Fellini, 1970), Compagnia Leone Cinematografica.

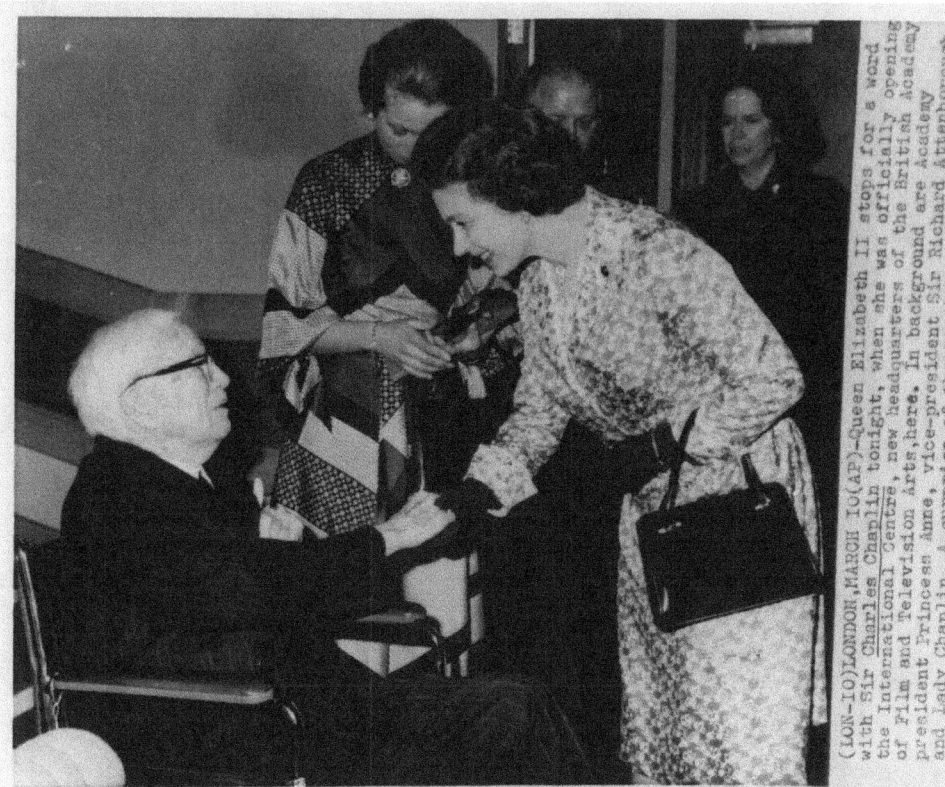

Chaplin receiving the British Academy of Film and Television Arts (BAFTA) Lifetime Achievement Award on March 10, 1976, one year after being knighted by Queen Elizabeth II.

reinterpretation of the art of circus, which had first brought them together. The moment is magically captured in Federico Fellini's film *I Clowns*, which was released at Christmas 1970 and captures Jean-Baptiste and Victoria in the wings, just setting out on their adventure, which was to become in succession *Le Cirque Bonjour*, *Le Cirque Imaginaire* and *Le Cirque Invisible*. In time it was to involve their children, Aurélia Thierrée and James Thierrée, who, with the guidance of Victoria's performance and design genius, went on to create their own wholly distinctive styles of performance.

Chaplin, of course, as the only person unaware that the film had been definitively abandoned, saw her departure and marriage as desertion, and said so. "Vicky… walked out on me,"* he told Richard Meryman during his momentous return to the United States in April 1972, almost twenty years since he had last set foot on American soil.

This long exile had been unplanned. On Wednesday, September 27, 1952, Chaplin and his family had embarked on the Queen Elizabeth for London and the premiere of *Limelight*. When they had been at sea for two days, the radio brought news that the recently appointed Attorney-General, Judge James McGranery, had rescinded Chaplin's re-entry permit and ordered the Immigration and Naturalisation Service to hold him for investigation should he

---

* Interview by Richard Meryman, op. cit.

Notepad with Chaplin's last writings, including the verses of *Ecce Homo* and notes on the dialogue of *The Freak*, c. 1977.

attempt to re-enter the country. McGranery, officially honoured by the Catholic church, and a dedicated enemy of Communism, served as Attorney-General for only ten months, but in that time he appointed as his special assistant Roy Cohn, who went on to be the right-hand man of Senator Joseph McCarthy in the House Un-American Activities Committee, and later Donald Trump's cherished personal lawyer and mentor from 1971 to 1986, when Cohn was shamingly disbarred, just before his death from AIDS. The Immigration and Naturalisation Service themselves advised that the Attorney-General's case was so shaky that any attempt to uphold it in the event of Chaplin's return "might well rock INS and the Department of Justice to its foundation." But they need not have worried: Chaplin chose not to return. Hollywood, terrorised by HUAC, did nothing to defend him.

Thus Chaplin's 1972 return to the United States seemed a historic gesture of reconciliation. A week or so before his arrival, his name was hastily added to the Los Angeles Walk of Fame. In New York he was honoured with banquets and a special show at the Philharmonic Hall. In Hollywood he met old friends, some of whom he scarcely remembered, and was awarded a special Oscar for his historic contribution to motion pictures. Always he responded with brief, simple, eloquent speeches. Two years later, in *My Life in Pictures*, he reflected, "I was touched by the gesture, but there was a certain irony about it somehow."[*]

Off-stage he seems to have been more hesitant in speaking, and though he always mentioned *The Freak* as an ongoing project which he was still trying to fund, his descriptions grew vaguer, though he invariably came to life when he described the character of Sarapha, and — invariably — vibrantly acted out Sarapha's reaction to the approach of non-winged humans. The distinguished critic and steadfast Chaplin fan William Wolf reported, for instance

> Occasionally there would be a glimpse of the old Charlie in the rapid way he'd snap his fingers, the beautiful manner in which he'd manipulate his shoulders to make a point, or his demonstration of how the half-woman, half-bird in his unproduced screenplay *The Freak* is supposed to claw at a man offering help. The sudden movements were pure Chaplin and he also laughed frequently and heartily.[†]

Show magazine quoted him:

> "I have a story called *The Freak* that I haven't been able to sell. It's a marvellous story, set on a strip along South America." At this point Chaplin exquisitely imitated a creature's clawing movements before continuing sadly. "But all that's gone now… I could do it beautifully. I know all the mechanics and everything. The only thing I want is a hand camera. That's the disadvantage of the modern age. Everything is so mechanical and so forth."[‡]

Richard Meryman, the celebrated *Life* editor and writer, who had conducted Marilyn Monroe's last interview two days before her death in 1962, secured an extended interview with Chaplin in his suite at the New York Plaza while in New York. Accompanied by Oona, ready to support his memory and speech, Chaplin reiterated his intention to shoot *The Freak*.[§]

---

[*] Charles Chaplin, *My Life in Pictures*, The Bodley Head, London 1974, p. 316.
[†] William Wolf, "Ready or Not, Fans, Here He Comes," *Los Angeles Times*, March 12, 1972.
[‡] "Chaplin at 83, America Rediscovered Hero," *Show*, June 1972.
[§] Interview by Richard Meryman, op. cit.

We know that Chaplin discussed the script with Ivor Montagu, who visited Vevey in early 1974, and seemed not to be in on the secret either, but believed the film was still to be made. Montagu was a remarkable figure—the communist son of an ennobled Jewish banking family of legendary wealth, zoologist, film director and producer (among other films of several early Alfred Hitchcock thrillers), world-class ping-pong player, friend of Sergei Eisenstein, and alleged Soviet spy. His suggestions for the script, in a letter of May 21, 1974, were very practical and positive: he proposed prolonging the healing of Sarapha's wings, injured when she landed on Latham's roof in the opening scene, until much later in the film. This would build anticipation of her eventual ability to soar into the sky—and at the same time reduce the amount of costly special effects work.*

In August 1974, Epstein, Victoria and Jean-Baptiste were at the Manoir, and it appears to have been Chaplin's own idea to take the wings out of storage. Epstein retrieved them from the cellar, where they were kept in bubble-wrap and plastic inside a coffin-like crate. Victoria strapped them on. Chaplin seemed magically reinvigorated, he abruptly stood up from the wheelchair in which he now generally moved around, and began to direct Victoria in some of her scenes. Jean-Baptiste, who venerated Chaplin but had never seen the wings or any work on *The Freak*, photographed the events, while Oona brought her 16mm film camera. Epstein recalled, "Charlie began rehearsing and composing set-ups for the film on the lawn. […] Afterwards Charlie, Josie, Vicky and I read the script aloud. Charlie got excited. He was ready to roll up his sleeves and start working. 'We're going ahead with the film', he said to me. Then he turned to Oona. 'Work out Jerry's deal' he said. Oona and I smiled at each other knowingly."†

Yet the myth was kept alive and periodically reported in the press. On March 4, 1975 Chaplin was in London to be invested by Queen Elizabeth II as Knight Commander of the British Empire. Geraldine told the *National Enquirer* that "her father, the legendary Charles Chaplin, at 86 is hard at work on his next film *The Freak*," Geraldine revealed that "Two of my sisters and I will be in it […] Its main character is a half-woman, half-bird, a complete farce. Daddy locks himself away every day to work on it."‡

The present writer met Chaplin on the day of the investiture. Miss Ford called and said, "We're having a little party at the Savoy in the evening, and wondered if you would like to come. Nothing special, I must warn you—just family." I knew nobody there—I had not even met Oona before that—but they did seem to be family and so close to Chaplin that they knew there was no point in bothering him. So I sat beside him where he was alone on a sofa. He seemed unsurprised and untroubled by my presence. He was still a handsome and elegant old gentleman, but it was quickly evident that a stroke had left him with expressive aphasia and, to

---

* Montagu writes: "I have an idea about the flying incidentally. Would it spoil Charlie's idea for the girl not to be airborne *throughout*? I mean: suppose she *had* been capable of flight, but in trying to get away from her exploiters—or even soon after the story begins—one wing had become injured. The movements of the other would be sufficient to establish her character as the angel?/freak? She would just as much constitute a gold mine to the would-be exploiters of her 'stunt' attraction in revivalism. Efforts on her part to recover strength in the damaged wing, the eagerness of the villains that she should, and her anxiety to conceal recovery from them […] would enable the action to be worked out just as timely but without any changes of theme. The theme basic to the plot could remain quite unchanged and intact." Letter from Ivor Montagu, May 21, 1976. Chaplin Archive, Ch06055.

† *Remembering Charlie*, op. cit., p. 207.

‡ Interview with Geraldine Chaplin, press clipping without header. Chaplin Archive, Ch16831.

Victoria Chaplin wearing the wings and rehearsing on the lawn of the Manoir, August 1974.

an indefinable extent, receptive aphasia also, so he could not respond with speech, and it was unclear if he absorbed what was said to him. But Geraldine was correct that his mind was not impaired. He could respond, with instantaneous momentary recovery, to some exceptional happening. In the course of the party there was a call from 10 Downing Street. Might the Prime Minister come to the Savoy to offer his personal congratulations? Ten minutes later the Premier, Harold Wilson (who had been instrumental in facilitating the belated knight-hood) arrived with Marcia Williams, his political secretary. Suddenly Chaplin was on his feet, the old "prop smile" illuminating his face, and his hand extended—an actor going on stage. Then Wilson turned to greet someone else, and Chaplin faded, his hand still held out. He was assisted back to his sofa.

I was with Chaplin again on Saturday, February 21, 1976. Again Miss Ford had called: "He will be at Anvil Studios on Saturday supervising the recording of the music for *A Woman of Paris*, if you would like to come." She was well aware it would be the last time he would ever enter a film studio.

He was in a little control room with Miss Ford and Oona. We sat on a row of chairs in front of the window which overlooked the studio. His condition seemed not much altered over the past year. Oona had her own, admirable way of minimising his incapacities. She determinedly treated him as if nothing at all was wrong, and lightly brushed off his unresponsiveness. When we were alone again, I tried: "Did it take long to write the music?" This produced an instant brisk response: "Not long. Inspiration mostly!"—which in retrospect can be seen as a smart PR comeback, because we have the testimony of the arranger/orchestrator Eric James that he had had a problematic task, building up the score by reworking old Chaplin themes, and filling in the gaps himself. He found that Chaplin's ability to communicate had "regrettably deteriorated tremendously" and that Chaplin himself told him he had no ideas for the music.

When the film was released in spring 1978, four months after Chaplin's death, Miss Ford prudently demanded a formal statement from James, asserting "that in my capacity of Music Associate to the late Sir Charles Chaplin I took down his melodies and melodic ideas and then helped him in the subsequent development and composition of his music to the very best of my ability as a trained and experienced musician. I deny most vehemently that I have ever claimed to be composer or co-composer of his music."

Chaplin died on Christmas Day 1977. But the myth of *The Freak* had been maintained to the end. In January 1975 Jerry told *Cinema and TV Today*, "Sir Charles was rehearsing the film all over Christmas with his two daughters, Victoria and Josephine. He told me to go over to Pinewood Studios and have talks there. I am certainly keeping my fingers crossed that the film will go ahead."* As late as July 1976, Epstein wrote to the Chaplins, reporting that the *Daily Express* had contacted him to ask about the impending divorce of Josephine Chaplin and her husband Nicholas Sistovaris (about which he pleaded ignorance), but also about the progress of *The Freak*: "I went on my merry way telling him the same stuff I told years ago—that you are working on the script, the wings have been made etc."†

When working, Chaplin liked to write on a distinctive style of note-pad, of large (approximately foolscap) format, with tear-off top hinging and yellow, lined paper. One of these is specially preserved and marked by Miss Ford as the last such pad he used. Miss Ford put no date on it, but it presumably was still on his desk at the time of his death. We do not know how late he continued to write—the writing here is now very much shakier and uncertain than before.

On this last tablet Chaplin has inscribed two quite separate passages. One (which we also find reproduced elsewhere in his late notes) is a song he had written in 1942 as a conclusion to his adaptation of Paul Vincent Carroll's 1934 play *Shadow and Substance*, whose theme— a devout but simple girl whose visions split the church and the community and result in her own death—has strong thematic similarities both to *The Freak* and to Wells' *The Wonderful Visit*. When he recalled the song here, for the last time, Chaplin somewhat muddled his original words, which were, as he had correctly written them, thirty-five years before:

> Ecce homo
> Ecce homo
> His crown
> Just a barren wreath of thorns
> There in the darkness
> He wore
> Just a barren wreath of thorns

---

* Press clipping without header. Chaplin Archive, Ch16799.
† Letter from Jerry Epstein to Oona and Charles Chaplin, July 2, 1976. Chaplin Archive, Ch06799.

But in the starlight
I saw
A rose
So red
Blooming on his crown of thorns
Glory
Glory
A rose
So red a rose
Blooming on his crown of thorns

Below this he has written out the brief scene from *The Freak* in which Sarapha, looking for Brook Street, London, lands beside a startled old drunk. This was to have been Chaplin's own last film role, for which £10 was allowed in the budget.

Cover of the screenplay of *The Freak*.

2
The Script

Three months after Chaplin's death, his business manager, Rachel Ford set about sorting the papers that had remained in his office, overlooking the lawns of the Manoir de Ban. She was confronted by thousands of pages in typescript or manuscript, largely unsorted, which represented the whole genesis and evolution of *The Freak*, from first sketches to the script from which the planned shooting would have been realized. The task was formidable, but so was Miss Ford, even in her eighties. The Chaplins had engaged her when they arrived at the Manoir de Ban in 1953, certainly awe-struck by her grandly patrician style. Her father was Franco-Irish and her mother, who died when she was six, French, but Rachel was educated in England during the First World War. In the Second World War she rose to the highest rank possible for a woman in the Free French Army, commanding two thousand women in the Army Medical Service. She was awarded the Croix de Guerre, with palm, and the Légion d'Honneur, and she knew the Best People. She told Kevin Brownlow of her job application to be "secretary" to Chaplin:

> I was a terrific fan and I only went to see him because I wanted to meet him, not because of the job. I told him I couldn't be a secretary because I couldn't spell and couldn't type but was hopeless with figures. I was wearing one man's ski boot and one woman's shoe, having suffered a burn, and I had lost my dog's lead. I kept saying, "I couldn't help you… I'd be no use at all. I know nothing about films."[*]

Chaplin hired her on the spot, with the caution, "I must warn you, you'll be mixing with the scum of the earth." Despite her protestations, Miss Ford was very soon In Charge. She did not mean to be intimidating, but she was—even sometimes to the Chaplins themselves. Eventually she was based in Paris where it was more appropriate to have the office, but visited Vevey frequently. It was on one of these visits that she sorted *The Freak* papers, permitting herself less than a week for the task, which she recorded with customary precision in her "Resumé of papers of CC that were in his library."

She listed eight copies of the script, a "parcel containing many spare numbered pages with handwritten corrections," as well as handwritten notes and photographs of Victoria.

---

[*] Kevin Brownlow, *Alla ricerca di Charlie Chaplin*, Edizioni Cineteca di Bologna, Bologna 2009, p. 18.

Charles Chaplin and
Rachel Ford, 1960s.
Photo by Maurice A. Aubry

Until now, we had assumed that the final script—the version presented to prospective financiers and used to estimate the budget—was one of three neatly bound copies in paper covers, apparently identical. In fact, only two of the three are identical and differ substantially from the third. Prior to 2015, none of the scripts preserved in the Chaplin Archive since Chaplin's death bore complete scene numbering; the meticulously handwritten sequence survived only in the script kept among Jerry Epstein's papers, which subsequently entered the Archive. With the exception of a handful of inserts, every one of the 364 scenes in this script aligns perfectly with the Breakdown, the scene-by-scene sketch that also records the method of shooting—location, glass shot, or studio set. This is the script which is reproduced in the following pages. The others are progressive earlier versions all including partial but radical variation from the final script, which are discussed in a subsequent chapter, "Evolution of a Script."

CHARACTERS IN ORDER OF APPEARANCE

Professor Edward Latham, 30-35 years old
Dr Piestroz, a Clergyman
Nagia, an old Indian housekeeper
Sarapha, the winged girl
Mrs Piesztroz
Alice, a young Indian polio sufferer
Alice's Father
Jackson
Ryman
Jackson's woman accomplice
London airport controllers, 1 and 2
Young Nun
Mother Superior

Father Donovin
Young Man going to confession
Screaming worshipper
Royal Opera House charlady
Newspaper Reporter in Westminster Cathedral
Margaret Latham
Dr James Gidson
Margaret's chauffeur
Margaret's Butler
Margaret's Second Butler, Henry
Sir Rex Horton
The Pentagons' Night Watchman
Lady Pentagon
Lord Pentagon
Countess Lebendoff
Guests and orchestra at Pentagons' ball
2 Plainclothes policemen accompanying Jackson
Doctor Everman
Margaret's Lawyer
Police Captain and other policemen.
Police Warder
Judge
Counsel for the Defence
Clerk of the Court
Foreman of the Jury
Quarantine Officer
Captain of the Fishing Boat

SYNOPSIS

Professor Edward Latham is a young English scholar and writer living on the coast of Chile, in a cliff-edge building once occupied by Trappist monks. As the film opens, he and his Indian housekeeper Nagia are seeing off Latham's guest and friend, Dr Piestroz.

That night Latham is awakened by Nagia. Something outside is being attacked by eagles. On the roof they find, injured and unconscious, a beautiful young girl—with wings. They put her on the bed in the guest room. Next morning she is awake, defensively hostile, and uncommunicative, but softens when food is offered—though enraged again when eggs are proposed. When after three days she eventually chooses to communicate, she proves to have a perfect command of idiomatic English. Soon she and Latham establish friendship, and she reveals that she is the child of English missionaries, now dead, and that the wings grew after she was born. Left alone she had lived with Fuegian Indians until she feared they were going to sacrifice her as propitiation to end a dry spell. In Latham's library, Sarapha finds an affectionate letter to his ex-wife Margaret, in which he praises Sarapha's beauty and attraction, but in a manner that she finds unfeelingly objective.

Sarapha finds that she can no longer fly.

Resumé of Papers of CC. that were in his library.   *Spares*

THE FREAK   31.3.78

     This is all I have been able to do in 5/6 days

A.   OK's script in black folders

B.   Two further folders - 1 black, 1 red, each containing what may prove to be a copy of OK'd script (A)

C.   Three copies of script, but these must also be checked with OK'd script as I know that many pages are wrong although numbers "run through".

Cbis   2 copies of script.

D.   Parcel containing many spare numbered pages with handwritten corrections. Note that the actual numbering of pages cannot be taken into account.

E.   Brown folder containing the story in prose.

F.   Parcel containing the story in prose.

G.   Hand written notes which I believe to be on Freak. Photographs of Vicky with wings. 1 folder with a few pages.

H.   Parcel containing designs etc.

With luck one should be able to find in D. copies of pages that are required to assemble true copies in B. folder and the 3 C sets. Otherwise photocopies of any missing/wrong pages will have to be done taking the GREATEST care if OK'd pages are used. Two people can check B and C fairly quickly.
When B. and C. have been checked and completed perhaps pages in D. that do not contain any hand written notes could be destroyed.
NOTE : I have kept everything.

List compiled by Rachel Ford of the material on *The Freak*
found in Chaplin's library after his death, March 31, 1978.

At the same moment as Latham and Sarapha see a train of caravans approaching, they receive an unexpected visit from Dr Piestroz and his wife. When Sarapha emerges from the clothes closet in which she has hidden, Dr and Mrs Piestroz take turns to faint. Meanwhile the caravan has arrived at the door. The long line of petitioners have learned from Nagia that Sarapha is an angel, and they have come to beg her to use her powers to heal Alice, a young girl suffering from polio. Sarapha touches her—and Alice rejoices that she is healed. As the train turns and leaves, it is clear that the girl's apparent recovery is a temporary illusion.

As Dr and Mrs Piestroz discuss Sarapha—and Dr Piestroz warns Latham to resist her very apparent attractions—a helicopter lands. Sarapha offers to go out and satisfy the new visitors' curiosity and get rid of them. Waiting for her are the shady Jackson and Ryman, who persuade her to enter the helicopter on the pretext of healing Jackson's polio-afflicted sister. Once inside she is tied up, and the helicopter, piloted by Ryman, takes off. Having drugged Sarapha, Jackson and Ryman discuss their multi-million plan to use their captive "angel" to exploit religious revivalism.

Tempera reworking of the preparatory drawings made by Gerald Larn.

At Paraguay, Sarapha is transferred to a private plane, bound for London.

When the plane arrives at London Airport, Jackson opens the door of the plane for the immigration officers—and Sarapha flies off into the night.

Sarapha flies over London and descends at the door of a church, which she enters. A young nun looks up from her praying, sees Sarapha and faints. As the Mother Superior comes to resuscitate her, Sarapha hides in a confessional.

The scene shifts in a church, where Father Donovin prepares to confess a young man. They find Sarapha in the confessional. Sarapha flies to the top of the nave and into the belfry, where she becomes entangled in the bell ropes, causing the bells to ring. Eventually she extricates herself and flies out of the Church. She reaches Covent Garden and sleeps on the roof of a market building.

In the morning—Sunday—she descends to the stage door of the Royal Opera House and is admitted by a friendly charlady, who supposes that she is a dancer. While Sarapha rests in a dressing room, she asks the charlady for directions to Brook Street.

Meanwhile, Father Donovin is giving reporters his account of the appearance of Sarapha in the church. The published report is subsequently read by Jackson and Ryman in their suite in the Savoy. Determined to recapture Sarapha, Jackson guesses correctly that she will seek out Margaret Latham—the wife of Professor Latham—at her home in fashionable Brook Street.

At midnight Sarapha leaves the Opera House and flies in search of Brook Street. She asks the way from a startled old drunk. He is no help, but Sarapha finds her destination, 27 Brook Street. Jackson and Ryman are there before her, keeping watch in the street below.

Sarapha flies to the window of the room in which Margaret is sleeping. The startled Margaret quickly recovers her composure, and the two rapidly achieve a sympathetic and confidential relationship. Their conversation is interrupted by a call from Jackson. Meanwhile Sarapha has noticed a photograph of Sir Rex Horton. Margaret explains that he is now her husband. She and Latham are divorced.

Jackson arrives, and says that in order to clear up the situation of Sarapha's immigration and quarantine status, her whereabouts must be known and that she must come and stay with them in the Savoy Hotel. She agrees to go, and despite Margaret's apprehension, at dawn next morning flies to the Savoy and enters the room they have designated. Later Jackson joins her and tells her that it will help her situation if they can establish she is an angel. Word of Sarapha's presence has already caused crowds in the hotel. Dr James Gidson, the revivalist preacher, joins them. He is at first awed by Sarapha, but quickly gets into fierce bargaining with Jackson about the economics of the coming event and the split of the profits. Sarapha disturbs the discussion by loudly chewing cornflakes, but eventually leaves the room. After Gidson leaves, Ryman tells Jackson that he has arranged for fake cripples to be at the revivalist event, to ensure miracles of healing will be witnessed.

Margaret calls Sarapha to tell her to be prepared to escape after the meeting, and to meet her at Hyde Park Corner, when they will drive to Margaret's country house.

The great revivalist event takes place at Earl's Court. At Sarapha's appearance the crowd becomes hysterical, crying out for miracles and for peace. Sarapha flies up and out of the skylight. She makes directly for Marble Arch and descends to find Margaret's car. They take off for Margaret's baronial mansion at Trent (a locality evidently invented by Chaplin, though there is a tiny village of that name in north-west Dorset). Sir Rex returns home, and though very struck by Sarapha, is tactless in proposing grouse for dinner.

Meanwhile, the issue has reached Parliament. The creature must be quarantined or expelled.

Two weeks after the arrival at Trent, Margaret asks Sarapha to accompany her to Lady Pentagon's fancy dress ball. There will be plenty of angels there, since her appearances have been so much in the news. Sarapha declines, but after she has gone to bed, she hears a car drive up. It is Jackson. She therefore takes off and finds her way to the Pentagons' house, where her elevated dancing causes a sensation.

Seeing Jackson in the ballroom, she takes off and lands in a little English village. In the town hall, Dr Everman is giving a lecture on Atheism. When Sarapha appears beside him on the stage, he faints, before she flies off into the night.

Sarapha returns to Margaret's country house and goes to her bedroom. Outside, Sir Rex in his car is watching her room with field-glasses. Now he comes up, makes an excuse to enter her room, and begins to assault her. She resists, and stabs him in the back and chest with scissors. Realising what she has done, she flies away.

In Margaret's country house, the police are hiding in Sarapha's room, confident that she will return. She does indeed come in the window of the darkened room, and is immediately caught.

Meanwhile, Latham suddenly returns to Britain, ready to support Margaret. The Lathams visit Sarapha in her police cell.

In the courtroom the defence persuades the jury to find Sarapha not guilty. The judge says that he will have to have her detained in quarantine until her status is established. After three weeks however, Latham succeeds in finding Sarapha's birth certificate in Somerset House. It shows that she is indeed the daughter of British missionaries. The Lathams extricate Sarapha from quarantine and take her to Margaret's home. She is listless and preoccupied, and talks of her wish to return to Chile.

At night she stands on the roof of Margaret's town house, and takes flight.

A fishing boat finds her body floating in the Atlantic.

Charles Chaplin's
The Freak

FREAK

CHARLES   CHAPLIN

The scene opens showing the extreme southern part
of the Chilian coast, with its debris of islands along its
lonely shore. The view is bleak from the sea, not a sign
of human habitation for miles around, save an adobe-looking
building perched on the very edge of a high cliff overlooking the sea. The building was at one time occupied by
Trappist monks, but abandonned, and is now occupied by
Professor Latham, a historian, and an old Indian housekeeper.

2   The CAMERA races up to the house.

3   DISSOLVE TO INTERIOR OF HOUSE. GUEST ROOM

In which Dr. Piestroz, a clergyman, forty-five, has just
finished packing.

HE EXITS to Professor Latham's sitting-room.

CUT TO PROFESSOR LATHAM's SITTING-ROOM

Professor Latham, attractive, about thirty to thirty-five,
has been working, correcting recondite matter for two
volumes he is writing on Chile for the Royal Geographical
Society.

ENTER Dr. PIESTROZ   PIESTROZ

Well, I'm off !

LATHAM

How are you going, by water or
land ?

PIESTROZ

I shall take the boat as far as Madre
de Dios and from there, I'll catch
the plane to Valparaiso.

ENTER NAGIA, AN OLD INDIAN HOUSEKEEPER.

NAGIA

Luggage strapped tight - nothing
fall off !

The first page of the final screenplay of *The Freak*.

1. The scene opens showing the extreme southern part of the Chilean coast, with its debris of islands along its lonely shore. The view is bleak from the sea, not a sign of human habitation for miles around, save an adobe-looking building perched on the very edge of a high cliff overlooking the sea. The building was at one time occupied by Trappist monks, but abandoned, and is now occupied by Professor Latham, an historian, and an old Indian housekeeper.

2. The CAMERA races up to the house.

3. DISSOLVE TO INTERIOR OF HOUSE. GUEST ROOM, in which Dr Piestroz, a clergyman, forty-five, has just finished packing.

4. HE EXITS to Professor Latham's sitting-room.

CUT TO PROFESSOR LATHAM's SITTING-ROOM.

Professor Latham, attractive, about thirty to thirty-five, has been working, correcting recondite matter for two volumes he is writing on Chile for the Royal Geographical Society.

ENTER Dr PIESTROZ.

> PIESTROZ
> Well, I'm off!

> LATHAM
> How are you going, by water or land?

> PIESTROZ
> I shall take the boat as far as Madre de Dios and from there, I'll catch the plane to Valparaiso.

ENTER NAGIA, AN OLD INDIAN HOUSEKEEPER.

> NAGIA
> Luggage strapped tight—nothing fall off!

> PIESTROZ
> Thank you, Nagia. (*tips her*) Well, Latham, I'm sorry to leave you alone with all this supernatural weather.

> LATHAM
> (*laughs*)
> I'll survive it until you get back.

PIESTROZ
I would like to stay longer—but Mrs Piestroz is alone in Valparaiso,
and she's not too well there.

LATHAM
(*as they walk to door*)
Then hurry back and bring her with you.

5. DISSOLVE TO VIEW OF COUNTRY THROUGH DOOR.

We see a Land Rover drive off, bouncing and bumping over the primitive track.

6. DISSOLVE TO BEDROOM. NIGHT TIME.

Latham asleep. The wind starts moaning and develops into screaming. The light of the moon brightens, then suddenly blackens as a cloud passes over it.

7. CLOSE UP. Latham stirs restlessly in his sleep. Suddenly he is awakened by a scream, then a sudden rapping at his bedroom. Latham sits up with a start.

NAGIA
It's Nagia!

LATHAM
Wait a minute!

He quickly gets out of bed and opens door.

ENTER NAGIA.

NAGIA
(*hysterically*)
Outside window, eagles—attacking.

LATHAM
Attacking what?

NAGIA
(*shakes her head*)
I don't know!

There is another scream. Then a cry for help! Then another thump against Latham's window.

LATHAM
Sounds like a human being!

NAGIA crosses herself.

> LATHAM
> Strange! This window is on the edge of a cliff overlooking the sea a hundred feet below!

Another thump and a scream… Then a faint cry for help!

> LATHAM
> (*clutching Nagia's wrist*)
> Listen! That's unmistakably the cry of a human being!

> NAGIA
> (*pointing upwards*)
> From the roof it came!

Latham quickly puts on his overcoat and slippers, takes an electric torch and EXITS, Nagia following him.

8. CUT TO ROOF.

A large flat space covering about a hundred square yards. The light of the moon sweeps across the roof, revealing a disordered heap by the chimney stack. Latham cautiously moves to see what it is: A supine figure lies breathing heavily.

Latham puts the torch light on it.

> LATHAM
> (*gasps*)
> Good heavens! It's a young girl! And she has wings!

She lies half clad in an old white sheep's skin, her left wing vertical against the chimney stack, her right wing lying flat upon the roof with a delicate white arm resting on it.

> NAGIA
> (*crossing herself*)
> Mio Deus!

Latham carefully turns the head, revealing the face of a beautiful young girl.

> LATHAM
> She's beautiful!

Nagia shakes her head forebodingly and again crosses herself.

> LATHAM
> (*incredulously*)
> It can't be a bird!

> NAGIA
> (*nods*)
> No. Angel! Bad angel fallen from heaven!

> LATHAM
> That's absurd! Here, take her feet!

Nagia shakes her head as she stoops to pick up the feet and together they EXIT below.

9. CUT TO GUEST BEDROOM.

Latham and Nagia ENTER carrying angel.

> LATHAM
> (*as he carries angel*)
> Too late to go to Madre de Dios for medical help—that's a hundred and twenty-five miles away… I don't think she's seriously injured. (*placing her gently on the bed, then placing her wings by her side and listening to her heart with a stethoscope*). Heart is a little fast—but, then, if it's a bird—that's normal! (*he gives her a sedative—handing stethoscope to Nagia*)

> LATHAM
> There is little we can do to-night. Sleep is the best thing, and we'll see what happens in the morning.

Latham EXITS.

Nagia puts things back in the medicine chest, then discovers she's alone with the angel, crosses herself and quickly leaves the room.

10. DISSOLVE TO SUN RISING OVER HORIZON.

11. CUT TO LATHAM.

Walking about in pyjamas. He has not been asleep. There is a knock at his door. Latham stops in his tracks.

> NAGIA'S VOICE
> Professor Latham? It's Nagia!

Sarapha. Drawings by John Rose.

> LATHAM
> Wait a minute! (*he unlocks the door*)
> How's our patient?

> NAGIA
> (*with a startled expression*)
> Awake! It wants to attack me!

> LATHAM
> (*putting on slippers and dressing-gown*)
> Nonsense! Did you speak to her in English or Spanish?

> NAGIA
> Spanish—but she no answer… She English angel—bad angel!

> LATHAM
> An English angel—impossible. Must be an American.

> NAGIA
> (*concerned*)
> No. English—bad luck angel!

> LATHAM
> How do you know?

> NAGIA
> I know. She brings bad luck to my people… No rain. Bad angel!

> LATHAM
> I don't think she's an angel. In fact I don't know what she is.

12. NAGIA AND LATHAM EXIT TO GUEST ROOM.

CUT TO GUEST BEDROOM.

LATHAM AND NAGIA ENTER.

CAMERA FOLLOWS THEM INTO ROOM where a young girl, extremely pretty, is sitting up in bed, her sensuous white neck and shoulders partly exposed, her wings hanging from each side of the bed, her large startled eyes staring at them. Professor Latham smiles; he decides to treat her as a human being.

> LATHAM
> Good morning. How do you feel? Nagia tells me you are English.

13. CLOSE UP ANGEL. There is no response.

14. SEMI-LONG SHOT OF THE THREE. ANGEL, NAGIA, LATHAM.

> LATHAM
> (*to Nagia*)
> We must find out if she has injured her wings.

15. CLOSE UP ANGEL.

As they approach her she snarls threateningly, showing her teeth and spreading her wings.

> LATHAM
> From such a response, I don't think there is much the matter with
> her… (*to Angel*) We are not going to hurt you! How are your wings?
> (*he shouts then pantomimes*) Wings! (*and becomes somewhat foolish*)

16. CLOSE UP GIRL.

She continues to stare, then slowly breaks into a smile.

> LATHAM
> Ah! We are progressing! Are you well enough to eat? (*shouts pointing
> to his mouth*) Eat!

He pantomimes a chicken laying an egg and eating it.

17. CLOSE UP ANGEL.

A look of horror comes over her face.

18. THREE-QUARTER SHOT LATHAM.

Points to grapes on side-board and shouts in Spanish.

> LATHAM
> Uva! Uva! Grapes! Grapes!

19. SEMI-CLOSE UP ANGEL.

She nods eagerly.

20. THREE-QUARTER SHOT LATHAM.

CAMERA follows him to side-board and back to Angel.

Latham cautiously offers her grapes to Angel which who snatches them and devours them, spitting the pips and skins all over the bed cover. Nagia hurriedly gets a plate and offers it to the Angel.

> ANGEL
> Don't bother, I can manage.

Nagia and Latham look at her, startled, then look at each-other.

21. DISSOLVE TO ROUGH SEA. Waves dashing against rocks, and throwing mountainous fan-like spray in the air…

22. TIME ELAPSE. DISSOLVE TO SAME SCENE, calm and sunny.

23. DISSOLVE TO ANGEL AND LATHAM walking on top of the plateau.

> LATHAM
> So you don't like Indians?

> ANGEL
> Oh—they're all right—but Nagia gets on my nerves.

> LATHAM
> Well, Nagia's gone now.

> ANGEL
> (*brightening up*)
> She's never coming back?

> LATHAM
> You can't tell with Indians. She said she must stay in Valparaiso as long as her father is ill there. And if he dies she must be there to bury him.

> ANGEL
> I hope he won't die for a long, long time yet!

> LATHAM
> (*laughs*)
> Just a few more questions, then I'll leave you alone. How is it that you have wings?

> ANGEL
> They grew after I was born.

LATHAM
Did your parents have wings?

ANGEL
No, they were missionaries.

LATHAM
Did they love you?

ANGEL
Oh yes, very much. But they were always sad when they saw me.

LATHAM
(*after thoughtful consideration*)
Well, you are a rare phenomenon. Your wings are possibly a form of
the stigmata

ANGEL
Stigmata?

LATHAM
Wounds on the crucified body of Christ—said to appear on the hands
and feet of religious young women—but in your case, you have
grown wings.

ANGEL
I hate them—people think I'm an angel.

LATHAM
What's wrong with that?

ANGEL
I don't like mystifying and frightening people. It gets on my nerves—
possibly it's the bird in me.

LATHAM
But you're not a bird.

ANGEL
You don't think so?

LATHAM
Of course not! You're a pretty young girl.

ANGEL
Thank you.

LATHAM
Then after you grew wings and were able to fly, what happened?

ANGEL
We lived with Fuegian Indians until my parents died.

LATHAM
They are dead?

ANGEL
They died when I was eight years old.

LATHAM
Oh! (*takes her hand and pats it sympathetically*) What happened after your parents died?

ANGEL
I lived with the Indians for a long time until there was no rain. Then, when I saw them dance one night, I felt that dance was for me.
(*she makes a sign, drawing her fingers across her throat*)

LATHAM
Did you think they would kill you?

ANGEL
I don't know—but I wanted to be sure they wouldn't.

LATHAM
(*laughs*)
You are very cautious.

ANGEL
But I get frightened as birds do.

LATHAM
You have a complex about being a bird. I insist you are a pretty young girl.

ANGEL
You think so?

LATHAM
However, after you thought they would kill you, what happened?

ANGEL
I flew away and lived in a cave, high up in a canyon.

LATHAM
Alone?

ANGEL
Yes, alone.

LATHAM
But why?

ANGEL
Because I am afraid of everyone and everyone is afraid of me.

LATHAM
(*thoughtfully*)
Life is a mystery!—As Schopenhauer said: "Life does not justify
reason or result."—

ANGEL
Why should it? I think that's asking too much.

LATHAM
(*laughs*)
You are a genius—a rare phenomenon. Where did you get all this
genius from?

ANGEL
(*with childish confidence*)
Oh just natural!

There is a silence and the music that has been playing softly becomes a little louder.

ANGEL
That music has been going through my head all the time. What is it?

LATHAM
Music?

ANGEL
Yes, that one you play on the record.

LATHAM
Oh, that's an old Chilean love song—over four hundred years old.

ANGEL
It's beautiful!

LATHAM
You like music?

ANGEL
(*smiles*)
Not much—not until now.

LATHAM
(*to avoid any hint of getting romantic*)
Let me see you fly.

ANGEL
(*shakes her head solemnly*)
I shall never fly again.

LATHAM
That's sad...

ANGEL shrugs.

LATHAM
Nothing is more exciting than to see you fly over the cliffs and glide down to the sea, and watch you skim the waves.

ANGEL
Seagulls do that.

LATHAM
But you're not a seagull. When you fly it is ethereally beautiful.

ANGEL
Well, if you talk like that—

24. She takes a running leap in the air and sails over the cliff.

25. CLOSE UP LATHAM.

He stands enthralled.

26 FADE TO LATHAM'S SITTING-ROOM.

MUSIC SWELLS.

The music of the phonograph comes to an end.

> ANGEL
> Do you mind if I play that again?

Latham is about to get up and rewind the phonograph.

> ANGEL
> Don't bother, I can wind it. (*she alights on the floor, and with two hops reaches the phonograph, and winds it, then returns and hops on the back of the settee*)

> LATHAM
> As you haven't a name, I think I shall call you Sarapha.

> ANGEL
> Thank you.

27. FADE INTO FULL MOON.

28. CUT TO LATHAM'S BEDROOM.

He is in bed asleep. There is a slight tapping at his bedroom door.

Latham turns on his pillow and opens his eyes, then quickly sits up. The tapping continues.

> LATHAM
> Who is it?

Latham goes to bedroom door.

> SARAPHA's VOICE
> Sarapha!

He hesitates, then opens the door and finds Sarapha standing there smiling at him.

29. CLOSE UP SARAPHA SMILING.

30. CLOSE UP LATHAM.

Looking sternly at her.

> LATHAM
> What is it?

> SARAPHA
> (*looks appealing at him, wanting to be embraced*)
> I can't sleep.

31. CLOSE UP LATHAM.

> LATHAM
> (*sternly*)
> Listen! You're too young not to sleep.

> SARAPHA
> (*quickly*)
> I'm eighteen!

> LATHAM
> Yes—but you need more sleep and a little more experience!
> (*he turns her around and walks her towards her bedroom*)

32. CAMERA follows them.

> LATHAM
> So now you go to bed like a good little girl, and see that you lock
> your door—otherwise I might weaken!

Sarapha, before ENTERING bedroom, turns and looks indignantly at him.

> LATHAM
> Quite so! But I happen to be a man!
> (*walks back to his room and laughs to himself*)

33. DISSOLVE TO LONG SHOT.

Showing magnificent scenery of land and sea. Storm clouds racing, rough seas beating against the coast.

34. INSERT CALENDAR.

It has changed from May to June.

35. CUT TO LATHAM's BEDROOM.

He's confined to his bed with a cold. Sarapha is taking his pulse. She looks at the clock.

> LATHAM
> I don't know what I'd have done without you—making beds,
> cooking, and darning my socks.

Sarapha smiles, makes a note of his pulse, then washes his face and gives him a piecemeal bath. After drying his back she soaps flannel and hands it to him. As he takes it, he catches her wrist and pulls her down, attempting to kiss her. She evades him.

SARAPHA
No, no, you are not well yet.

LATHAM
Yet!

SARAPHA
You must get well and finish your book.

LATHAM
I've almost finished the second volume.

SARAPHA
Then what are you going to do?

After a silence, LATHAM smiles wistfully.

LATHAM
Write another book, I suppose. Or go to London—and take you with
me.

SARAPHA
If you take me to London, I'll have my wings removed.

LATHAM
(*indignantly*)
What! Have your wings cut off? I should say not.

36. DISSOLVE TO LATHAM's LIBRARY.

Sarapha is busy dusting and putting books back into the library shelves. She kisses each book, and in this manner, clears up his desk. Putting notes in their proper box on the shelf, she notices a letter addressed to Mrs Margaret Latham. She picks it up and is tempted to open it, but hesitates, then tears it open and reads:

"My dear Margaret, I have had a fantastic experience—I have encountered a freak—a beautiful creature with wings! Whom I found wounded on the roof of the house—An Angel as Nagia insists she is—a wicked angel! But it's a bird with a human body! Quite beautiful! What a romance I could have! If I were not in love with the most beautiful wife in the world. Your devoted husband, Edward."

Sarapha can read no further. She puts the letter back in its envelope, leaves it on the desk, and continues her work.

The flight of Sarapha from the cliff. Storyboard by Gerald Larn.

37. FADE INTO EXTERIOR OF HOUSE. SEMI-CLOSE UP.

Sarapha, steeped in sadness, spreads her wings and exercises them. She breasts the wind as she accelerates them, then starts to run for the purpose of flying, but she cannot get off the ground. Eventually, she falls.

38 CUT TO LATHAM'S LIBRARY .

He is watching Sarapha from the window.

39 CUT TO SARAPHA.

She gets up and tries again, accelerating her wings then running, but stumbles again.

40 CUT TO LIBRARY. SEMI-LONG SHOT.

Latham leaves window hurriedly and EXITS out of room.

41 CUT TO WHERE SARAPHA HAS FALLEN. SEMI-LONG SHOT.

LATHAM appears and lifts her gently to her feet. She looks haggard and sad.

> SARAPHA
> (*tearfully*)
> I'll never be able to fly again!

Latham, in silence, leads her towards the house.

MUSIC SWELLS.

42 DISSOLVE TO TRAIL OF CARAVAN. Indians following.

43 CUT TO EXTERIOR OF HOUSE.

CLOSE-UP OF SARAPHA watching caravans approaching. She turns and hurries inside, CAMERA PANNING with her.

44 CUT TO LATHAM'S SITTING-ROOM.

Sarapha ENTERS breathlessly.

> SARAPHA
> People are coming!

45. SEMI-CLOSE UP LATHAM.

He gets up, takes his field glasses and EXITS to door, where he stands.

46. CUT TO OVAL SCENE THROUGH FIELD GLASSES.

Showing the trail coming towards the house.

> LATHAM
> (_laughs ironically_)
> They're coming all right—and in this direction.

He turns and hurries into sitting-room, followed by Sarapha.

47. MEDIUM LONG SHOT. CAMERA FOLLOWS.

> LATHAM
> (_as he is hurrying_)
> If this is the press they'll undoubtedly make a scandal. Nagia's away
> and this will give them ample opportunity for their opprobriums.
> (_looking at Sarapha_) You'd better not be seen.

At this moment there is a knock at the front door. Sarapha flutters her wings and leaps into a clothes closet. Latham in the excitement quickly feels his coat pocket and adjusts his handkerchief, then goes to the door and stealthily opens it.

48. CUT TO CLOSE UP DR PIESTROZ AND WIFE.

> LATHAM
> (_closes door and leads way into sitting-room_)
> Come in, come in!

> PIESTROZ
> I warned you I should bring my wife!

> LATHAM
> (_unconsciously whispering_)
> Delighted, upon my word to be sure. How did you come?

> PIESTROZ
> By boat, this time. The sea is quite calm, you know.

> LATHAM
> (_as he helps to take off Mrs Piestroz's cloak_)
> How are you, Mrs Piestroz? The doctor told me that in Valparaiso
> you were not feeling well.

> Mrs PIESTROZ
> Oh I'm much better now. All I need is a change of air. I was awfully nervous in Valparaiso.

> LATHAM
> Well, you'll find the air very relaxing here. I hope you'll stay a little longer this time.

She gives her cloak and hat to Latham who goes to hang them in clothes closet and absent-mindedly opens door revealing Sarapha. Latham jumps back quickly.

> LATHAM
> Oh! It's Sarapha!

49. SEMI-CLOSE UP SARAPHA.

She emerges cautiously spreading her wings and shaking off a few feathers.

50. CUT TO TWO SHOT.

Piestroz and his wife watching with astonishment.

51. THREE SHOT LATHAM AND PIESTROZS.

> LATHAM
> Oh, this is Sarapha. (*turning to Sarapha*)
> My friends, Dr and Mrs Piestroz.

52. TWO SHOT PIESTROZS.

The doctor bows gravely. Mrs Piestroz laughs in a silly way, then staggers backwards and faints on sofa.

53. CAMERA PANNING WITH HER.

Sarapha and Latham run towards her and try to revive her.

54 CUT TO SEMI-CLOSE UP DR PIESTROZ.

He also faints.

55. CUT TO THREE SHOT.

Latham ENTERS with glass of water. Sarapha gently lifts up Mrs Piestroz's head and gives her some water.

56. LARGE CLOSE UP Mrs PIESTROZ.

She drinks water. Now she recovers and opens her eyes.

CAMERA PULLS BACK.

She sees Sarapha bending over her with a glass of water, gives a weak "oh!" and faints again.

57. CUT TO LONG SHOT SITTING-ROOM. Mrs Piestroz is partly revived and is about to sit up when she hears the surge of solemn voices singing hymns. She faints again.

58. CUT TO SEMI-CLOSE UP Dr PIESTROZ.

He also faints, falling into armchair.

59. CUT TO SARAPHA.

She moves from window to Latham, who sees that the doctor has fainted. He EXITS to help doctor.

60. CUT TO PIESTROZ.

Latham ENTERS and lifts Piestroz up.

> PIESTROZ
> (*feebly*)
> My wife is very nervous! — Where is she? What's it all about?

> LATHAM
> It's a long story. I'll explain later.

There is a knock at the front door.

> LATHAM
> (*hysterically to Sarapha*)
> Keep out of sight. I'll try and get rid of them

61. CUT TO SARAPHA.

She steals away into kitchen.

62. CUT TO LATHAM.

He goes to door muttering.

> LATHAM
> This is Nagia's doing. I'll get rid of them.

He strides over to front door and quickly opens it.

63. THREE SHOT.

He is confronted with a smiling young Indian girl, crippled, in a wheel chair, her Indian father and mother, half-breeds, standing behind her.

> MOTHER
> Sorry, sir, we're from Madre de Dios, and this—is our daughter (*pointing to smiling girl*) who has polio. When we heard that an angel had descended on your house, we all came together, for we are believers, sir.

> LATHAM
> (*interrupting*)
> Who told you about this?

> MOTHER
> The lady who worked for you.

> LATHAM
> Nagia!

> MOTHER
> Yes, Nagia. No one believed her, but Alice did. She convinced us all. Alice believes that if she could just touch her, just see her, it would give her strength to get well.

64. CUT TO BIG CLOSE UP YOUNG GIRL.

She nods eagerly.

65. CUT TO CLOSE UP SARAPHA.

In kitchen listening as if possessed. She EXITS.

66. CUT TO FRONT DOOR INTERIOR.

Sarapha ENTERS and appears at door. There is a little scream of excitement at her appearance.

67. CUT TO GROUP. SEMI-LONG SHOT.

They immediately kneel and cross themselves.

68. CUT BACK TO SARAPHA. REVERSE SHOT. FRONT DOOR.

Sarapha gently strokes head of the child then lifts her hand and kisses it. There is a murmur of appreciation, then more chanting.

> SARAPHA
> If you have faith, all things are possible, you will cure yourself.

Sarapha EXITS forward to CAMERA's right.

69. CUT TO INDIAN GROUP. LONG SHOT.

One patient endeavouring to sit up. Another, smiling, tries to lift her arms.

70. CLOSE UP CRIPPLED INDIAN GIRL.

Struggling to lift her arms.

> YOUNG GIRL
> Look! Look! Already I am better!

71. CLOSE UP LATHAM.

Watching in silence.

72. CLOSE UP INDIAN MOTHER.

Weeping with joy.

73. CLOSE UP INDIAN FATHER.

Wiping his tears as he shouts to Sarapha.

> FATHER
> (*in Spanish*)
> God bless you! God bless you! You have cured my daughter

74. CUT TO THREE SHOT. LATHAM, AND PIESTROZ.

> PIESTROZ
> What is he saying?

> LATHAM
> God bless you! You have cured my daughter! Life is tragic!

75. CLOSE UP SARAPHA.

> SARAPHA
> (*with emotion*)
> No! No! Life is not tragic—If I have wings, it is to give those poor people hope—And if that hope never leaves them, then they must get well! They *will* get well!

During the above dialogue, voices outside rise in a hymn of thanks.

76. CUT TO EXTERIOR. FULL SHOT.

Showing Indians singing.

77. CLOSE UP CRIPPLED GIRL.

Smiling, she continues to lift her arms.

78. LONG SHOT.

The Indian pilgrims are leaving. As the trail winds its way, the father and mother pause and turn chair towards house, then cross themselves.

79. CLOSE UP CRIPPLED GIRL.

She attempts to cross herself but fails.

FADE INTO

80. SITTING-ROOM.

CLOSE UP Mrs PIESTROZ.

> Mrs PIESTROZ
> (*half convinced*)
> She can't be an angel!

> LATHAM
> We don't know what she is!

> Mrs PIESTROZ
> But those wings!

> LATHAM
> As Goethe says: "There is no logic in Nature."

Mrs PIESTROZ
How is it she speaks English?

LATHAM
(*humorously*)
Who knows! There could be English angels in heaven—but she
doesn't claim to be an angel. At times she feels she is a bird.

Mrs PIESTROZ
That's bizarre! Absurd!

LATHAM
The absurd and bizarre are quite evident under a microscope!

Mrs PIESTROZ
Every time I see her, she gives me the creeps!

PIESTROZ
(*intercepting*)
My dear, if she has aroused the spirit of religion—

Mrs PIESTROZ
(*indignantly*)
Religion! What religion?

PIESTROZ
Well... Let's say: Totemism.

Mrs PIESTROZ
Totemism! That's something to do with a totem pole! You're getting
very Freudian, Dr Piestroz!

She gets up and looks at herself in mirror.

Sarapha ENTERS, and is ready to lay table.

Mrs Piestroz sees her through mirror and suddenly jumps with fright.

Mrs PIESTROZ
Hallo!—Oh! I've forgotten to comb my hair!
(*EXITS hurriedly*)

CAMERA FOLLOWS HER TO

81. PASSAGE LEADING TO KITCHEN AND UPSTAIRS BEDROOM.

She turns to find Sarapha still following her. Then she runs upstairs.

82. CLOSE UP SARAPHA looking innocently after her.

83. CUT TO SITTING-ROOM.

> PIESTROZ
> (*thoughtfully*)
> I must say she is very pretty.
>
> LATHAM
> (*solemnly*)
> Oh she's quite beautiful! And abnormally bright.
>
> PIESTROZ
> It could be a throw-back of the pterodactyl type.
>
> LATHAM
> The disturbing thing is that she has a terrific attraction for me.
>
> PIESTROZ
> I must say, she's very appealing with her wings—but that thought must never enter your head. (*he gets up and abruptly looks out of window*) Hallo! What's this?
>
> LATHAN
> (*gets up quickly and goes to window and looks out*)
> A helicopter! This is the beginning of the end! I'm afraid the whole world will be trailing to our doorstep!
>
> PIESTROZ
> I'll get rid of them at once.
>
> LATHAM
> They'll never leave until they have seen Sarapha.

84. CLOSE UP SARAPHA laying table.

> SARAPHA
> I'll get rid of them.
>
> PIESTROZ
> That's a good idea. After they've seen you, their curiosity will be satisfied—I hope!

SARAPHA. FROM THE COURTYARD GATE SEES THE INDIANS APPROACHING —

LATHAM'S P.O.V. —

LATHAM'S COURTYARD THRONGED BY PILGRIMS— THE
DOOR OPENS.

SARAPHA APPEARS ON THE STEPS. THE MEN SNATCH OFF
THEIR HATS. +

THE PLEADING RELATIVES MOVE BACK - CAMERA WIDENS ANGLE
TO REVEAL THE GIRL —

CHILD'S P.O.V. OF SARAPHA AS SHE DESCENDS - ARMS &
WINGS EXTENDED - FROM VERANDAH INTO THE SUNLIGHT!

SARAPHA'S HANDS ENTER FRAME THE CHILD EXTENDS
HER OWN & SLOWLY RISES FROM THE WHEELCHAIR.

SARAPHA'S HANDS DROP FROM FRAME — C.V. ON HAPPY
CHILD — SHE TURNS TO CROWD — " I AM CURED!".

SARAPHA RETIRES INDOORS THE CHILD IS LIFTED UP.

THE CHILD'S MOTHER AND FATHER REACT TO
THE MIRACLE

THE CHILD DANCES WITH JOY — SOME HAPPILY ATTACK THE
WHEELCHAIR —

SOME SING HYMNS · OTHERS PROSTRATE THEMSELVES &
WRITHE IN ERSTACY

THE DEPARTING INDIANS TAKE A BACKWARD LOOK & CROSS
THEMSELVES — THE CHILD MANIFESTS SUDDEN DISTRESS —

— SHE CANNOT WALK!

> SARAPHA
> You go on with your lunch. Don't wait for me.

Sarapha EXITS.

85. CUT TO HELICOPTER LANDING. LONG SHOT.

The engines are turned off and two men jump down from cock pit. Business-like, they start ploughing and pulling until a stretcher appears.

86. CUT TO INTERIOR SITTING-ROOM.

Latham looking out of window.

> LATHAM
> Look at them! It's as though Pandora's box had suddenly opened.

> Mrs PIESTROZ
> I'm afraid you'll have to finish your book in London.

87. CUT TO HELICOPTER IN BACKGROUND. SEMI-LONG SHOT.

ENTER Sarapha.

88. CLOSE UP JACKSON AND RYMAN.

Aged about thirty-five. They stand frozen, then cross themselves. Both are dressed in business suits. Jackson's eyes are perhaps too close together, but for that, he is handsome.

> JACKSON
> (*states solemnly*)
> You must give us time to recover! This is an experience I shall never forget. It is indeed a privilege—I don't know how to address you!

89. SEMI-CLOSE UP SARAPHA.

> SARAPHA
> (*simply*)
> My name is Sarapha.

90. CLOSE UP JACKSON AND RYMAN.

They cross themselves.

> JACKSON
> This is Mr. Ryman, and my name is Jackson.

There is a moan from inside the helicopter.

> JACKSON
> We are from Madre de Dios, and when we heard the wonderful news
> of your faith healing, we flew here to beg you to cure my sister.

> SARAPHA
> What's the matter with her?

> JACKSON
> Polio! She's inside the helicopter, too ill to come out. If you could just
> pray with her, she believes she would be cured.

VOICE from inside the helicopter can be faintly heard praying.

> VOICE
> "Holy Mary, full of grace…"

91. CLOSE UP SARAPHA.

Listening.

Before prayer is finished, she decides to ENTER helicopter.

The steps are down ready. The moment Sarapha steps inside she is grabbed by the two men
close behind her.

92. CUT TO INSIDE HELICOPTER, showing men suddenly grabbing Sarapha's arms.

While Jackson is struggling with Sarapha, the invalid, a big woman, gets up from the stretcher
and helps Jackson, while Ryman hurriedly closes door and starts engines.

93. LONG SHOT.

Sarapha flaps her wings in all directions, hitting out at everybody. Jackson gets ropes and in
tying her down gets finger bitten.

94. CLOSE UP JACKSON NURSING HIS FINGER.

CAMERA PULLS BACK. Tying is almost complete.

95. SEMI-CLOSE UP SARAPHA.

Looking pathetic as she lies at side of helicopter like a trussed chicken.

> JACKSON
> (*still nursing his finger*)
> Now if you behave yourself, no harm will come to you.

CLOSE UP SARAPHA looking indignantly and threateningly at woman and Jackson.

> JACKSON
> First of all, you must realise that if you behave yourself, you'll be
> well treated.

CLOSE UP SARAPHA.

Still looking threateningly at all of them.

> JACKSON
> On the other hand—we can make it very uncomfortable for you!

> SARAPHA
> I am being kidnapped!

> JACKSON
> Oh no you're not! We don't kidnap birds—We catch them!
> There's nothing you can do about it! But if you co-operate, you'll be
> treated as a human being—It's up to you.

96. CLOSE UP SARAPHA.

She begins to weep quietly.

CLOSE UP WOMAN.

She looks at Sarapha feeling sorry for her.

> WOMAN
> We want to be your friends. If you promise not to fight or struggle,
> we will undo those ropes.

97. CLOSE UP SARAPHA.

She looks sadly at woman and nods, acquiesing.

Woman starts to untie her.

Sarapha notices magazines strewn about the floor.

> WOMAN
> Mr Jackson is in the advertising business.

Sarapha, now free, picks up one of the magazines and thumbs through it casually.

98. INSERT PICTURES OF NUDE GIRLS.

Another page shows a woman's arm enlarged and bent to look like the checks of a woman's buttocks, and several other types of photographs suggesting pornography.

> WOMAN
> Mr Jackson is a rich man, so if you co-operate, you'll be well treated.

> SARAPHA
> I'm thirsty.

> WOMAN
> Would you like some orange juice?

> SARAPHA
> (*nods*)
> Thank you.

Woman gets up and nudges Jackson.

> WOMAN
> The lady would like some orange juice.

99. DISSOLVE TO RYMAN SPEAKING IN A WHISPER.

> RYMAN
> Kidnapping is a risky business.

> JACKSON
> There is no kidnapping—she's a bird!

> RYMAN
> What's she doing now?

> JACKSON
> Asleep—she wanted a drink, so we gave her orange juice with the business in it. She's out like a light!

100. CUT TO CLOSE UP SARAPHA SLEEPING.

101. CLOSE UP RYMAN.

>RYMAN
>(*solemnly*)
>It's risky! But there's a lot of dough in it.

>JACKSON
>This is bigger than dough. With the right publicity we can rule the world!

>RYMAN
>(*impressed*)
>I'd break it all in the newspapers at once if I were you. Then follow it
>up in all the important magazines — *Life*, *Time*, *Playboy*, *Vogue*!

>JACKSON
>*Vogue*? She's no fashion plate! This kid has got something.

>RYMAN
>Keep away from sex —

>JACKSON
>(*waves disparagingly*)
>That commodity is cheap. Today people want to believe in some-
>thing. If we handle this right, we can revolutionise the whole world!

>RYMAN
>Don't you think we should concentrate a little more on the dough,
>instead of revolutionising the world?

>JACKSON
>You must think in big terms, Ryman! This is a ten million dollar a year
>proposition! Money'll come from lectures, collections, gifts, legacies. We'll
>print our own Bible! That alone is a hundred million dollar proposition.

>RYMAN
>Can she talk?

>JACKSON
>She doesn't have to talk. We can get Dr James Gidson, the revivalist,
>to do that.

>RYMAN
>(*nods approvingly*)
>Have you told her all this?

> JACKSON
> Yep!

> RYMAN
> What does she say?

> JACKSON
> (*with a disparaging gesture*)
> She's an animal—knows nothing about money!

Ryman looks cautiously over his shoulder.

102. CLOSE UP SARAPHA.

Still sleeping.

> RYMAN
> Well, she'd better learn.
> (*lowering his voice*) Otherwise she'll end up in the zoo!

103. CUT TO HELICOPTER LANDING AT PARAGUAY. LONG SHOT.

Midnight. Ryman looking out of window.

104. LONG SHOT.

Sarapha is carried off helicopter and taken into plane.

FADE.

105. DISSOLVE TO INTERIOR OF PLANE.

CLOSE UP SARAPHA.

Waking up. She is in a daze and looks out of porthole.

106 CUT TO LARGE BODY OF WATER.

107. CUT TO WOMAN AND SARAPHA. TWO SHOT.

> WOMAN
> (*smiles*)
> We are out in the middle of the Atlantic Ocean.

108. CLOSE UP SARAPHA still in stupor from sleeping drugs. She does not answer.

109. SEMI-LONG SHOT.

Jackson appears from cockpit and sits beside Sarapha.

> JACKSON
> How do you feel?

110. CLOSE UP SARAPHA.

She opens her eyes and nods.

> JACKSON
> We're on our way to London—I think you'll like it there.

CLOSE UP SARAPHA.

She tries to smile.

> JACKSON
> I'm sorry we've had to do this, but when we heard about you and
> your wings, we decided to investigate.

> SARAPHA
> So you kidnapped me?

111. Jackson looks at her searchingly.

> JACKSON
> Frankly, yes: We kidnapped you—but not for mercenary reasons;
> I got all the money I want—I'm in the advertising business. But now,
> I want to do something constructive: This world is cynical, decadent!
> Nobody tries any more. They just fool round with sex and drugs. But
> you can change all that.

112. CLOSE UP SARAPHA.

She looks at him, then down at floor. There are pornographic magazines lying around.

> JACKSON
> (_pointing to magazines_)
> That's to make money. But I've got other ideas—If—if only you'll
> co-operate—It's up to you!

113. CLOSE UP SARAPHA.

She looks at him with an inscrutable expression of contempt.

CLOSE UP JACKSON.

Looks at his watch.

> JACKSON
> (*as he gets up*)
> I must see Ryman

114. CUT TO COCKPIT. ENTER JACKSON.

> RYMAN
> (*whispers*)
> Did you talk to her?

> JACKSON
> (*nods*)
> I think I've sold her the idea!

> RYMAN
> What are you going to do when we get to London?

> JACKSON
> Talk to the immigration officer. Then if there's passport trouble,
> I'll claim she's a bird and that's she's my property.

> RYMAN
> If they quarantine her?

> JACKSON
> We can wait and see—whatever happens, we're in the money.

> RYMAN
> (*doubtfully*)
> Well, you know best.

115. DISSOLVE TO LONDON AIRPORT NIGHT TIME.

116. CUT TO AIRPORT TOWER. FULL SHOT.

> FIRST MAN
> Hallo! What's that?

> SECOND MAN
> (*listening with earphones*)
> Private plane. From Paraguay, wants clearance.

Sarapha flies over the rooftops of London. Storyboard by Gerald Larn.

> FIRST MAN
> Call up Immigration.

> SECOND MAN
> Hallo! Immigration?

117. CUT TO JACKSON'S PRIVATE PLANE, FULL SHOT.

Ryman stops engines then EXITS into cabin.

> RYMAN
> (*after listening with ear phones*)
> Immigration is coming!—Fingers crossed!

Jackson leaves Sarapha to open door and turns to Ryman.

> JACKSON
> Here, give me a hand!

Cabin door eventually opens. Jackson jumps out and Ryman EXITS into cockpit.

118. CUT TO CLOSE UP SARAPHA.

Like a flash, she darts out and flies up into the night.

119. DISSOLVE TO SARAPHA FLYING HIGH ABOVE LONDON.

120. CUT TO VIEWS OF LONDON AND RIVER THAMES FROM ABOVE.

121. DISSOLVE TO SARAPHA.

Her wings are still, giving the effect of gliding.

122. LONG SHOT OF CHURCH.

Lit up, showing figures filing out and going their respective ways.

123. SEMI-LONG SHOT.

Sarapha alights on the tower, CAMERA following.

124. CLOSE UP TO SARAPHA.

Looking about her.

125. CUT TO CHURCH ENTRANCE.

It is now empty.

126. CUT TO SARAPHA. SEMI-LONG SHOT.

She flies down.

127. CUT TO ENTRANCE.

Sarapha lands, looks about cautiously; then looks inside and tip-toes up nave.

128. CUT TO FIGURE KNEELING. SEMI-CLOSE UP.

Facing altar, her back to Sarapha.

129. CUT TO SARAPHA.

She stops suddenly, rooted!

130. CUT TO KNEELING FIGURE. SEMI-CLOSE UP.

She finishes praying and turns round.

CAMERA moves in to LARGE CLOSE UP.

A young face tightly enshrouded in a white cloth covered with black hood. She sees Sarapha, gives a little scream, then faints.

131. CUT TO SARAPHA SEMI-CLOSE UP.

She turns to run out of church, but outside there is a policeman with his back to her.

132. CUT TO CHURCH ENTRANCE.

Showing policeman's back near street lamp.

Sarapha stops quickly then turns.

133. REVERSE SHOT.

Showing nave and Sarapha running towards altar.

134. CUT TO SMALL CHAPEL OFF SIDE OF CHURCH.

MOTHER SUPERIOR PRAYING. SEMI-LONG SHOT.

She looks up quickly, crosses herself and EXITS to where she heard scream.

135. CUT TO YOUNG NUN LYING IN NAVE.

Mother Superior ENTERS, runs to nun, and 1ifts her head.

> MOTHER SUPERIOR
> My child! What's the matter?

> NUN
> I saw an angel!

> MOTHER SUPERIOR
> Where?

> NUN
> (*dramatically*)
> Here! Standing there, before me!

> MOTHER SUPERIOR
> (*sympathetically*)
> My dear, you have been studying too hard. Perhaps it's the heavy food you've been eating. You must watch your diet and get more sleep.

136. CUT TO SARAPHA.

She peeks from behind an altar and sees a chance to hide in a confessional box. She EXITS hurriedly. On her way she passes several candle-lit altars and is seen by Mother Superior, who passes quite close to her but pays no attention, as though she hasn't seen her, and EXITS through a door.

137. THREE-QUARTER SHOT.

Sarapha cautiously opens door of confessional, then quickly EXITS into it.

FADE.

138. DISSOLVE INTO DAWN OVER WESTMINSTER, Parliament, Big Ben, and Westminster Cathedral.

SYMPHONIC MUSIC.

139. CUT TO FATHER DONAVIN. THREE-QUARTER SHOT.

CAMERA follows him arriving at Church entrance. He looks at his watch.

140. CUT TO LONG VIEW OF CHURCH.

Several worshippers are in pews.

141. CUT TO CANDLE-LIT SHRINES.

>WORSHIPPER
>Can I talk with you a moment?

>FATHER DONAVIN
>(*looking at watch*)
>I have many dispensations to make, you'd better see me after mass.

He walks on down nave.

142. CUT TO CANDLE-LIT SHRINES. FULL LENGTH SHOT.

Several shadowy figures take candles, light them, and place them amongst others.

143. CUT TO FATHER DONAVIN. FULL LENGTH SHOT.

CAMERA pulls back until he reaches the confessional box where Sarapha is sleeping. Outside the confessional, a young man is waiting. As Father Donavin approaches, he bows respectfully. With a gesture, Father Donavin refers him to confessional while he ENTERS the one next to it.

CAMERA moves into

144. THREE-QUARTER SHOT.

The young man goes towards confessional. He opens the door and Sarapha, who was asleep, is suddenly awakened. She looks startled and gives a little cry.

145. CLOSE UP YOUNG MAN.

Looking startled, rigid, and wide-eyed.

146. CUT TO SEMI-CLOSE UP FATHER DONAVIN.

>FATHER DONAVIN
>(*putting ear close to small hole*)
>What's that?

>SARAPHA'S VOICE
>Sorry! I fell asleep!

FATHER DONAVIN
What?
(*after a pause*)
Who is this?

147. CUT TO CLOSE UP SARAPHA.

SARAPHA
My name is Sarapha.

148. CUT TO SEMI-CLOSE UP FATHER DONAVIN.

FATHER DONAVIN
Sarapha! Sarapha! Who's Sarapha? Where's the young man?

Father Donavin steps quickly out of confessional and sees the young man still struck dumb, his startled eyes wide open.

Father Donavin immediately opens door of confessional.

FATHER DONAVIN
(*shouts*)
Oh! (*after seeing Sarapha he backs away a pace*)

Sarapha steps cautiously out of confessional.

SARAPHA
I beg your pardon! Forgive me, I didn't mean to disturb you.

149 REVERSE SHOT.

Showing priest and young man looking startled, wide-eyed, and rigid.

150. CUT TO LONG SHOT.

Showing centre of nave.

151. CLOSE UP WORSHIPPER NEAREST CAMERA.

She has been praying and as she lifts her head she sees an angel talking to Father Donavin and the young man.

152. CUT TO CLOSE UP OF WOMAN.

Finishing praying and looking up. She blinks and shakes her head as though having hallucinations which she wants to hide, so goes on praying.

153. CUT TO CLOSE UP ANOTHER YOUNG GIRL.

She has finished praying, looks up then screams.

154. CUT TO THREE SHOT. FATHER DONAVIN, SARAPHA, YOUNG MAN.

Sarapha backs away from them, bewildered, as screaming continues. Unnerved, Sarapha takes off.

155. LONG SHOT. SARAPHA FLYING ABOVE NAVE OF CHURCH.

156. CUT TO SEMI-LONG SHOT. BELFRY.

Sarapha ENTERS flying, but there is no place to land. She eventually clings to narrow window slits.

157. CUT TO FATHER DONAVIN. FULL LENGTH SHOT.

He has fainted and young man is trying to revive him.

158. SEMI-CLOSE UP SARAPHA.

INSERT her robe gets entangled with bell rope. Trying to release herself, she rings bell.

159. CUT TO EXTERIOR OF CHURCH.

Pedestrians walking by look up surprised by bell ringing.

160. CLOSE UP.

One looking at his watch.

161. CUT TO ENTRANCE.

Several people going into church.

162. CUT TO BELFRY.

Sarapha still clinging and struggling to release her frock.

163. INSERT OF ROPE.

Frock released.

164. CUT TO FULL LENGTH SHOT.

Sarapha EXITS flying.

165. CUT TO LONG SHOT.

Sarapha flying towards CAMERA then she turns and flies away from CAMERA.

166. CUT TO SIDE DOOR OF CHURCH. FULL LENGTH SHOT.

Sarapha EXITS from church and flies upwards.

167. DISSOLVE SEMI-CLOSE UP SARAPHA flying over London.

She looks down and sees that a mist is enveloping the Thames. She decides to glide down.

168. DISSOLVE TO COVENT GARDEN from the sky.

Sarapha ENTERS from above and lands on glass roof of market building next to the Royal Opera House with its facade of Doric columns, etc.

169. CUT TO FULL LENGTH SHOT.

She walks on the rim of the glass roof CAMERA following her.

170. CLOSE UP SARAPHA she stops and looks down.

171. CUT TO DESERTED STREET OF COVENT GARDEN.

Vegetable carts and baskets are in untidy array. She decides to rest and sleep on roof.

172. DISSOLVE TO BIG BEN.

Striking nine o'clock.

173. CUT TO SEMI-CLOSE UP SARAPHA.

She awakes. She stands and looks down at the deserted streets and decides to land on the pavement.

174. CUT TO FULL-LENGTH SHOT STAGE DOOR.

A life-size poster is plastered on the wall of the building. It reads: "Royal Opera House, Covent Garden, presents The Angel. A spectacular production supported by the Royal Ballet."

Sarapha ENTERS from the top of scene and after reading poster she stands for a moment to collect her wits. Suddenly door rattles from inside. Bolts are drawn and the door opens. A charwoman appears sweeping.

175. CUT TO FULL SHOT.

>   CHARWOMAN
>   (*cheerfully on seeing Sarapha*)
>   Good morning, dear.

She goes on sweeping into gutter where she stops and looks at Sarapha.

>   CHARWOMAN
>   Have you been waiting long, dear?

176. CLOSE UP SARAPHA.

She shakes her head.

177. CLOSE UP CHARWOMAN.

>   CHARWOMAN
>   I'm sorry, I didn't know there was a dress rehearsal Sunday morning.
>   I'll unlock your dressing room. (*she pauses*) Let me see, you're on the
>   top floor.

178. CUT TO TOP FLOOR. TOP OF STAIRS.

Charwoman and Sarapha come to top of stairs and EXIT towards CAMERA.

179. CUT TO REVERSE SHOT. DRESSING ROOM PASSAGE.

Charwoman and Sarapha ENTER from back of CAMERA.

>   CHARWOMAN
>   (*mumbling and unlocking dressing room door*)
>   They never told me a thing about a Sunday rehearsal. I'm expected to
>   be a mind reader!

180. CUT TO INTERIOR DRESSING ROOM.

As charwoman ENTERS. She turns and looks at Sarapha.

>   CHARWOMAN
>   Why don't you take those heavy wings off? Then you could lie down
>   on the sofa and rest until rehearsals. What time are they?

181 CLOSE UP SARAPHA.

She shakes her head.

As Charwoman approaches Sarapha, CAMERA PULLS BACK.

182 TWO SHOT.

Sarapha makes a pretense of getting her wings off.

> CHARWOMAN
> Here, let me help you.
> (*she struggles to free Sarapha from her wings*)
> My heavens! You'd think they were real! I can't find the straps!
> What are they made of—plastic?

> SARAPHA
> (*laughs*)
> Don't bother, I'll get them off!

> CHARWOMAN
> Well you put them on—I suppose you can take them off.

EXIT Charwoman, CAMERA PANNING WITH HER.

183. CUT TO SARAPHA THREE-QUARTER SHOT.

CAMERA FOLLOWING.

She looks round the room. A glass stands on the wash basin. She turns on tap and drinks two glasses of water, then hops on to back of couch and squats.

184. CUT TO FULL LENGTH SHOT ANOTHER DRESSING ROOM.

Charwoman is pottering about. She takes boiling water and pours it into tea pot.

185. CUT TO THREE-QUARTER SHOT.

Sarapha is perched on edge of couch. She is dozing. Suddenly there is a knock at the door. Sarapha flaps her wings and jumps off edge of couch.

> SARAPHA
> Come in.

186. THREE-QUARTER SHOT.

Charwoman ENTERS carrying tray with a cup of tea on it.

> CHARWOMAN
> I thought I'd bring you a cup of tea and some biscuits. When you're through with the tea things, just leave them on the dressing table. I'll collect them in the morning. I know what Sunday morning rehearsals are. I used to be in the ballet myself.

Charwoman is about to leave.

> SARAPHA
> Thank you, you're very kind. Oh, please, could you tell me where 27 Brook Street is?

187. THREE-QUARTER SHOT.

Charwoman pauses at door.

> CHARWOMAN
> Let me see, that's up towards the end of Park Lane. You know where Marble Arch is?

188. CLOSE UP SARAPHA.

She shakes her head.

> CHARWOMAN
> You know where Piccadilly is? It's north from here. (*points in direction*) It's all lit up—you can't miss it.

> SARAPHA
> (*shaking her head*)
> I'm sorry but I'm a stranger here!

> CHARWOMAN
> (*looking at her doubtfully*)
> Gawd! Where do you come from?

> SARAPHA
> Chile! (*smiles*)

> CHARWOMAN
> Chile! That must be somewhere outside London.

Without comment Charwoman produces a pencil.

> CHARWOMAN
> (*she draws on newspaper covering dressing table*)
> You know where this theatre is? And the Strand? Well, you go right
> up the Strand until you come to Trafalgar Square. Then ask for Picca-
> dilly—go right up along Piccadilly and you'll come to Hyde Park.
> Anyway, one of the girls can tell you.

> SARAPHA
> (*looking at drawing*)
> Thank you very much.

Charwoman EXITS.

Sarapha looks about the room, yawns, then hops on to the back of sofa and goes to sleep.

FADE.

189. DISSOLVE TO CHURCH. SEMI-LONG SHOT.

Several newspaper men are interviewing young nun.

190. SEMI-CLOSE UP FATHER DONAVIN.

> FATHER DONAVIN
> If it were not that this young man and myself witnessed this phenom-
> enon, we should dismiss the matter as hysteria! However, several
> others can testify that it was not an apparition but a physical fact—an
> angel!—with wings flew up and down the nave of the church, and
> rang the bell!

> REPORTER
> Have you any idea where she went?

> FATHER DONAVIN
> The angel flew out of the church and disappeared in the morning
> mist. Several witnesses here will verify the fact.

191. DISSOLVE TO SUITE OF ROOMS AT SAVOY HOTEL. SITTING-ROOM. FULL
SHOT.

Jackson is walking up and down and Ryman is in an armchair reading aloud.

> JACKSON
> Just read the headlines.

RYMAN
(*reading*)
"The Kingdom of Heaven is at hand." I think they're kidding it.

JACKSON
Read on.

RYMAN
"In the small hours of the morning, an angel or whatever it was—appeared flying up and down the nave of Westminster Cathedral, witnessed by astounded worshippers attending early morning mass. The Reverend Father Donavin, and many others saw it and fell on their knees as they watched, awed and fascinated, the angel ringing the church bell, then disappearing into the heavens…" (*puts down newspaper*) She's gone nuts!

JACKSON
(*laconically*)
The first thing is to find out where she is, before she ends up in the zoo.

RYMAN
Frankly, if it were my property, I'd go directly to Scotland Yard.

JACKSON
(*irritably*)
That's silly. And have her shipped back to Chile. (*he picks up a large book from table*) What's that man's name? (*turning pages of* Who's Who, *he runs his index finger down to Professor Latham*) Here it is! Professor Latham, 27 Brook Street.

RYMAN
What makes you think she'll be there?

JACKSON
It's just a shot in the dark.

192. DISSOLVE TO FULL LENGTH SHOT.

Sarapha is perched on the head of the sofa.

193. CUT TO BIG BEN.

Striking twelve o'clock.

194. CLOSE UP SARAPHA.

She opens her eyes, listens, stretches her wings and hops down from sofa. She looks round fugitively, goes to dressing table and studies the Charwoman's drawing.

195. INSERT CRUDE DRAWING OF THE THEATRE and a drawn arrow pointing north.

196. BACK TO FULL LENGTH SHOT.

She goes to northern window, opens it, and steps out on window sill.

197. FULL LENGTH SHOT.

She pauses to see the sky lit up in a northern direction.

She lifts herself, flaps her wings, and disappears in the direction of the lighted sky.

198. FADE INTO SARAPHA FLYING OVER LONDON. NIGHT TIME.

She keeps repeating "Brook Street! Brook Street!" She looks, stops her wings, then glides down.

199. CUT TO QUIET STREET CORNER. FULL LENGTH SHOT.

A drunk staggers round corner, stops abruptly to steady his balance.

200. SARAPHA ENTERS FROM THE TOP OF THE PICTURE BESIDE HIM.

> SARAPHA
> (*to drunk*)
> Pardon me, but could you tell me where Brook Street is?

201. CLOSE UP DRUNK. The man's eyes bulge.

202. CUT TO SARAPHA. FULL LENGTH SHOT.

> SARAPHA
> (*impatiently*)
> Oh don't bother!

She takes off and flies up into the night, leaving drunk flabbergasted.

203. CUT TO CLOSE UP SARAPHA.

Flying over the roofs, occasionally looking down.

204. CUT BACK TO CLOSE UP OF DRUNK still standing, his eyes still bulging.

205. CUT TO SARAPHA FLYING.

She stops, hovers, then descends an empty street. Sarapha lands below. She looks up and down street, then looks at numbers.

206. INSERT BROOK STREET.

207. INSERT NUMBER 23.

208. BACK TO SARAPHA. FULL SHOT.

She skips and hops along until she gets to number 27.

209. INSERT NUMBER 27.

210. CLOSE UP SARAPHA. She looks up, then EXITS upwards.

211. CUT TO FIRST FLOOR WINDOW.

Sarapha ENTERS from below, slowly flapping her wings and looking in. No, she decides to fly up to next floor.

212. CUT TO STREET BELOW.

Two shadowy figures stop in front of the house and look up.

> JACKSON
> (*whispering*)
> There she is!

> RYMAN
> What are you going to do?

> JACKSON
> Wait! (*they steal off in the night*)

213. CUT TO OPEN WINDOW. FULL LENGTH SHOT.

Sarapha flies up and holds on to window sill, and knocks gently on the side of the window frame.

214. CLOSE UP MARGARET LATHAM IN BED ASLEEP.

She is rich, and beautiful—a young Barbara Hutten type. She sits upright with a start and quickly looks at window, then gives a little scream, her large brown eyes wide open. Sarapha holds on to window sill, her wings flapping.

Sarapha arrives flying at Margaret's house. Storyboard by Gerald Larn.

SARAPHA
Pardon me. I'm sorry to disturb you, but aren't you Margaret
Latham, wife of Professor Latham?

MARGARET
I was!

SARAPHA
I know the Professor very well.

MARGARET
Good heavens! Is he dead?

SARAPHA
Oh no! I'm Sarapha, you might have heard of me.

MARGARET
(*transfixed*)
Sarapha! My God—it's true! I thought he was crazy! You, you actually exist!

SARAPHA nods and smiles with relief.

MARGARET
(*reaches for her smelling salts*)
I'll come to in a minute! (*putting her hand to her brow*) You know,
your wings are lovely—

SARAPHA
(*turns*)
I hate them! If people see me, they think they are either dead or in
heaven!

MARGARET
Well, frankly, I am a little confused myself. (*sniffs her smelling salts*)

SARAPHA
(*smiles and shakes her head negatively*)
No—I am not an angel—and I'm not from heaven.

MARGARET
Thank God for that!
(*puts down smelling salts and puts her hand to her brow*) But tell me,
what is it that is supporting you?

> SARAPHA
> (*smiling*)
> I'm holding on to your window sill.
>
> MARGARET
> (*confused*)
> Heavens! Wait a minute—I'll open the front door, downstairs.
>
> SARAPHA
> Don't bother, I can manage.

Sarapha jumps lightly through open window and stands by the curtain. For a moment they gaze at each other.

215. IN THIS MOOD CUT TO CLOSE-UPS BACK AND FORTH.

> MARGARET
> But you're beautiful!
>
> SARAPHA
> Thank you. So are you!
>
> MARGARET
> Won't you sit down—or—or something?
>
> SARAPHA
> Thank you! (*looks about her*) If it doesn't disturb you, may I jump
> on the head of your sofa? Sitting on chairs is difficult because of my
> wings.
>
> MARGARET
> (*over polite*)
> Please do.

SARAPHA jumps and lands lightly on the head of the sofa and sits. Margaret is slightly startled, but recovers.

> MARGARET
> It's like Christmas or something. (*tense*) But there are so many ques-
> tions I want to ask you that I don't know where to begin. (*turns*) You
> came from Chile? How did you get here?
>
> SARAPHA
> I was kidnapped, drugged, and brought to England, but I escaped in
> London.

MARGARET
How did you manage? Where did you sleep?

SARAPHA
Everywhere! In a church—in the Royal Opera House, and now I'm
being pursued. That's why I came here to ask if you could give me
shelter for the night.

MARGARET
Of course, of course! But tell me more about yourself. How is it you
have wings?

SARAPHA
They grew after I was born.

MARGARET
Oh! (*after a pause*) Your mother must have been thankful for that!
(*again using smelling salts*)

MARGARET
Did your parents have wings?

SARAPHA
No they were missionaries.

MARGARET
(*nods, tensions drops*)
I see. However, tell me about the people who kidnapped you.

SARAPHA
They are scoundrels. They say I have no status as a human being, and
that if I go to the authorities; they would claim me as their property.
That I am a bird, and have escaped into the country.

MARGARET
But you are not a bird. You can claim that you were kidnapped and
that you are English.

SARAPHA
(*shrugs*)
I have no proof.

MARGARET
But you speak English.

SARAPHA
(*thinks*)
I believe my parents were English—English missionaries. But when they died, I lost all account of who I was.

MARGARET
Your parents are dead?

SARAPHA
Yes. They died when I was eight years old.

MARGARET
(*sympathetically*)
Oh! (*placing her pillows for comfort*) Tell me more—more!

SARAPHA
Then I lived with the Indians… Then there was a dry spell, so when I saw them dance one night—I knew what to expect. So I flew away.

MARGARET
They would have killed you?

SARAPHA
(*with solemn assurance*)
Oh yes—if I'm mixed up in their religion. Look what they did to Jesus!

MARGARET
Then what happened?

SARAPHA
I lived in a cave, high up in the mountains.

MARGARET
Alone?

SARAPHA
Yes, alone.

MARGARET
Fantastic! (*lost what to say next and putting her hand to her forehead*) But eh—getting back to the people who kidnapped you… But here I am plying you with questions—and you must be hungry. (*Sarapha nods eagerly*) What would you like?

SARAPHA
A glass of milk, please.

> MARGARET
> (*makes a wry face*)
> Milk?

Telephone rings. They both jump.

216. CLOSE UP MARGARET AND SARAPHA.

They are frightened and look at each other questioningly.

> MARGARET
> Who the hell can that be at this time of night? (*she quickly puts her hand to her mouth and turns to Sarapha*) Pardon me!

> SARAPHA
> (*smiles*)
> Don't apologise. I'm tired of people kneeling and praying to me, so that a little word like hell is welcome at times!

The telephone rings again and Margaret deliberates a moment, then picks up the telephone.

> MARGARET
> Hallo! Who is it?

> VOICE OF JACKSON
> I would like to speak to Sarapha, please.

> MARGARET
> I don't understand.

> VOICE OF JACKSON
> The creature who flew up to your room a moment ago—I have a very important message for her from the quarantine authorities.

Margaret is about to become indignant, but covers the telephone with her hand and turns to Sarapha.

> MARGARET
> You heard what he said?

217. CLOSE UP SARAPHA.

She nods.

> MARGARET
> (*to Sarapha*)
> I think we should listen to what they have to say. (*turns back to telephone without waiting for answer*). Where are you now?

> VOICE OF JACKSON
> We're at the Piccadilly Hotel—quite near.

> MARGARET
> Will you please be here in half an hour.

> VOICE OF JACKSON
> Oh yes, we'll be there.

MARGARET hangs up telephone and sits down before an elaborate dressing table, retouches her make up and perfumes herself.

> MARGARET
> We'll talk to them in the boudoir and see what they have to say.

> SARAPHA
> I know what they'll have to say. They believe I am a bird and that they have the right to claim me as their property.

> MARGARET
> (*indignantly*)
> Property! I never heard of such a thing! You're a human being! You're not a bird—

> SARAPHA
> Well (*shrugs humourously*) sometimes a jackdaw feeling comes over me—so you'd better hide your jewelry! (*they both laugh*)

In the silence, Sarapha looks round and sees a photograph in a silver frame.

> MARGARET
> That's Sir Rex Horton. (*Sarapha nods politely*) Now I'll tell you something about myself. Professor Latham and I are getting a divorce and I'm going to marry Rex.

Sarapha nods silently.

> MARGARET
> You see, I'm a spoilt brat. My parents died and I was left an orphan, and ever since, I've done what I liked—that's the penalty of being rich! Life is a terrific struggle for happiness. One gets involved in marriage and divorce!

Storyboards by John Rose.

Storyboards by Gerald Larn.

SARAPHA
(*almost to herself*)
A divorce will break Professor Latham's heart.

MARGARET
(*looking at her with amusement*) Has he broken yours?

SARAPHA
Me? No, What would he want with a freak! Half bird and half woman.

MARGARET
(*humourously*)
Oh, you have many possibilities! However, you can stay here as long as you like.

SARAPHA
(*earnestly*)
I am sorry to inconvenience you.

MARGARET
Not at all! I shall make a career of protecting you. But tell me about the people who kidnapped you.

SARAPHA
They terrify me. One is named Jackson, and the other, Ryman.

MARGARET
Kidnapping is a very serious offence!

SARAPHA
(*nods forlornly*)
I know it, but what can I do? They threaten to have me put away as an animal.

There is a ring at front door. Margaret jumps—they both jump.

MARGARET
Don't be afraid, no one will harm you.

She EXITS from the room.

218. DISSOLVE INTO MARGARET'S BOUDOIR.

As Jackson and Ryman ENTER Sarapha stands facing them.

> JACKSON
> (*coldly*)
> Good evening!

Sarapha snarls and shows her teeth and slightly spreading her wings. Margaret, on the contrary, makes an effort to be amiable.

> MARGARET
> Can I offer you a drink of some kind?

> JACKSON
> (*coldly*)
> No thank you. (*addressing Sarapha*) The police and the immigration have been on my neck ever since you escaped into the country. They insist that you are a bird, and that you have stolen into the country without going through quarantine.

> MARGARET
> (*indignantly*)
> Ridiculous! She happens to be a human being!

THREE-QUARTER SHOT.

219. JACKSON AND RYMAN ignore the remark.

> JACKSON
> As to your status, a hearing will come up in the lower Courts. I have managed to have it postponed for two weeks. In the meantime, I've booked rooms for you at the Savoy Hotel. Because you have no passport, the Immigration authorities will want to know where you are at all times, so be there tomorrow morning at nine o'clock sharp!

> SARAPHA
> What room is it?

> JACKSON
> The sixth floor. To avoid trouble, I suggest you fly in through the open window as you did, here, tonight.

Sarapha is lost and looks at Margaret for an answer.

> MARGARET
> (*ignoring their presence*)
> I think it is wise to let the immigration people know where you are at all times.

> SARAPHA
> (*to men*)
> I shall be there.

> JACKSON
> (*menacingly*)
> If you try to escape again, the police are bound to find you.

> SARAPHA
> (*turning to men*)
> I shall be there at dawn.

> JACKSON
> Good. Then we'll get the matter cleared up. (*turning to Sarapha*)
> Do you know where the Savoy Hotel is?

220. CLOSE UP SARAPHA.

She shakes her head.

Ryman produces a map and lays it on the table.

> RYMAN
> Just follow the river (*tracing with his finger*) until you get to Waterloo
> Bridge. It's on the right, next to the Shell Oil Company.

221. TWO SHOT.

Jackson turns to Margaret.

> JACKSON
> I must apologize for this intrusion, but it's all for this—this creature's
> benefit.

> MARGARET
> Frankly, I should think it's for everyone's benefit!

Jackson, ignoring her remark, bows, then turns to Sarapha.

> JACKSON
> Don't forget, nine o'clock sharp, the middle suite on the sixth floor of
> the Savoy Hotel. (*EXITS*)

222. CUT TO STREET DOOR.

JACKSON AND RYMAN EXIT.

Margaret closes door after them then runs upstairs.

223. CUT TO BEDROOM. MARGARET ENTERS, her eyes sparkling.

> MARGARET
> That Jackson is a monster! The sooner you get away from him, the better.
>
> SARAPHA
> But what can I do? I can't fly away again! I'm afraid! The thought of being arrested and put in quarantine with other animals terrifies me.
>
> MARGARET
> That's a bluff! (*indignantly*) Afraid? Afraid of what? You are a human being!
>
> SARAPHA
> But I have no proof of it! I've lived in a cave all my life—I must go to this hotel…
>
> MARGARET
> I wouldn't.
>
> SARAPHA
> I daren't disobey them—I daren't!
>
> MARGARET
> Then leave your window open, in case you want to make a quick get away. You know where this house is? You're always welcome.
>
> SARAPHA
> I'm sorry to drag you into all this.
>
> MARGARET
> I enjoy a fight.
>
> SARAPHA
> (*pleading*)
> Please come to the hotel—I don't want to be alone with those people.
>
> MARGARET
> Don't worry, I'll be there!

224. FADE INTO DESERTED BROOK STREET. LONG SHOT.

The dawn is potential of summer, the atmosphere is soft.

The CAMERA PANS to 27 Brook Street then races up to fourth floor where Sarapha stands on window sill, ready to take off. She leaps into the air and accelerates her wings as she sails off in the direction of the Savoy Hotel. Sarapha descends on to the branch of a large tree. A tramp, asleep on a bench, awakes—he sees Sarapha on a tree.

225. CLOSE UP SARAPHA.

She looks up at sixth floor, Savoy Hotel, then leaps up to it.

226. CLOSE UP TRAMP. He takes it big.

227. THREE-QUARTER SHOT EXTERIOR HOTEL.

228. SARAPHA ENTERS from below and ENTERS room through window.

229. FULL-LENGTH SHOT.

Sarapha ENTERS room and looks about it with a lost expression. She finds a stool and sits on it, looking utterly dejected.

230. DISSOLVE TO ROOM CLOCK. It is 9 o'clock.

Telephone rings. Sarapha picks up the receiver.

> VOICE OF JACKSON
> Sarapha, are you there?

> SARAPHA
> (*hesitates*)
> Yes!

> VOICE OF JACKSON
> (*sarcastically*)
> I just wanted to be sure that you hadn't lost your way.

> SARAPHA
> I'm hungry.

> VOICE OF JACKSON
> Of course! What would you like?

> SARAPHA
> Anything but eggs or meat. Perhaps some cornflakes and cream.

231. CUT TO SITTING-ROOM JACKSON'S SUITE. FULL SHOT.

> JACKSON
> (*to woman secretary who helped kidnap Sarapha*)
> Ring for a waiter from your room and order cornflakes and cream.

> SECRETARY
> (*repeating*)
> Cornflakes and cream. (*EXITS*)

> JACKSON
> (*EXITS then ENTERS Sarapha's suite*) I've just been on the phone
> to Immigration; they are debating whether you are a human being or
> a bird! They say there's no record of your identity in Chile—but it
> might help your case if the public believe you are an angel. Dr James
> Gidson, the revivalist, also thinks so, and he is interested in your
> cause and has great influence.

Telephone rings.

> JACKSON
> Hallo! Oh yes, have him come up. (*to Sarapha*) That's the Reverend
> James Gidson now! If we can get him interested, it will be a great
> triumph. He is a brilliant orator, and you an angel from heaven…
> (*knock at the door, the secretary ENTERS with cornflakes*)

JACKSON, worried, walks up and down. He turns to the Secretary.

> JACKSON
> Are those crowds still around the hotel?

> SECRETARY
> Yes, sir. It's difficult to keep a secret like this for long!

> JACKSON
> (*worried*)
> It's getting a little out of hand.

232. KNOCK AT THE DOOR.

JACKSON opens it CAMERA PANNING with him.

ENTER Dr Gidson with gusto and a smile.

> Dr GIDSON
> I've managed to have the case postponed for three weeks, so it will give us time to organize as it were. (*he turns and rubs his hands with satisfaction, but is suddenly checked on seeing Sarapha*) Oh!

> JACKSON
> (*interposes*)
> This is Dr Gidson, the celebrated minister, and this is Saint Sarapha.

Dr Gidson, overcome, sits in a chair.

> Dr GIDSON
> I'm overwhelmed! Let me get my breath first... Those wings, are they real?

> JACKSON
> Yes, sir. The real thing! And she can fly too!

> Dr GIDSON
> (*gets up*)
> This is indeed a privilege—to meet an angel!—Even in my business! (*he laughs, perhaps too loudly*)

Jackson points perfunctorily to settee and Dr Gidson sits down.

> SARAPHA
> (*bows*)
> Pardon me! (*returning to cornflakes*).

> Dr GIDSON
> I hope I haven't come at an inopportune time.

> JACKSON
> Not at all. It's been a little hectic with the crowds outside, but an angel must be fed, you know!

As Jackson speaks, the chewing of cornflakes is heard.

> JACKSON
> As our time is limited, Dr Gidson, I think we should get to the point.

> Dr GIDSON
> (*clears his throat*)
> Ah!

233. CUT TO SARAPHA STILL EATING CORNFLAKES.

Jackson looks once or twice in her direction.

> JACKSON
> Although I'm a business man, I'm interested in religion and in the cause of humanity... (*munching of cornflakes is heard, but Jackson continues*) In these kinetic times of radio activity, man is in danger of destroying himself. He needs religion! He needs the dogma of religion to bring back his faith in Christianity. That's why we need Saint Sarapha's presence.

During Jackson's speech ("He needs religion"):

234. CUT TO SINGLE SHOT. SARAPHA STILL EATING CORNFLAKES.

She stops chewing when she hears the word "dogma," then continues chewing.

235. CLOSE-UP Dr GIDSON FEIGNING CONVICTION.

> Dr GIDSON
> Absolutely no question of doubt.

236. CUT TO JACKSON.

> JACKSON
> (*with excitement*)
> If you two get together, it will be the greatest revival in the history of mankind!

> Dr GIDSON
> Without doubt—

> JACKSON
> *You* are a brilliant speaker, and you, an angel from heaven! It will be the salvation of mankind! You can write your own ticket.

237. CUT TO Dr GIDSON GETTING IMPATIENT.

Crossing and uncrossing his legs.

> JACKSON
> (*carried away*)
> With the right publicity, you can rule the world!

238 CUT TO Dr GIDSON.

He looks at his watch.

239. BACK TO JACKSON.

> JACKSON
> One nation! One people! No more wars! It's frightening. (*he takes the hint*) All right! Let's get down to business.

> Dr GIDSON
> Ah!

CUT TO JACKSON SINGLE SHOT.

> JACKSON
> In the first place, I'll finance the proposition, put up the money — then we'll split, fifty, fifty.

240. CUT TO Dr GIDSON CLOSE UP.

> Dr GIDSON
> Of the gross.

> JACKSON
> Oh, no, no, not the gross — the profits.

There is an uncomfortable silence.

241. CUT TO CLOSE UP SARAPHA.

Chewing cornflakes.

242. CUT TO SINGLE SHOT.

> Dr GIDSON
> (*looking at Sarapha*)
> I'm sorry but I am beholden to a committee that would never accept a participation in the profits — unless we limit the expense.

243. CLOSE UP JACKSON.

> JACKSON
> (*covering his irritation*)
> Well, we can't limit the expense of a project of this nature! It will require thousands and thousands of dollars.

Dr GIDSON
I loathe saying this, but in the past we have had some very unpleasant experiences participating in profits—they even charge us for the wear and tear of the office carpets.—No. We'd sooner take less of the gross. (*turning to Sarapha*) You'll pardon me for bickering this way, but I'm beholden to members of my committee. And after our unfortunate experiences, they would never think of anything less than a percentage of the gross.

JACKSON
(*scowling*)
O.K., fifteen percent of the gross.

244. CUT TO CLOSE UP Dr GIDSON.

Dr GIDSON
(*slowly shaking his, head and turning to Sarapha*)
My committee would never accept anything less than twenty percent of the gross.

Dr GIDSON
(*he turns to Sarapha and smiles*)
I must apologise for this irksome business.

245. CLOSE UP SARAPHA.

Chewing cornflakes. Feeling she is in the way, she gets up.

SARAPHA
I think I'll finish them in the next room. (*EXITS*)

JACKSON nods and closes door after Sarapha's EXIT, then turns abruptly to Gidson.

JACKSON
O.K., twenty percent!

Dr GIDSON
Of the gross—good! Then I'll have my lawyer go over the details of the contract with your lawyer. So, I'll be off.

JACKSON
O.K., but there's one favour I'd like to ask you. If the press want to know how you became associated with Sarapha, I suggest being vague, non-committal. She came to you in a dream as it were! But the less said the better. (*Gidson EXITS*)

246. ENTER RYMAN.

RYMAN
The hotel management is complaining about the crowds in the lobby—the guests can't get to their rooms.

JACKSON
(*light heartedly*)
Well! It may be a nuisance, but it's wonderful publicity.

RYMAN
(*rubbing his hands, whispers*)
Where's the dame?

JACKSON
(*laconically*)
You mean Saint Sarapha? She's in her room eating cornflakes!

RYMAN
(*whispering*)
Everything settled?

JACKSON nods and puts his fingers to his mouth.

RYMAN
(*whispering*)
I've got an agent negotiating for one or two cripples in chairs to be in the audience, who'll get up and walk at the right time.

JACKSON
(*looks concerned*)
Be careful!

RYMAN
We're in the clear… This is done wholly through an agent.

JACKSON
She won't go for that.

RYMAN
Who?

JACKSON
The Angel.

RYMAN
She's dumb enough to go for anything! She thinks she can cure
people.

JACKSON
I'll take a look at her. (*EXITS, and ENTERS Sarapha's room*)
Hallo, how do you feel?

Sarapha, for answer, looks inscrutably at him as she chews her cornflakes.

JACKSON
At the meeting, there'll be a number of cripples who will have come
to you for help. Now's your chance to do something for humanity,
and incidently, do something for yourself. (*he EXITS*)

DISSOLVE. PHONE RINGS.

247. SARAPHA GOES TO TELEPHONE.

248. CUT TO CLOSE-UP MARGARET.

MARGARET
I'm sorry I won't be there at the meeting. Are you alone?

SARAPHA
(*looks around*)
Yes… but…

MARGARET
After the meeting, come to my house in Brook Street.

SARAPHA
But I can't come alone.

MARGARET
Listen! After the meeting, fly to Hyde Park Corner.

SARAPHA
But I'll be recognised.

MARGARET
(*excited*)
Fly to the top of Marble Arch—I'll meet you there. I mean I shall
have the blue Rolls Royce waiting for you down below. (*goes closer to
phone*) I don't want to say too much on the phone—Brook Street is
out, I shall drive you to my house in the country.

249. FADE INTO EARL'S COURT. NIGHT TIME. CROWDS MILLING ABOUT OUTSIDE.

250. DISSOLVE TO DRESSING ROOM.

Dr Gidson is thoughtfully walking up and down.

Jackson is also walking up and down.

Sarapha is sitting alone, sad and bewildered.

Voices are heard singing hymns. The sound rises like a tidal wave when the door is opened.

> JACKSON
> I wish they wouldn't sing so loud.

Ryman ENTERS full of enthusiasm and excitement.

> RYMAN
> We're packed! Not a seat to be had! We've arranged loud speakers outside so that thousands will not be disappointed.

> JACKSON
> (*to Sarapha*)
> That's why you must learn your speech. They want to hear you talk. (*reading from speech*): "I've come to bring you tidings of joy and happiness from our Heavenly Father, and to tell you that he so loved the world that he gave his only begotten son." (*turning to Gidson and handing him script*) Here, you know more about this than I do!

> Dr GIDSON
> She'll never learn that! She must depend on inspiration! (*begins to walk up and down*)

251. CLOSE UP SARAPHA.

Looking morose and sad.

252. CLOSE UP Dr GIDSON.

Placidly walking up and down.

> JACKSON
> (*worried and emotional*)
> What a night!

Dr GIDSON
(*continues walking up and down*)
Yes, quite pleasant. I hope it continues this way for the next few weeks.

JACKSON
(*in an agony of nerves*)
Where's Sarapha?

RYMAN
I don't know—She was here a moment ago. She seems to have disappeared.

FLUSHING OF A TOILET can be heard.

JACKSON
(*relieved and embarrassed*)
Oh!

253. As Doctor ENTERS and opens door of the auditorium, a tremendous roar of hymn singing is heard.

Dr Gidson ENTERS and the audience keep singing while he prays.

After prayers-he stands up. The singing then comes to an end, and silence pervades.

254. CUT TO FULL SHOT.

Showing audience.

255 CLOSE UP Dr GIDSON.

Dr GIDSON
This is an era of epical events. An era in which we have seen the world from the viewpoint of the moon. As I looked at this little round earth— partly enveloped in clouds, I realised that not a sign or trace of human history could be seen or felt. No past culture—no religion has left the slightest trace upon our little earth—and for the moment, I felt I had lost God! Yet, in that vast, black mystery of space, the eminence of God is more deeply felt than in all the words of the gospel… Most of you have recently read in the newspaper of the holy visitation that occurred at the London Cathedral. This night, at an immense cost, we have hired this hall for another visitation, and while we wait, I shall pass among you with the collection box. So let us sing a hymn of gladness.

> All things bright and beautiful,
> All creatures great and small,

> All things bright and beautiful,
> The Lord God made them all.

256. CUT TO DRESSING ROOM.

Jackson and Ryman are walking up and down.

As Jackson is about to EXIT:

> RYMAN
> Where are you going?

> JACKSON
> To keep an eye on the collection boxes!

256a. As Jackson EXITS the organ and choir begin to sing and the sound rises and swells.

When the door opens a gigantic wave of singing rises as Sarapha makes her entrance.

> While shepherds watch'd their flocks by night,
> All seated on the ground,
> The Angel of the Lord came down,
> And glory shone around.

257. CLOSE UP SARAPHA.

A look of terror is on her face as she appears.

During the second verse the singing ceases and in the silence a woman screams: "Look! Look!—The Angel of the Lord!"

258. CUT TO SECTION OF AUDIENCE.

They look where the screams come from. Some faint.

259. CLOSE UP SARAPHA.

Looking terrified. Eventually the noise subsides and Sarapha speaks.

> SARAPHA
> I don't know if I'm an angel or not. We are all a mystery… But I do
> know that life is a desire! I see it in the trees, their branches spreading
> and reaching upwards (*inspired*) and that desire is in us all! To those
> I speak who have come for help: If that desire is within you, and is
> strong enough, it will cure you. You're bound to get well!—You must
> get well!

In the pause that follows, a woman shouts: "I'm cured!—I'm cured!" Another screams and stands up in an invalid chair. Then another. Some are genuine, some are fakes. The following scene is a pandemonium of hysteria.

260. CUT TO FULL SHOT.

A cripple standing in a chair.

> CRIPPLE
> I am cured! I have the will to walk! I will walk!

261. SHOUTS AND EXCLAMATIONS.

"Hallelujah!"

262. CUT TO ANOTHER SECTION.

"Life is Desire! Desire is Life!"

263. CUT TO ANOTHER SECTION.

Somebody throws up their hands: "I have the desire to walk—I will walk!"

264. CUT TO ANOTHER SECTION.

Someone is shouting: "Peace—no more wars!!—No more sorrow!"

265. CUT TO ANOTHER SECTION.

They are chanting: "No more wars—no more sorrow—We shall have peace!! Peace is in the mind and soul!—Peace in the mind—in the soul!!"

266. CUT TO ANOTHER SECTION.

Someone shouts: "Do you want your sons killed? Do you want them crippled? Armless sons, legless sons? Then pray for peace!"

267. CUT TO ANOTHER SECTION.

"We shall have peace! If you don't want your sons killed—then pray for peace!"

268. CUT TO SOMEONE SHOUTING.

"Pray for peace—no more wars—no more sorrow!"

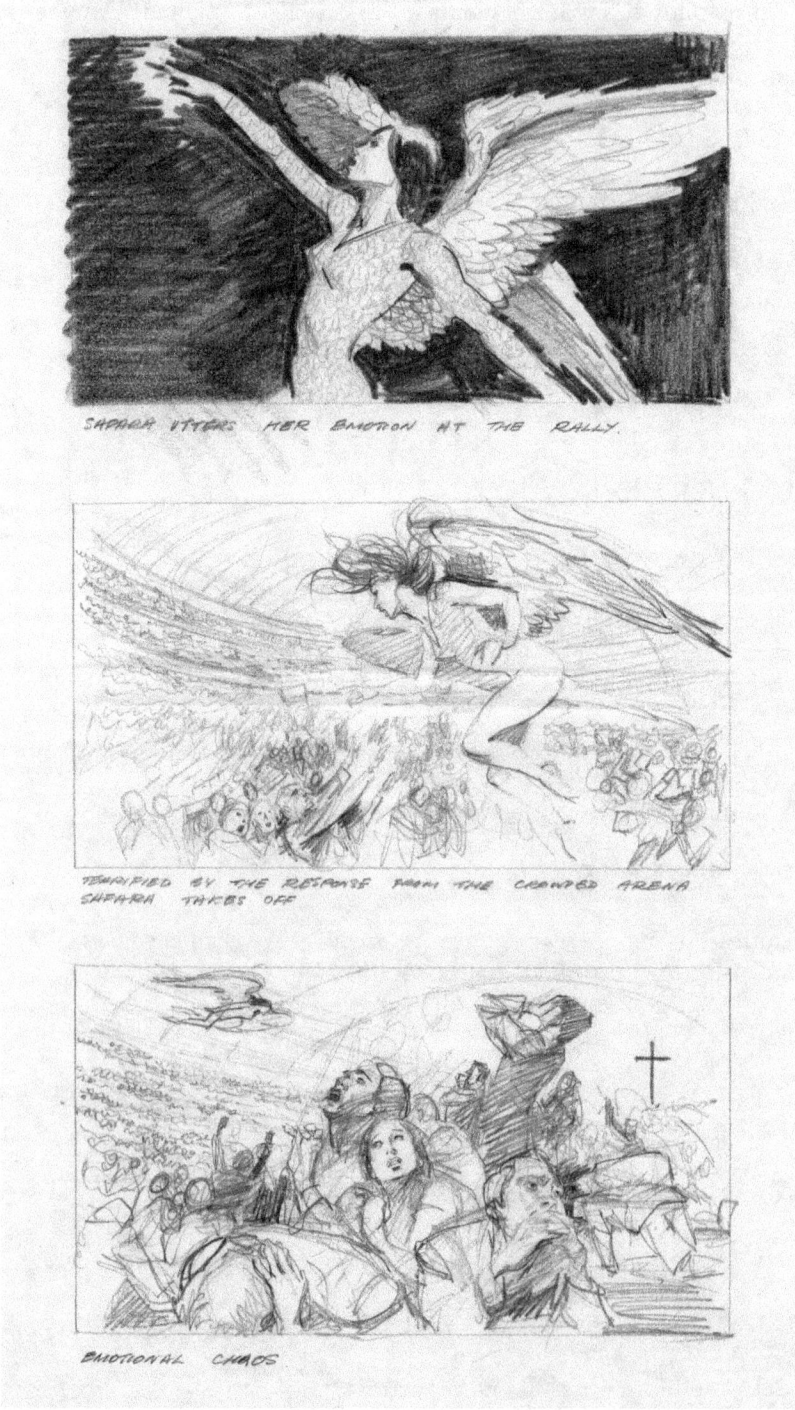

The revivalist gathering at Earl's Court. Storyboard by John Rose.

269. CUT TO ANOTHER SECTION.

They start singing hymns, which is taken up by everyone. The people around begin chanting: "No more wars, no more sorrow! The Angel of Mercy has spoken!" Some begin to fall on their knees and pray. Others scream and act like holy rollers, chanting, throwing their hands in the air, and falling and rolling on the ground.

270. CUT TO FULL SHOT.

Wave after wave of growing hysteria and increasing screams and shouting: "The Angel of Mercy has spoken—No more wars!"

271. MEDIUM SHOT SARAPHA.

Looking frightened. Her wings flutter and she begins to flit and hop about.

272. CUT TO AUDIENCE. FULL SHOT.

This evokes more hysteria, screams, and chanting.

273. CUT TO MEDIUM SHOT SARAPHA

Suddenly she takes off and flies over the heads of the audience.

274. CUT TO AUDITORIUM. FULL SHOT.

After circling once or twice, Sarapha flies out through the skylight and disappears. Sarapha circles up into the night, flaps her wings, then spreads them to catch the breeze which lifts her upwards into a cloud.

275. CUT TO SKY SHOT. OXFORD STREET LIT UP.

276. CUT TO MARBLE ARCH FROM SKY.

277. CUT TO CLOSE UP SARAPHA.

Recognising Marble Arch.

Sarapha eventually alights on the top of it unnoticed, and stands at the side of the statue, she peers intensely, looking for Margaret's blue limousine. At last she sees it.

278. CUT TO LOW SHOT.

Car moving over to curb.

279. CLOSE UP SARAPHA.

On top of Marble Arch. She is nervous and impatient, almost in tears, ready to jump.

280. CUT TO LIMOUSINE.

Door opens.

281. CUT TO TOP OF MARBLE ARCH.

Sarapha flies down and leaps into limousine. She is too emotional to pay attention to her wings. She flings her arms round Margaret's neck and bursts into tears.

> SARAPHA
> I'm afraid!—Afraid!—I want to go back to Chile—to my cave!

> MARGARET
> There there! I'll take you home—to my house!

282. CLOSE UP CHAUFFEUR.

Looking through small mirror of car. He is amazed.

283. CLOSE UP MARGARET.

> MARGARET
> (_shouting to chauffeur_)
> Trent!

284. CUT TO CHAUFFEUR.

He jumps, touches his cap, and starts car.

285. CUT TO INTERIOR LIMOUSINE.

Sarapha continues weeping. Her sobbing ceases into sporadic catching of her breath, until, eventually, she dozes off to sleep, much to Margaret's discomfort as Sarapha's wings are propped under her chin.

286. DISSOLVE TO HOUSE AT TRENT.

A typical Georgian country mansion.

287. CUT TO FULL SHOT.

Margaret getting out of car, followed by Sarapha.

CAMERA following them into house.

288. CUT TO VIEW OF HALL AND BARONIAL STAIRCASE.

289. CUT TO MEDIUM SHOT.

Sarapha looking round the baronial hall as Margaret talks to the butler. Butler, looking startled, crosses himself, as he listens to Margaret, and hands her a telegram.

> MARGARET
> (*tearing open telegram*)
> Miss Sarapha will sleep in the main guest room (*then she reads telegram*). Oh dear! "Will arrive Thursday Victoria station 12.30 Love Rex." I wish he'd stay hunting for another week or so. (*turning to Sarapha*) However, you must be very tired, so I will show you to your room.

290. CUT TO THREE-QUARTER SHOT.

As they ENTER bedroom

CAMERA PANNING with them.

> MARGARET
> I don't know how you sleep with those wings, but this is the best I can offer you (*pointing to bed*)—unless you prefer a perch or something.

> SARAPHA
> (*politely*)
> Thank you. I can manage.

> MARGARET
> Poor dear! You've been through a terrible ordeal. What with being kidnapped, and that depressing meeting—

> SARAPHA
> (*smiles*)
> It's my nerves—birds are nervous creatures you know!

Margaret sits in a chair and studies her.

> MARGARET
> How old are you?

> SARAPHA
> (*wearily*)
> I don't know—I'm supposed to be eighteen. I believe I'm very young.
>
> MARGARET
> (*laughs*)
> Never lose that belief. (*looking at Sarapha on the bed and shaking her head*) You're going to have many problems when you marry! However, don't count your chickens before they're hatched. Now what am I saying! (*EXITS*)

291. FADE INTO HOUSE OF COMMONS.

A few members are listening, and are bored with the speaker. One or two are asleep.

> M.P.
> This creature has aroused a degree of public hysteria posing as an angel. We must defer this matter until we have positively established this creature's identity. First, we must determine whether it is a bird or a human being! This will require the Royal College of Surgeons to decide. If it is a bird, then this House must act at once and have it quarantined. There are many legal processes which will have to be decided. If it should bite someone, there is the danger of rabies. It might be efficacious to have the police put out a warning that this bird—or animal—is still at large. Anyone bitten by it should go to the nearest hospital for first aid, and then notify the police.

FADE INTO

292. MARGARET'S COUNTRY HOUSE. SITTING-ROOM.

293. CLOSE-UP SARAPHA.

Looking pensive.

294. CUT TO MARGARET ENTERING.

> MARGARET
> My dear, you look sad. This confinement is not very conducive to your health or happiness. You need exercise—Tonight is the Pentagons' fancy dress ball, and we've been invited. I think it's a grand idea, being fancy dress, no one will recognise you.
>
> SARAPHA
> I don't want to embarrass you.

MARGARET
Not at all—You'll be perfectly safe there. Since your appearance
at Earl's Court angels have become quite fashionable. There'll be a
profusion of them at the ball tonight.

SARAPHA
You think it's safe?

MARGARET
Of course. The Pentagons don't know you, and as for the rest of the
guests, there'll be angels everywhere.

SARAPHA
Perhaps I'd better stay home.

MARGARET
Whatever you wish—but I don't want to leave you alone in this
house.

SARAPHA
(*smiles*)
Please don't worry! I'm used to it!

MARGARET
Well, if you should change your mind, you'll find a map on the back
of this, showing the directions. (*she produces an invitation card*) The
Pentagons' house is about sixteen miles from here as the crow flies—
there I go again!

SARAPHA
(*wistfully with emotion*)
You're wonderful!

Margaret laughs and dismisses the remark with a wave of her hand as she EXITS.

Sarapha hears the great doors open and close, the starting of car and changing of gears, the
acceleration of the engine and the noise fading into the distance.

295. DISSOLVE TO HOUSE ON THE CLIFF.

Sarapha is asleep. She is awakened by Chilean music.

296. Latham ENTERS her bedroom and they embrace.

DISSOLVE.

She has dozed off, and is awakened by a car coming into the drive and stopping outside the door. She looks at the clock and is shocked when it strikes twelve.

> SARAPHA
> Perhaps it's Margaret!

She runs to the door and sees three men getting out of the limousine.

297. CLOSE SHOT THREE MEN.

One of them is Jackson. She slams door quickly and runs upstairs. There is a long open window on the first floor. As she dives out of it, she hears the front door bell ring. In her excitement, she has forgotten the letter of directions.

> SARAPHA
> (*mumbling to herself*)
> I must have left it in the library.

Instinctively she flies in a westerly direction.

298. SKY SHOT. SHOOTING DOWN.

She recognises a large house, all lit up.

> SARAPHA
> This must be it.

299. LONG SHOT. FROM SARAPHA ABOVE.

She glides down on to the roof of Lord and Lady Pentagon's house.

300. CLOSE UP SARAPHA.

She peers down and sees a number of guests arriving.

301. LONG SHOT.

Guests arriving.

302. CUT TO ROOF.

She runs along the edge of it and stops. It is the back of the house. She softly alights below, just as a man appears round the corner of the house.

303. CUT TO CLOSE UP NIGHT WATCHMAN.

He peers at Sarapha, then approaches.

304. TWO SHOT.

> SARAPHA
> I've lost my way.
>
> NIGHT WATCHMAN
> Where do you want to go, Miss, back to the ballroom?
>
> SARAPHA
> Yes.
>
> NIGHT WATCHMAN
> I'm afraid you'll have to go through the main entrance—if you don't
> want to get lost again—I'll be happy to show you the way.

305. TRAVELLING SHOT.

He walks her to front of house where many guests are standing near the main entrance, laughing and chatting. As the two pass, nobody pays any attention to them. The night watchman points to the entrance.

> SARAPHA
> Ah! Thank you. Now I know my way.

306. FULL SHOT

She ENTERS facing the grand staircase. Three other angels pass her on the stairs. She pauses a moment.

307. CLOSE UP MARGARET.

Recognising her. She EXITS to greet Sarapha.

308. TWO SHOT.

> MARGARET
> (*smiling*)
> So you changed your mind?
>
> SARAPHA
> (*looking pale and frightened, smiles*)
> Yes.

MARGARET
First you must meet our hosts.

They EXIT.

309. CUT TO BALLROOM. FULL SHOT.

Buffet at one end, and dancing and gaiety going on.

310. CLOSE UP LADY PENTAGON.

At a table near buffet. She recognises Margaret approaching and gets up from table.

311. CLOSE THREE SHOT LADY PENTAGON.

LADY PENTAGON
Margaret, darling, do come and join us.

MARGARET
Lady Pentagon, this is Miss Sarapha.

LADY PENTAGON
(*to Sarapha*)
How do you do—Please sit down.

CAMERA follows them as they sit at the table.

312. TWO SHOT LADY PENTAGON AND SARAPHA.

LADY PENTAGON
My dear, your wings are divine. They look almost real!

The butler now pours champagne into all their glasses and offers Sarapha a glass of champagne. Sarapha looks at it questioningly.

MARGARET
Champagne! You need a little to relax you.

Sarapha sips it carefully, frowns, then nods approvingly at Margaret. Lord Pentagon approaches table. The butler draws up a chair for him.

MARGARET
This is Lord Pentagon—Miss Sarapha.

SARAPHA DANCES WITH LORD PENTAGON AT THE COSTUME BALL

AND TAKES OFF ABOVE HIS HEAD —

The masked ball of Lady Pentagon. Storyboard by John Rose.

> LORD PENTAGON
> How do you do? I've met so many angels tonight, I feel I'm in heaven.
> (*turns to Sarapha*) Are you with it?

Sarapha looks at Margaret.

> MARGARET
> (*nods*)
> Of course.

> SARAPHA
> I'm not so very good!

> MARGARET
> You must try. When you've finished, come to the pink room. We shall
> be there.

313. CUT TO BALLROOM. FULL SHOT.

> LORD PENTAGON
> It's the first time I've ever danced the bumps with an angel!

Other angels are dancing around. Nobody pays much attention to Sarapha. His Lordship raises his hands to the level of his ears and undulates in a peculiar fashion. Sarapha, feeling the effects of the champagne, falls into the mood of the dance. In the excitement, she gyrates with a slight desperation, doing the bumps better than the rest of the guests. Many of them stop dancing and watch her with amusement, forming a circle around her.

During the above, the CAMERA goes into

314. TWO SHOTS, CLOSE UPS, and moves about with Sarapha and Lord Pentagon. The music is ugly with its electric bass tones urging on the guests.

315. CUT TO GUESTS amused and watching.

Sarapha, stimulated by the champagne, forgets herself entirely, flutters her wings and rises several feet in the air. Now everyone stops, amazed, except His Lordship, who, with his back towards her, is absorbed in the merriment of dancing and does not notice that Sarapha's elevation is quite high.

316. CUT TO ORCHESTRA.

It stops playing and watches Sarapha, who is too carried away to notice anything. The music terminates, the guests applaud. Sarapha thanks His Lordship and leaves him to find her way to the pink room.

317. CUT TO PASSAGE leading to pink room. Sarapha ENTERS.

318. THREE-QUARTER SHOT.

She stops suddenly looking down at floor.

INSERT OF DIAMOND EAR RING.

319. CLOSE UP SARAPHA.

She stares as though under the spell of a magpie. Quickly she snatches up the ear ring and EXITS into pink room and innocently fastens it to her left ear, then looks in the mirror.

Margaret and Lady Pentagon ENTER.

> LADY PENTAGON
> (*looking concerned*)
> Someone has lost an ear ring. I wonder if she left it here.

320. TWO SHOT.

Sarapha is standing in a position which prevents Margaret from seeing her left ear ring.

CAMERA follows them as they search the pink room. When Margaret turns, Sarapha innocently turns too, so that the left ear cannot be seen.

321. CUT TO COUNTESS LEBENDOFF ENTERING. MEDIUM SHOT.

> LADY PENTAGON
> We've looked everywhere, but there's not a particle sign of it.

322. CUT TO MARGARET AND SARAPHA.

They both look bewildered. Margaret turns quickly to Sarapha who innocently turns in a direction that still hides her left ear from Margaret.

> MARGARET
> (*to Countess Lebendoff*)
> Are you sure you lost it here?

> COUNTESS LEBENDOFF
> Well, I'm not sure…

> MARGARET
> Then we must go on looking for it.

> COUNTESS LEBENDOFF
> Oh please don't bother—it's insured.

Suddenly Margaret turns and sees the ear ring dangling from Sarapha's left ear.

> MARGARET
> (*astonished*)
> Sarapha, may I speak to you a moment? (*turning to Countess*)
> Will you excuse me, I'll join you later.

323. TWO SHOT.

Margaret leads Sarapha away.

324. CUT TO HALL.

Margaret and Sarapha ENTER.

> MARGARET
> (*stops, turns, and confronts Sarapha*)
> My dear, where did you find that ear ring?

> SARAPHA
> (*innocently*)
> I picked it up.

> MARGARET
> Give it to me quickly. I'll give it to one of the servants. He can say he
> found it.

Sarapha innocently hands the ear ring to Margaret. Margaret hurriedly leaves Sarapha. At that moment, music of the bumps starts again and Lord Pentagon arrives. With Sarapha, he takes the position for starting to dance. Then Sarapha sees Jackson, with two other men, standing in the entrance. She immediately recognises Jackson and makes an excuse to Lord Pentagon.

> SARAPHA
> Excuse me! (*she EXITS rapidly to the grand staircase*)

325. DISSOLVE. Sarapha finds herself in an ante-room. She tries to lock the door, but it won't lock. There is a knock at the door from outside. Sarapha quickly puts a chair under the door handle then opens the window. She EXITS through the window as knocking continues.

326. CUT TO ROOF.

Sarapha alights on it.

327. DISSOLVE INTO SAME SET.

Sarapha appears behind a chimney stack. She creeps to the edge of the roof and looks over, listening to the dogs barking and cars driving up.

328. CUT TO BELOW. FRONT OF HOUSE.

Hunting dogs and blood hounds are sniffing about and barking, led by policemen and men. More police cars arrive.

329. CUT TO ROOF.

In a medley of the barking dogs and arrival of police cars, Sarapha takes off and flies up into the night.

330. DISSOLVE TO A QUIET PICTURESQUE ENGLISH VILLAGE.

Sarapha has lost her way. She alights on a building opposite a town hall.

331. CUT TO FRONT OF TOWN HALL.

There are typical announcements of meetings, political and otherwise. One announcement is for tonight: "Dr Everman, Atheist, will speak on Religion."

332. CUT TO SARAPHA ON OPPOSITE BUILDING.

Far off the rumbling of thunder is heard. There is a frightful stab of lightning overhead, then crash of thunder, and large raindrops begin to fall. The rain increases into a cloud burst as thunder strikes and lightning flashes. Lost and terrified, Sarapha decides to find shelter out of the storm.

333. CLOSE UP SARAPHA.

Looking frightened as storm increases. She looks across at an open window, and flies over to it, hanging on to the window sill to look inside.

A voice can be heard: "I do not believe in the Bible! Neither in the Old Testament, nor in the New Testament. In fact, I do not believe in spiritual manifestations of any kind…"

334. CUT TO INTERIOR OF CHAMBER.

Window at the back showing Sarapha looking in from the outside. The room is empty, possibly a committee room. Sarapha looks to find a place to hide—but is undecided.

Suddenly thunder strikes and a bolt of lightning makes her decide quickly!

She hops into the empty committee room. She hears voices and footsteps approaching and seeing a door open, quickly hides behind it. A typical committee member walks in. As he closes the door, he catches sight of Sarapha hiding behind it. But he only blinks, as though something is wrong with his eyesight, takes a tablet from his pocket, then pours a glass of water from a jug and swallows the pill.

335. CUT TO SARAPHA STEALTHILY CREEPING OUT OF THE ROOM.

336. CUT TO PASSAGEWAY WITH STAIRS LEADING DOWN TO SOMEWHERE.

Sarapha, startled, ENTERS and looks around, hears voices and footsteps approaching, and quickly darts into a hall leading downstairs.

337. CUT TO LECTURE HALL.

Where Dr Everman is lecturing.

> Dr EVERMAN
> As Professor Einstein said, he does not believe in mystic manifesta-
> tions unless witnessed by twelve other scientists. How can there be
> a heaven, as the Bible will have us believe, when three young men
> having touched the moon must isolate and sterilise themselves for
> three weeks against X-ray bacteria and radio activity. How can there
> be a heaven with angels sitting on clouds, playing harps?

Suddenly there is a gasp of emotion from the audience.

338. CUT TO CLOSE UP SARAPHA.

She finds herself on the lecture platform. She has a startled expression.

339. CUT TO Dr EVERMAN.

He turns and sees Sarapha, then faints before she flies upwards, through the transom, and escapes into the night.

340. DISSOLVE TO MARGARET'S COUNTRY HOUSE.

Then to

341. INTERIOR OF SITTING-ROOM.

Sir Rex Horton is having supper.

BUTLER
I have placed your bags and laid out your clothes in the blue guest
room, sir. The principal guest room is occupied by Miss Sarapha as
you were not expected until the twenty-first.

REX
Miss Sarapha? Who's she?

BUTLER
The angel, sir.

REX
(*looks up from his supper*)
Angel?

BUTLER
Yes, sir.

REX
Have I met her?

BUTLER
I don't think so, sir. She is the lady with wings. There has been quite
a lot about her in the papers. You might have read about the Earl's
Court meeting—the lady is reputed to be an angel!

REX
An angel indeed!—She's staying here?

BUTLER
Yes, sir. But she has gone with Madam Margaret to Lord and Lady
Pentagon's house, to stay the night. They are having a charity ball
there.

REX
Then I won't wait up for them. You have put my clothes in the blue room?

BUTLER
Yes, sir. Is that all, sir?

REX
That's all, James.

BUTLER
Good night, sir.

>REX
>Good night, James.

342. DISSOLVE TO WINDOW. NIGHT TIME.

Sarapha alights on the roof of Margaret's house and makes her way along the ledge until she comes to her room. The window is open, she ENTERS quickly through it, then accidentally closes it down with a bang.

343. CUT TO SIR REX HORTON'S ROOM.

He picks up the telephone.

>REX
>Someone is moving about in the guest room.

>BUTLER
>It might be Miss Sarapha, sir. She may have returned through the window.

>REX
>(*dispelling his sense of incredibility*)
>Will you please find out and phone me back.

>BUTLER
>Yes, sir.

Rex puts the phone down and a moment later it rings.

>BUTLER
>Miss Sarapha is home, sir.

>REX
>Put me on to her room will you, please.

>BUTLER
>Yes, sir.

344. CUT TO SARAPHA'S ROOM.

A moment later. Telephone rings. She answers it hesitatingly.

>SARAPHA
>Yes?

REX
I am Sir Rex Horton. I understand that you are our distinguished
guest.

SARAPHA
How do you do, sir.

REX
How do you do—I thought that you were staying the night at Lord
and Lady Pentagon's House.
SARAPHA
I was—but I had a sudden headache.

REX
Too bad. I'm sorry, I hope you are rid of it by now.

SARAPHA
Thank you.

REX
Is Margaret with you?

SARAPHA
No. I think she is staying the night at Lord and Lady Pentagon's
house.

REX
And what are you doing?

SARAPHA
I'm about to go to sleep—I hope to have the pleasure of meeting you in
the morning. Good night, sir. (*she replaces phone and prepares for sleep*)

345 DISSOLVE TO SAME ROOM. SARAPHA ASLEEP.

There is a gentle tapping at the door. Sarapha sits up with a start. Yes! She sees the handle of
the door quietly turning.

346. CUT TO INSERT DOOR HANDLE TURNING.

REX's VOICE
Don't be alarmed, it's Rex. Open the door a moment.

SARAPHA
(*coldly*)
What do you want?

> REX
> I left important papers in the desk by the window.

Reluctantly she opens the door and Rex looms up in the doorway. He has evidently been drinking.

> REX
> I'm sorry to awaken you, but I just wanted to see what an angel
> looked like.
> SARAPHA
> (*coldly*)
> I'm not an angel!

> REX
> You have the world believing you are, and they're not easily fooled.

> SARAPHA
> I don't wish to fool anyone! I am a freak, half bird, and half woman!

> REX
> Exciting!

> SARAPHA
> There is very little that's exciting about me.

> REX
> Don't believe it—You are quite beautiful.

He ENTERS the room and boldly sits on the end of her bed. She quickly gets out the other side.

> SARAPHA
> Please, I want to sleep.

> REX
> (*with a grin on his face as he approaches he*r)
> I thought we'd do something sacrilegious!

> SARAPHA
> Please!

He catches her by the wrist and tries to kiss her. She fights and screams, shouting: 'I hate you!' He places his hand over her mouth. Immediately she bites it. In the struggle that follows, he twists her arm, but with her free arm she manages to reach the dressing table, upon which is a pair of scissors and stabs him in the back and chest. Then, seeing what she has done, she opens the window and flies away.

347. FADE INTO JACKSON'S APARTMENT.

Ryman is reading a newspaper.

Jackson is having his breakfast.

> RYMAN
> (*reading from newspaper*)
> "Sir Rex Horton, fiancé of Mrs Margaret Latham, was found
> stabbed to death in one of the guest rooms at Mrs Margaret Latham's
> country house. According to investigations, the crime must have
> been committed while Mrs Latham was visiting Lord Pentagon's
> house. Developments were uncovered by the police, who are now
> looking for Sarapha, the reputed angel, whose appearance at Earl's
> Court created a sensation. Since the discovery, Sarapha, a guest of
> Mrs Latham has been missing. The angel is wanted by the police for
> questioning."

> JACKSON
> Sooner or later, they'll find her. She's too conspicuous to be flying
> around free…

> RYMAN
> (*continues reading*)
> "The butler said that he served supper to Sir Rex and later heard
> screams coming from Sarapha's room, and discovered that Sir Rex
> had been stabbed to death with a pair of scissors. The police are still
> searching for Sarapha." Well, I think we should be glad to be rid of
> our property!

348. CUT TO MARGARET'S COUNTRY HOUSE.

One of the top rooms has a window wide open. Police are stalking about stealthily, some are
carrying rope nets. Police Captain with two other men ENTER.

> POLICE CAPTAIN
> (*whispering*)
> All the windows are closed. This is the only way she can get into the
> house.

> DETECTIVE
> Don't you think we should keep the kitchen window open? She's
> bound to get hungry.

JACKSON ASSAULTS SARAPHA —

SHE PICKS UP THE SCISSORS —

Above, right and over: storyboards created in June 1969 by John Rose,
from a version of the script in which Jackson assaults Sarapha.

THE POLICE WAIT AS SARAPHA ENTERS MARGARET'S TOWN HOUSE

THEY SWITCH ON THE LIGHTS AS THEY ATTACK—

SAPARA STRUGGLES WITH MARGARET'S BOY-FRIEND —

STABS HIM WITH THE SCISSORS.

> POLICE CAPTAIN
> We've had it open ever since Mrs Latham left, and she hasn't turned
> up there yet!

> POLICE CAPTAIN
> Besides, it's too obvious, the kitchen! Like setting a trap for mice with
> food in it! (*a shadow from the moon flies by*) Hallo! What's that? Turn
> off the light! You'd better be careful, she's dangerous. Remember
> she's an animal!

At last the waiting is rewarded. A flying shadow passes along the wall. The men quickly back
out of sight. Some get behind curtains. Sarapha flies down to window sill and looks in, her
wings flapping slowly, to see if anybody is inside. Satisfied that no one is around, she hops in.
Immediately, the police catch her and she begins to cry like a seagull.

FADE INTO

349. POLICE CELL.

Sarapha is huddled in a corner with a rope net over her.

> WARDER
> (*to Margaret*)
> I wouldn't go too near, Madam, she's dangerous.

> MARGARET
> I'm not afraid. Sarapha! This is Margaret.

Sarapha does not answer.

> MARGARET
> Professor Latham has come to see you.

Sarapha looks up in a daze, and recognises Latham.

> SARAPHA
> Did you finish your book?

> LATHAM
> (*smiles*)
> Yes. And now, I've come to help you and to tell you that Margaret
> and I have an excellent Counsel for you, so don't worry.

350. DISSOLVE TO COURTROOM.

Sarapha is listening to the Counsel for the defence, who is just finishing his plea.

> COUNSEL FOR THE DEFENCE
> My Lord, there are many extenuating circumstances. (*to the jury*)
> Witnesses have testified that Sarapha is a freak, half woman and half
> bird. She was anybody's property. What happened was in defence of
> this poor creature's honour. With these words, I leave her fate in your
> hands.

351. DISSOLVE TO SAME COURT ROOM.

> CLERK OF COURT
> Everybody stand up, please.

The Jury files in. The Judge ENTERS.

After the usual formalities:

> JUDGE
> Ladies and Gentlemen of the Jury, what is your verdict?

> FOREMAN
> Not guilty!

352. CUT TO CLOSE UP SARAPHA.

She is expressionless.

353. CUT TO CLOSE UP JUDGE.

> JUDGE
> Miss Sarapha, the jury has found you not guilty, but because of the
> peculiar circumstances of your case, I shall have to place you in
> custody until the quarantine department has decided what to do with
> you. Therefore, you will be detained in quarantine until that matter is
> settled.

FADE INTO

354. MARGARET'S TOWN HOUSE. SITTING-ROOM.

Margaret is nervously walking up and down.

Butler ENTERS and announces Professor Latham.

> LATHAM
> (*elated, and after embracing Margaret*)
> Good news! Somerset House has turned up the records of Sarapha's

birth certificates. The records show that her family were English missionaries for three generations.

MARGARET
We must go at once and tell Sarapha. (*she gets up and rings bell for Butler*) Poor dear, she'll be so happy to get out of that horrible quarantine.

Butler ENTERS.

MARGARET
Will you please have the limousine ready as soon as possible.

BUTLER
Yes, Madam.

MARGARET
That poor child! Three weeks she's been in that wretched place!

LATHAM
Now that she is free, what are you going to do about her?

MARGARET
Look after her as well as we can, I suppose.

355. DISSOLVE TO OFFICES OF QUARANTINE DEPARTMENT.

It is very much like a zoo: dogs barking etc. Hundreds of photographers and reporters are milling about, waiting for any minor incident.

ENTER Margaret and Latham.

QUARANTINE OFFICER
Good morning, Madam. Congratulations!

MARGARET
Thank you. Has Miss Sarapha heard the news?

QUARANTINE OFFICER
Not yet. She's still asleep.

MARGARET
Poor dear, she needs all the rest she can get. How is she this morning?

QUARANTINE OFFICER
Much better! Occasionally, she weeps. But normally, she is very sweet.

Margaret turns round and sees all the reporters and photographers.

> QUARANTINE OFFICER
> I've tried to keep them from bothering her. We have extra police for
> that.

> LATHAM
> (*to Margaret*)
> You'd better take these release papers.

> MARGARET
> Thank you, my love. (*turns to officer*) Well, I believe we have the
> documents you want.

> QUARANTINE OFFICER
> Thank you, Madam. (*after reading them*) Everything is in order. This
> way, Madam.

He opens door into a room that could be private except for the bars and cage-like effect in
front of the window.

Photographers and reporters rush to get a snapshot or a glimpse of Sarapha.

Margaret and Latham ENTER.

Sarapha is asleep in the corner, her face buried in her arms.

> MARGARET
> (*gently touches Sarapha's shoulder*)
> Sarapha! This is Margaret, and here is Professor Latham.

Sarapha looks up, then seeing the Professor she half smiles.

> MARGARET
> We've come to take you home.

Sarapha looks listlessly at Margaret and Latham.

> MARGARET
> Don't you understand? You're free now!

Sarapha slowly buries her face in her arms and goes off to sleep again.

> MARGARET
> (*looking tearfully at Latham*)
> It's awful! She doesn't want to leave!

356. FADE INTO SITTING-ROOM OF MARGARET'S TOWN HOUSE.

> LATHAM
> (*sits down, exhausted*)
> That's a big place, Somerset House, and I've been all over it. (*he takes tea from butler and Margaret pours another cup*) What are we going to call Sarapha. By her family name?
>
> MARGARET
> She prefers to be called Sarapha, the name you gave her.

Latham nods then becomes thoughtful.

> LATHAM
> What are we going to do about her?
>
> MARGARET
> I don't know. She worries me. She's so preoccupied.
>
> LATHAM
> We should go away somewhere.
>
> MARGARET
> She keeps talking about Chile. How beautiful it is there.
>
> LATHAM
> But that's too far.
>
> MARGARET
> She's not happy here. (*there is a timid knock at the door*) Sarapha?
>
> SARAPHA
> May I come in?
>
> MARGARET
> Of course. Like some tea? (*she hands her a cup of tea*)

SARAPHA turns and sees LATHAM.

> SARAPHA
> (*cheerfully*)
> Ah! Professor Latham!

She smiles. But as she puts her cup down, it rattles from her trembling.

> MARGARET
> My dear, we were just deciding that we all need a holiday, and should
> get away from these awful reporters and photographers, so we
> thought of taking the yacht and going to Cornwall, the air is bracing
> and it will do you good.

> SARAPHA
> (*enthusiastically*)
> That's towards Chile!

> MARGARET
> Yes, darling, but Chile's too far. We'll go there another time—Besides,
> Edward's book will be out shortly, and we all want to be here for
> that.

Sarapha smiles and sips her tea.

FADE.

357. FADE IN. NIGHT TIME.

Sarapha stands on the roof of Margaret's town house. The night is pale and the moon is clear, and Sarapha spreads her wings and takes off.

358. DISSOLVE TO THE MIDDLE OF THE OCEAN. CHILEAN MUSIC IS PLAYING.

359. CLOSE UP SARAPHA.

Flying in pale moonlight.

360. DISSOLVE TO MIDDLE OF THE ATLANTIC OCEAN.

The sun shines fiercely, the morning is hot and sultry, and the ocean looks stale and inactive. Far off is a fishing boat.

There is a spot on the horizon. The Captain of the fishing boat takes his binoculars and looks:

> CAPTAIN
> What's that?—Could be amber grease. We'll go take a look!

He moves the steering wheel in that direction.

361. DISSOLVE TO BOAT NEAR THE FLOATING DEBRIS.

362. CUT TO CLOSE UP SARAPHA.

Her body floating, her wings spread, her face downwards.

> CAPTAIN
> (*with excitement*)
> Lower the skiff!

363. DISSOLVE TO NEWSPAPER HEADLINES.

"The Freak found dead in the middle of the Atlantic Ocean."

364. DISSOLVE TO MARGARET'S SITTING-ROOM.

She has been weeping.

LATHAM puts down the newspaper thoughtfully and goes to her side.

> LATHAM
> Poor Sarapha! Her life was impossible. Now her problems are over.

FADE.

THE END.

The Flight of Sarapha. Drawings by Gerald Larn.

Charlie Chaplin in *The Kid* (1921).

The Lure of the Winged Humanoid

Oddly—given the cinema's life-long delight in tricks and special effects—Chaplin's conception of a winged humanoid has been a comparative rarity in cinema. Roger Vadim's *Barbarella* (1968) had Pygar (John Philip Law), a blind angel who had lost the will to fly. In 1974, Marcel Carné, at the final extreme of his creative decline, made an unworthy adaptation of H. G. Wells' *The Wonderful Visit* (*La Merveilleuse Visite*, 1974), about the misfortunes of a straying angel, exposed to human nastiness. These were winged: but most airborne cinema protagonists have found other contrivances to achieve flight—Superman and Batman their miraculous cloaks, and Mary Poppins her umbrella. The angels in Wim Wenders' *Wings of Desire* (1987) and Brad Silberling's 1998 Hollywood remake, *City of Angels*, had no need for wings, though Wenders' poster cheekily conferred a pair on Bruno Ganz.

With the close of the 20th century, however, generously be-winged angels won greater presence on the screen. In the title role of Nora Ephron's *Michael* (1996), John Travolta boasted archangelic wings which are somewhat at odds with his enthusiastic embrace of a saucily human life-style during a visitation to rural Iowa. In Kevin Smith's *Dogma* (1999) Alan Rickman was the seraph Metatron. In the title role of Luc Besson's 2005 *Angel-A*, Rie Rasmussen reveals her splendid wings at the moment when she must rescue the incorrigible loser André (Jamel Debbouze) from fatal despair. Tilda Swinton embodies a curly blonde Archangel Gabriel in the comic-book-inspired *Constantine* (2005, directed by Francis Lawrence).

The most ambitious film filled with winged humanoids, however, suffered the same fate as *The Freak*, and never came to light. In 2004 Philip de Blasi and Brian Willinger wrote a script for a film adaptation of Milton's *Paradise Lost*, which was accepted by producer Vincent Newman and Legendary Pictures. The final script was largely the work of Rupert Hazeldine. The synopsis was simple:

> Lucifer and Michael, the two most powerful archangels, are bound by deep friendship until God creates Man, his greatest work. Lucifer, unable to remain submissive to God should this mean lowering himself before mankind, begins his dark decline and is cast out—devoting himself from then on solely to revenge.

The director was to be Alex Proyas, of Greek origin, and an agreement was made with Warner Bros. for production and financing. From the beginning it was assumed that Bradley Cooper would play the leading role of Lucifer, assisted by an all-star cast. Proyas on his part planned to shoot in 3D. The electrifying visual impressions created by set designer Owen Patterson and talented concept artist David Woodland give an idea of what the film could have been.

Jackie Coogan and Charlie Chaplin in *The Kid* (1921).

Forty years after *The Freak*, the authors of *Paradise Lost* wouldn't have had to struggle, as Chaplin had, with mechanical harnesses and swan feathers imported from South Africa. The free flight of the archangels could have been profitably entrusted, at some cost, to computer generated imagery. The weeks and months-long post-production on CGI was the biggest item of budget expense. A start date was set for January 2012 in Sydney, but at the last moment Legendary suspended work, in an attempt to reduce the $120 million budget to a figure closer to the initial $100 million. In early February, the project was finally abandoned.

However, silent cinema had afforded one memorable instance of multiple winged humanoids—in Chaplin's own 1921 masterpiece, *The Kid*. Having lost his adopted Kid, and exhausted by the search, Chaplin the Tramp falls asleep on his doorstep, and dreams of Paradise, with all the characters of the film—bully, cop, orphanage officials, stray dog and the Kid himself—transformed into genial winged angels. But sin and temptation creep in, in the form of a flirtatious angelic seductress, played by 12-year-old Lillita MacMurray, who four years later, as Lita Grey, was to become Chaplin's second and most problematic child-wife. The sequence divided contemporary critics: Sir James Barrie, of all whimsical writers, charged Chaplin with whimsy; but the Irish-born Francis Hackett (1883–1962), in *The New Republic*, celebrated the sequence as "a simple man's version of the Big Change, made up from the few properties with which a simple man would be likely to be acquainted."[*]

---

[*] Francis Hackett in *The New Republic*, Vol. XXVI, no. 338, p. 136.

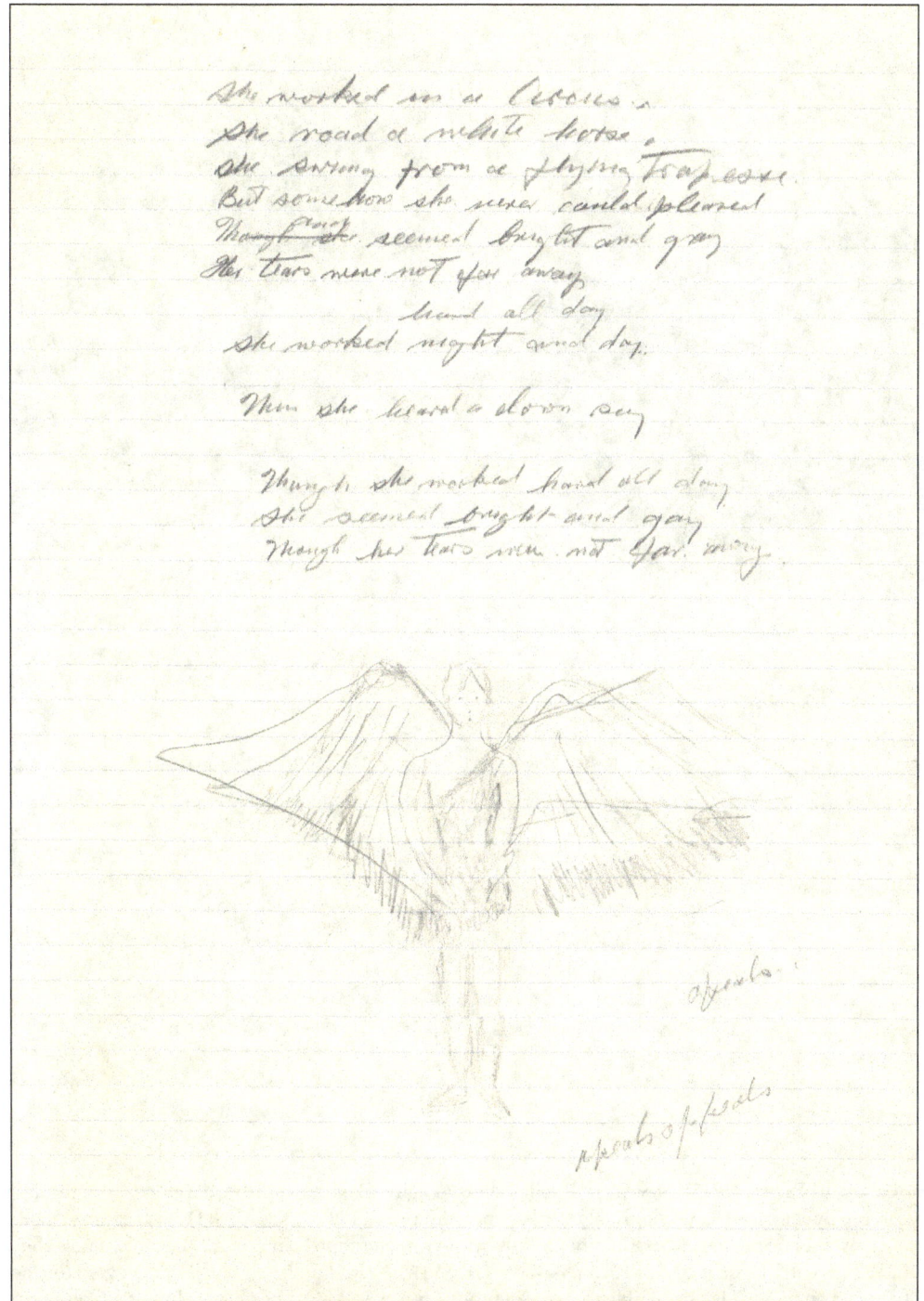

Notes for the opening song of 1968 reissue of *The Circus* (1928),
which Chaplin was working on at the same time he conceived *The Freak*.

Above: "Icarus Fallen" (1845), New York Public Library Digital Collections/Edvard Munch, "Harpy" (1894) Clarence Buckingham Collection/"Ulysses Passing the Sirens" (1894), New York Public Library Digital Collections. Right: Six-winged Seraph, from a 12th-century manuscript/Ivan Bilibin, "Bird of Paradise Sirin," (1905)/Terracotta statuette of a mermaid, Ancient Greece, Museum Purchase Fund/Engraving on the foot of Tutankhamun's golden shrine/Henri Fantin-Latour, "Réveil" (1886), The Charles Deering Collection/ "Nemesis," 1502, The New York Public Library Digital Collections/"Apollo in chariot drawn by two winged horses; Sphinx, panther, griffin and lion, 1844–1861," New York Public Library Digital Collections.

If Sarapha is a *rara avis* in cinema, universal mythology on the contrary is overrun by creatures with human bodies but borne on wings, from Nemesis with her whip, to the Sirens. Abrahamic religions have their orders of Angels: the name Sarapha is evidently derived from the title of the highest order of Christian angelology, the six-winged Seraphim. On the verso of an orphan page from a draft of *The Freak*, someone (not Chaplin) has gone to the trouble of writing the individual names of the Seraphim, but this line of research seems not to have been pursued further.

The most celebrated winged human, Icarus, relied of course, on a fabrication. His father Daedalus constructed the wings, using feathers and wax, to facilitate their escape from Crete. Daedalus warned his son not to fly too low lest the damp from the sea clog his wings, or too high, where the sun might melt them. Icarus flew too high, and fell, like Chaplin's Sarapha, to die in the ocean.

The earliest pictorial depiction of a winged humanoid, dating from the 14th century B.C., only came fully to light in 2019, when Tutankhamun's coffins, discovered almost a century before, were removed from the tomb for restoration, to reveal that the foot of the golden inner coffin bore an exquisite engraving of a winged humanoid of uncertain sex.

In literature, the mother of all winged humanoids is Youwarkee, in a mysterious masterpiece published in 1751, *The Life and Adventures of Peter Wilkins, A Cornish Man.* Not until 1835—with the discovery of the original publisher's contract—was the author, "R.P." eventually identified as Robert Paltock (1697–1767), an obscure resident of Clement's Inn, London. The book had only a single critical notice on its appearance, in *The Monthly Review*, which

Peter Wilkins.
Life and Adventures.
Illustration by Phiz
(George Vickers, 1862).

-8a-

as days went by

~~Days that followed~~, Sarapha's sadness deepened. She consoled herself, however, with the bitter thought that whatever happened, ~~he~~ could never enjoy the pleasures of fleetness, flying above clouds and skimming the sea. He was confined to legs that dragged one after the other – *and neither joy* that depended on automation to get him somewhere.

In spite of herself, her ornithological urge began to grow. She wanted to fly ~~again~~, to lift her feet off the ground and soar to the sky and breathe fresh mountain air, to fly away from sadness.

She had not flown since she was in love. She needed practice. She stood a moment exercising her wings, closing her eyes, and breasting the wind. Then ~~she~~ ran – but she could not get off the ground. – After several attempts, she stumbled and fell.

The Professor had witnessed the scene from the library window and ran to her aid. They never spoke, he understood.

"I wonder if I will ever fly again," she said sadly.

Page of preparatory notes for *The Freak*.

dismissed it as a poor derivative of the imaginary expeditions of *Robinson Crusoe* and *Gulliver's Travels*, though conceding that "if the invention of wings for mankind to fly with is sufficient amends for all the dullness and unmeaning extravagance of the author, we are willing to allow that his book has some merit, and that he deserves some encouragement at least as an able mechanic, if not as a good author."

Later generations were to revalue the book, whose extravagant invention and engaging first-person narrative were highly regarded by Scott, Coleridge and Leigh Hunt and their contemporaries, and *Peter Wilkins* has remained in print ever since. An anonymous dramatisation was a success at the Theatre Royal, Covent Garden in 1827, and Wilkins became a favourite theme for pantomimes during the first half of the nineteenth century. The special attraction of the story remains Paltock's invention of the *Gawry,* or flying people, the most beautiful of whom, Youwaakee, becomes Peter Wilkins' spouse.

Youwaakee's arrival in the story is startlingly like Sarapha's descent on Latham's cliff house in the opening scenes of *The Freak*. Wilkins suspected he was about to be attacked by some unknown force:

> I had scarce got the gun in my hand… when I felt such a thump upon the roof of my antechamber as shook the whole fabric and set me all over into a tremor. I then heard a sort of shriek, and a rustle near the door of my apartment; all of which seemed very terrible. But I, having before determined to see what and who it was, resolutely opened my door and leaped out. I saw nobody; all was quite silent, and nothing that I could perceive but my own fear amoving, I went then to the corner of the building, and there looking down, by the glimmer of my lamp, which stood in the window, I saw something in human shape lying at my feet.[*]

---

[*] Robert Paltock, *The Life and Adventures of Peter Wilkins, a Cornish Man*, Reeves & Turner, London 1884.

Paulette Goddard and H. G. Wells in Palm Springs, 1940.

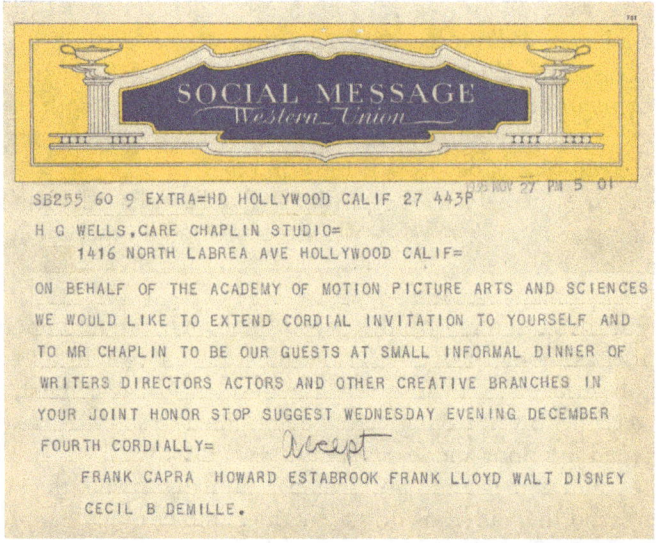

Telegram addressed to Wells at Chaplin's studios
during his stay in Hollywood, November 27, 1935

Just as in *The Freak,* this human shape proves to be a beautiful young woman, injured and unconscious, whom Wilkins nurses back to health, and teaches to communicate with him. Still without any awareness of Youwaakee's aerial capability, Wilkins takes her into his home. They fall in love and decide to marry—a ceremony informally but expediently accomplished by simply getting into bed together. In bed, Peter is bewildered to find, as he believes, that Youwaakee remains fully dressed. Then he realizes that what he takes to be a garment is her "*graundee,*" the wings that closely enwrap her when not in use. This is explained and Youwaukee graciously withdraws her *graundee,* "till putting my hand again to the softest skin, and most delightful body, free from all impediment, presented itself to my wishes, and gave itself up to my embraces."* The marriage unsurprisingly goes on to produce plentiful off-spring, endowed only with vestigial wings, sadly inadequate for flight.

Leigh Hunt's rhapsody on Youwaakee could have described Sarapha's place in Latham's home and heart as Chaplin conceived it in early drafts of *The Freak*:

> Now a sweeter creature [than Youwarkee] is not to be found in books; and she does him [Paltock] permanent honour. She is all tenderness and vivacity; all born good taste and blessed companionship. Her pleasure consists but in his. She prevents [i.e. anticipates] all his wishes; has neither prudery nor immodesty; sheds not a tear but from right feeling; is the good of his home and the grace of his fancy.[†]

Did Chaplin know *Peter Wilkins*? The stage versions were long before his time, but the book has always been accessible and eminently readable. In 1928 Dent and Dutton issued the most beautiful edition, one of the first books illustrated by the young Edward Bawden, which might well have tempted Chaplin for his library.

Another notable literary work, however, closer to home, is likely to have been a stronger inspiration for the spirit of *The Freak*, if not for specific incident. Its author, H. G. Wells, had remained a valued friend of Chaplin since 1921, when Chaplin impetuously stopped work in his Hollywood studio, to take a trip to Europe. He had left England on October 2, 1912 as the young rising star of a touring vaudeville company. He returned on September 9, 1921 as the most recognised and best-loved figure in the world. In London he found himself lionized by the great figures of society, literature, theatre and the arts in general. He particularly looked forward to meeting H. G. Wells, who had written to him in concern when he read that Chaplin had suffered burns while shooting *The Idle Class*. Now Wells wrote to him:

> I've just discovered that you are in town. Do you want to meet Shaw? He is really very charming out of the limelight. I suppose you are overwhelmed with invitations, but if there is a chance to get hold of you for a talk, I will be charmed. How about a weekend with me at Easton, free from publicity and with harmless, human people. No phones in the house.[‡]

---

* *The Life and Adventures of Peter Wilkins*, a Cornish Man, op. cit.

† Leigh Hunt, *Of Peter Wilkins and the Flying Woman*, in "Leigh Hunt London Journal," November 5, 1934.

‡ All quotations on this page are from Charles Chaplin, *My Trip Abroad*, Harper & Brothers, New York & London, 1933, pp. 89, 96, 100 (first edition 1922). Correspondence preserved in the Chaplin Archives shows that Chaplin hired Louis Monta Bell as his ghostwriter for the book.

BUT SHE WOULD NOT BE A LADY

by

H. G. WELLS

Christabel Grace is an orphan. Her mother died when she was seven and she has been brought up chiefly by her maternal uncle who runs a wayside garage in Connecticut. She has never known who her father is/ The uncle is a clever mechanic and a bit of an inventor. His wife is a nonentity and the child is brought up as a boy with no feminine associates. She happens to have a natural aptitude for mechanism. She has no dolls and she is never happier than when she has a monkey wrench in hand and a well smudged face.

She is first seen in trousers and with a blackened face helping her uncle take down an engine, and she is evidently a competent and trusted assistant.

But Christabel, none the less, has a father. He is a very rich man indeed, the great speculator, Mr. Robert Paragania. He has married and divorced his wife, and he is childless. He is a vain, jealous, self-tormented imaginative man. He has one outstanding romantic incident in his past. He lived with Ruth Grace, the mother of Christabel, for a time but he would not marry her because she was a dancer. He kept her in a flat, left her alone for days at a time and was tormented by jealousy. Gradually his moods and suspicions killed her love for hi,. He couldn't believe that he was the father of her child, though he had no sound reason to suspect her, and she left him in a storm of indignation and returned to her brother, the garage

Page from the treatment of *She Would Not Be a Lady* by H. G. Wells, preserved in the Chaplin Archives.

"I left no time in accepting such an invitation," recalled Chaplin. They met in advance of the planned weekend, when they were brought together at a preview of Harold M. Shaw's film of Wells' *Kipps*. Both had mixed feelings about the film, but Chaplin was touched by Wells' kindness in whispering "Say something nice to the boy": *Kipps* was the debut of 22-year-old George K.Arthur, who sat beside them. The subsequent weekend was mostly spent playing games, indoor and outdoor, with Wells' clever young sons. Afterwards Chaplin pondered, "As I speed into town I am wondering if Wells wants to know me or whether he wants me to know him. I am certain that now I have met Wells, really met him, more than I have met anyone in Europe. It's so worth while."

The friendship remained strong over the years. On his 1931 visit to England Chaplin spent a good deal of time with Wells, and they met again in Juan les Pins, with Chaplin's romance of the moment, May Reeves. In November 1935, Wells was invited for a four-week stay at Chaplin's home, but in fact saw little of his host who was battling with the music for *Modern Times*; he spent much of his time dictating letters to Chaplin's secretary, Catherine Hunter, refusing pressing invitations for celebrity speaking engagements. His last visit, in 1940, to stay for a fortnight in the course of a lecture tour, was also unfortunately timed. Chaplin and Paulette Goddard were in the process of breaking up, and following the premiere of *The Great Dictator*, Chaplin had remained in New York, leaving Paulette to host Wells—which no doubt she did with charm. Perhaps Wells and Chaplin had at some time discussed possible film projects: an enigmatic survival in the Chaplin archives is a rough treatment (in four copies) by Wells for a projected film on womens' liberation, *She Would Not Be a Lady*.[*] Wells died, at 80, in 1946.

Chaplin commemorated his 1921 European trip with a lively memoir, published in America as *My Trip Abroad*. For the British edition, however, he changed the title to *My Wonderful Visit*. Was this in fact a tribute to his friend Wells, one of whose earliest novels, published in 1895, was *The Wonderful Visit*, which related the apparition in an English village of a winged humanoid—a self-confessed angel? It seems impossible that Chaplin would not have read this marvelous, haunting little book and that it would not have coloured his conception of Sarapha's troubled encounters with earthbound humans. Wells' story was inspired by a remark of Ruskin, that an angel appearing in Victorian England would be shot on sight, a reflection echoed by the Spanish-born film maker Luis Buñuel about the time that Chaplin was working on *The Freak*: "If Christ came back they would crucify him all over again."[†]

The Wonderful Visit is set in the little English village of Siddermouth. One night a strange light appears in the sky and there are reported sightings of a large luminous bird. Next day the Reverend Hillyer, Vicar of Siddermouth, a scholarly ornithologist, sets out with his gun in hopes of a rare specimen for taxidermy. He sights the creature and fires, only to discover that his bullet has pierced the wing of an iridescent angelic youth:

> Slight of figure, scarcely five feet high, and with a beautiful, almost effeminate face such as an Italian Old Master might have painted... He was robed simply in a purple-wrought saffron blouse, bare-kneed and bare-footed, with his wings (broken now, and a leaden grey) folded behind him.

---

[*] Chaplin Archives, Ch00323.
[†] Joan Mellen (ed.), *The World of Luis Buñuel: Essays in Criticism*, Oxford University Press, Oxford 1978, p. 8.

Sarapha. Drawings by John Rose.

> Let us be plain. The angel of this story is the Angel of Art, not the one that one must be irreverent to touch—neither the Angel of religious feeling nor the Angel of popular belief.[*]

The Vicar attempts to stem the bleeding, and helps the Angel—experiencing terrestrial distresses of pain and hunger entirely new to him—to the vicarage. Arriving there, they are confronted by the curate's wife and daughters, who make the worst assumptions about this creature with free chestnut hair, feminine visage and a skirt reaching hardly to the knee. The ladies flee in shock and disgust.

The anxious vicar has the Angel change into his own best suit, thereby hiding his wings, and giving him the appearance of a hump-back. Dr Crump is called to attend to his injuries, and devises a lot of rational anatomical explanations for the unaccustomed growths from the young person's back. The curate comes to protest at the insult to his family, and though he accepts that the stranger is not a woman, he also ridicules the notion that the young person could be an angel.

When they are alone, the Angel spots a violin, takes it up and plays heavenly melodies which thrill and stir the Vicar.

Next morning the Angel explores the village alone, and meets only open hostility, from the villagers, and from two itinerant tinkers. The village boys pelt him with stones until he is rescued by Dr Crump, who happens to pass by, still stubbornly diagnosing his wings as a lamentable deformity.

Meanwhile Lady Hammergallow, the lady of the manor, visits the vicarage with her ineffectual ear-trumpet, and delightedly decides that the angel must be the vicar's illegitimate son, conceived before he took orders. "I never suspected you were nearly such an interesting man… It is most romantic." She plans to give a concert to exploit the stranger's musical gifts.

Returning to the vicarage the Angel meets the little servant girl Delia, in whom he first recognizes kindness in a human. He discusses with the Vicar the compulsion of humans to inflict pain. The Vicar agrees about the universal presence of pain in the human world.

At Lady Hammergallow's concert at Siddermorton House, the Angel's heavenly music intrigues the guests, but he is disgraced when it is discovered that he is unable to read printed music. He is still further shamed by his courtesy to the servants, and his incomprehension of the flirtatious advances of a friend of the curate's wife. Back at the Vicarage, Constable Horrocks complains that the Angel has destroyed the barbed wire around the estate of the local squire, Sir John Gotch, after seeing it injure some passing stranger.

The Angel plays his violin again: "For a week now he had known pain and rejection, suspicion and hatred." In the village he again meets Dr Crump, to whom he declares, "It's impossible for you to know who I am. Your eyes are blind, your ears are deaf, your soul is dark, to all that is wonderful about me. It's no good my telling that I fell into your world."

Sir John Gotch tells the Vicar the Angel must be gone in a week. The Vicar's staff concur: the creature is no gentleman. Sadly, the Vicar buys supplies and packs bags for the Angel, ready to dispatch him to London and his own fate.

The angel meanwhile has met Sir John Gotch in the woods and as "encroaching proof of his encroaching humanity," has whipped Sir John into unconsciousness. He supposes he has killed him.

---

[*] This and the following quotations are from H. G. Wells, *The Wonderful Visit* (1895), The Floating Press, Auckland, 2012.

Theodore Kosloff, Bluebird in *The Sleeping Beauty*, ca. 1900.
In 1909 Kosloff was part of the corps de ballet of the Ballets Russes' first Paris season alongside
Nijinsky. In the 1930s Chaplin hired him to give dance lessons to Paulette Goddard in preparation for
his project on Nijinsky, which later evolved into *Limelight*.

"Philharmonic Auditorium." Program of Anna Pavlova and her company's U.S. tour, February 1921. The New York Public Library Digital Collections.

Ariel the Flying Dancer, lithograph by Joseph E. Baker, ca. 1880. Huntington Digital Library.

"Truly this is no world for an angel" said the Angel. "It is a World of War, a World of Pain, A World of Death. Anger comes upon one… I, who knew not pain or anger, stand here with blood stains on my hand. I have fallen. To come into this world is to fall. One must hunger and thirst and be tormented with a thousand desires. One must fight for foothold, be angry and strike.

He returns to the vicarage to find the house is burning, on account of the vicar's carelessly throwing a lighted match into his waste paper basket while igniting his patent incandescent reading lamp.

The bystanders tell the Angel that Delia has just rushed back into the house—to save his violin.

For a moment the Angel stood staring. Then in a flash he saw it all, saw this grim little world of battle and cruelty transfigured in a splendour that outshone the Angelic Land, suffused suddenly and insupportably glorious with the wonderful light of Love and Self-Sacrifice. He gave a strange cry, and before anyone could stop him, was running into the burning building… Then the Angel was hidden by something massive (no one knew what) that fell, incandescent, across the doorway. There was a cry of "Delia" and no more. But suddenly the flames spurted out in a blinding glare that shot upward to an immense height a blinding brilliance broken by a thousand flickering gleams like the waving of swords. And a gust of sparks, flashing in a thousand colours whirled up and vanished. Just then, and for a moment by some strange accident, a rush of music like the swell of an organ, wove into the roaring of the flames.

The Renaissance philosopher Giovanni Pico della Mirandola reflected in 1486, "If we burn with love for the Creator only, his consuming fire will quickly transform us into the flaming likeness of the Seraphim."[*]

Concluding *The Wonderful Visit,* Wells tells us that two crosses in Siddermorton churchyard bear the names of Thomas Angel and Delia Hardy, but the graves are empty: and that the Vicar survived, unhappy and unkempt, only for another year. "But little Hetty Penzance had a pretty fancy of two figures with wings that flashed up and vanished among the flames... Until Crump took her in hand and cured her with fattening dietary, syrup of hypophosphites and cod liver oil."

There are few narrative parallels between *The Wonderful Visit* and *The Freak*. The Angel's experience of the world is a quiet English village; Sarapha's the great metropolis of London. Sarapha has come from a solitary existence in the wilds of Chile; the Angel has somehow fallen from Heaven—mankind's Land of Dreams.

"In some incomprehensible manner I have fallen into this world of yours out of my own!" said the Angel, "into the world of my dreams, grown real.

The Angel is an authentic and self-confessed Angel, repudiated by the human world; Sarapha vehemently disclaims any angelic status, but the world around her insists upon bestowing it upon her, for their own generally devious purposes. The Angel is more and more persecuted, while Sarapha is finally rescued from the various threats and afflictions to which she has been exposed. Yet both in the end choose to quit the human world, in the solitude of water or the glory of fire. Just one scene is common to both stories. In *The Wonderful Visit,*

The Angel lay upon the summit of the cliff above Bandram Bay, and stared out at the glittering sea. Sheer from under his elbows fell the cliff, five hundred and seven feet of it down to the datum line, and the sea-birds eddied and soared below him... The swell frothed white on the flinty beach, and the water beyond where the shadows of an outstanding rock lay, was green and purple in a thousand tints and marked with streaks and flakes of foam.

Presently the angel stopped sobbing, and stared with a tear-stained face at the beach below him. "This world," he said, "wraps me around and swallows me up. My wings grow shrivelled and useless. Soon I shall be nothing more than a crippled man, and I shall age, and bow myself to pain, and die... I am miserable. And I am alone."

---

[*] Giovanni Pico della Mirandola, *Oratio de hominis dignitate* (1486).

Later that night, Delia looks out of her bedroom window at the moonlit garden and sees a figure come out of the house:

> It was the Angel. But he wore once more the saffron robe, in the place of his formless overcoat. In the uncertain light this garment had only a colourless shimmer, and his wings behind him seemed a leaden grey. He began taking short runs, flapping his wings and leaping, going to and fro amidst the drifting paths of light and the shadows of the trees. Delia watched him in amazement. He gave a despondent cry, leaping higher. His shriveled wings flashed and fell. A thicker patch in the cloud-film made everything obscure. He seemed to spring five or six feet from the ground and fall clumsily. She saw him in the dimness crouching on the ground and then she heard him sobbing.

In *The Freak,* Latham similarly watches Sarapha in his garden:

> FADE INTO EXTERIOR OF HOUSE. SEMI-CLOSE UP.
>
> She is depressed. Sarapha sadly spreads her wings and breasts the wind as she accelerates them, then starts to run, but she cannot get off the ground. Eventually she falls, gets up, and tries again, accelerating her wings, then running, but she stumbles again.
>
> CUT TO LATHAM'S LIBRARY. SEMI-LONG SHOT.
>
> Latham is watching Sarapha from the window. He leaves window hurriedly and EXITS from room.
>
> CUT TO WHERE SARAPHA HAS FALLEN. SEMI-LONG SHOT.
>
> Latham appears and lifts her gently to her feet. Her attitude has changed towards him, she becomes distant and formal. She looks haggard and sad.
>
>> SARAPHA
>> (*tearfully*)
>> I'll never be able to fly again!
>
> Latham, in silence, leads her towards the house.

Finally, the Angel was more fortunate than Sarapha, when ultimately he saw "this grim little world of battle and cruelty transfigured in a splendour that outshone the Angelic Land, suffused suddenly and insupportably glorious with the wonderful light of Love and Self-Sacrifice." Sarapha was denied such ecstasy.

The fascination with winged humanoids has sometimes extended to theatre and music. Around the turn of the twentieth century it may have been the pervading excitement with heavier-than-air aviation that stirred the Russian Imperial Ballet costumiers to equip *premiers*

The English actress Viola Tree in the role of Ariel in *The Tempest* by William Shakespeare.
Poster by Charles Buchel, London, 1904. Courtesy of Jennie Bissett.

danseurs in the roles of the Blue Bird in *The Sleeping Beauty* and the Genie of the Sea in *The Little Humpback Horse* with substantial wings. The fashion does not seem to have lasted long: wings are not advantageous to line and style in classical dance, though the costumes were otherwise exquisitely flattering. Around the same time, the Russian painter Sergei Sergeyevich Solomko (1867–1928) drew a group of winged humanoids that, reproduced on postcards, gained international popularity.

One theatrical manifestation of a winged humanoid, however, is likely, from all circumstantial evidence, to have entered Chaplin's singular attic-memory sixty years before he embarked on *The Freak*. Sir Herbert Beerbohm Tree (1852–1917) had opened the palatial new Her Majesty's (later His Majesty's) Theatre in 1897, and, alongside contemporary works that included Shaw's *Pygmalion*, notably embarked on a succession of spectacular and popular Shakespearean productions, following his principle that "Everything that tends to aid illusion, to stimulate the imagination of an audience, is legitimate on the stage." These shows fascinated the young Chaplin: "As a boy of fourteen I had seen Tree in many of his great productions."[*] At fifteen, he more than likely saw Tree's production of *The Tempest*, which opened on September 14, 1904. The moment was particularly favourable: throughout September and October, between tours of *Sherlock Holmes*, in which he played Holmes' page, Billy, the young Chaplin was "resting" in London. Even if he did not see the production from the gallery of His Majesty's during these weeks, he must certainly have been aware of the exquisite poster designed for the production by the painter Charles Buchel (1872–1950), who worked for Tree for many years. The poster depicts Tree's daughter Viola in the role of Ariel. (*The Pall Mall Gazette* ungallantly found her "too big and strapping," but Buchel counters that.)

Ariel is true to the song, "On the bat's back I do fly," yet at the same time he/she boasts his/her own spread wings. Is it too extravagant to see in the romantic allure of this enchanted figure a first inspiration for Sarapha?

---

[*] Charles Chaplin, *My Autobiography* (London: Penguin Books, 2003), 195. First published 1964 by The Bodley Head.

Victoria Chaplin, Shepperton Studios.

Chaplin at work in his studio at the Manoir de Ban. Photo by Yves Debraine, 1958.

4

Evolution of a Script

The quantity of surviving working papers for the conception of *The Freak* is greater than for any of Chaplin's other films or projects like *The Great Dictator* or *Limelight*, and Rachel Ford's brave effort to organise them three months after his death, in six days, was inevitably limited in its success. The mass remains bewildering, with innumerable detached orphan pages. It is often hard to conjecture the chronological development of the work in progress.

Yet this does not diminish its value as insight into Chaplin's creative mind and method. A phrase he often used, in differing contexts, was "ideas keep popping into my head." When an idea popped in, he seems to have seized it, saved it and tried it out. It might be discarded immediately, or elaborated and tried again... The early notes and drafts are comparable in their process to the precious out-takes from his Mutual films of 1916–17. Fifty years later, this is still the same creative mind at work, tirelessly experimenting, rejecting, re-moulding until the moment of recognition that it has Come Right.

Chaplin laboured over the composition of *The Freak* from September 1967 to the early summer of 1969, constantly rewriting, revising, rejecting. The first stage was to relate and develop his story in the form of a past tense narrative treatment, until—apparently in late September 1968—he decided he was ready to move on to writing a formal script. This seems to coincide with the moment that the definitive title was adopted. Each surviving copy and version of the script carries the title, apparently previously unmentioned, "THE FREAK by CHARLES CHAPLIN."

Some 1,400 pages from the narrative treatments survive, many duplicated. None of these narratives carries the story beyond the Pentagon ball, and Sarapha's sudden flight after seeing that enemies have infiltrated the Pentagon mansion. There is no anticipation of the coming dramatic climax and resolution of the story; these seem only to have been considered and conceived in the subsequent script process. Among these pages, a unique near-complete type-script of the narrative treatment, with careful page-numbering (including many inserted pages with supplementary alphabetical ordering), seems to represent the final version of the treatment, ready to be converted into script form.

One sequence remains consistent, from the earliest draft treatment to the definitive script: the description of Latham's Chilean cliff dwelling and the arrival of Sarapha and first steps in taming her. Often, through the years, when he spoke to the press about *The Freak*, Chaplin went out of his way to express special satisfaction in its location—at least for the opening episodes—on the coast of Chile. There is no evident record as to what led him to this exotic choice. In the earlier 20th century the English-reading public showed little curiosity about the topography or the shifting politics of that country. The only popular books available when Chaplin was at work were Brenda Hughes' *Folk-tales from Chile* (1962) and Lois Bianchi's *Chile in Pictures* (1965), though Chaplin could also have consulted classics such as *Wanderings in Patagonia* (1879) by Victorian explorer Julius Beerbohm or *A Naturalist's Voyage around the World*, in which Charles Darwin makes specific reference to the Fuegini Indians, an indigenous population of Tierra del Fuego. In October 1969, *National Geographic Magazine* republished passages from Darwin's writings. Victoria recalls that there were often copies of *National Geographic* in the Chaplin home, though she does not know if there was a regular subscription.

In 1970—the year *The Freak* was to have been filmed—the advent of Salvador Allende and his subsequent Washington-supported overthrow by Augusto Pinochet's brutal military junta brought Chile's administration to international attention.

However, in other ways Chile had come into the news in the 1960s. May 22, 1960 saw the Valdivia earthquake, the most powerful seismic event in recorded history, whose resultant tsunami brought damage and deaths as far away as Japan. In 1966 a border dispute between Chile and Argentina was brought before the Court of Arbitration in London, and when adjudicated would have required the signature of Queen Elizabeth II. These events excited the international press in different degrees, and stimulated articles and pictures in many illustrated journals of the day.

However, having settled on his location, Chaplin is inclined to invent his own Chile. The script makes reference to Valparaiso, the capital, but the nearest town to Latham's cliff-edge retreat is named as Madre de Dios, a hundred and twenty-five miles distant. The place appears to be Chaplin's fiction: the only recorded Madre de Dios is an island in the Magallanes Region, mainly occupied by skeletons of whales and people who lived three or four millennia ago. Chaplin invents his own mysticism also. In early drafts of his story—though not in the final script—he propounds an origin for his winged protagonist:

> She had come from a remote valley somewhere in the Andes. Her family, like herself, had wings and were by nature nocturnal and lived on grapes which they picked from the vineyards at night. In fact they belonged to a small flock of the same breed that inhabited the valley. The legend, according to a few Indians who had seen them, was that they were avenging angels sent down upon earth to punish those who disbelieve in the Bible. Occasionally, an Indian came upon them and would cross himself and pray. They were left alone because Indians were superstitious, and believed that if they told others they would bring a curse upon themselves. By devious means, they had kept out of the way of European people. Her family migrated with the building of a hydrogen plant, which caused them to suffer air pollution. Then her family flew away and she was left behind.[*]

A variation on this description adds:

> They lived in caves in a steep, narrow canyon where no one could reach them. They kept away from people because their nature was such. According to an old Indian legend, they were an ancient race of winged people whose appearance had influenced the writers of the Bible.

---

[*] Chaplin Archive, Ch00047. Unless otherwise indicated, all quotations are taken from this file, in which Rachel Ford compiled handwritten and typed notes for the treatment and various drafts of the screenplay.

Above: *Tabula Magellanica
qua Tierrae del Fuego: cum
celeberrimis fretis a E. Magellano
et I. Le Maire detectis Novifs et
accuratisim descript exhibetur*,
1652. Biblioteca Nacional de
Chile.

Left: Inhabitants of Tierra del
Fuego, illustration by Alexander
Buchan, 1769. British Library
Collections.

Chilean cliff, backdrops painted by Gerald Larn.

In one early treatment, describing the villainous Jackson's decision to kidnap Sarapha, Chaplin writes, "He had heard of the fabulous legend of the Aconagua angels, and had paid little attention to it, until he heard Nagia's story." Any record of such legend is to say the least elusive and it is likely again to be Chaplin's invention. Aconagua is the highest mountain in the Americas, 15 kilometres outside Chile's border with Argentina. It is known as the Mountain of Death, both for the high level of climbing accidents and the perils from unmanaged human waste.

One of the special appeals of the treatments is the series of brief sketches of the principal characters on their first introduction. Edward Latham developed (and aged) from draft to draft.

A young man of twenty-eight years, attractive-looking, studious. Attractive, adventurous, perhaps prone to too many worldly distractions, but talented. Hence his self-exile to this remote and God-forsaken place to study, above all things, morphology.

Professor Latham was a young scientist of thirty-three whose morphological studies had kept him for the past year living on this plateau collecting recondite data for two volumes on archaeology which he was writing for the Royal Geographical Society of London.*

Professor Latham was an attractive young man, who was of a reputable middle class family. He considered his sense of propriety was not snobbish, not conformed to ordinary standards of social behaviour—most of his relatives were of the cloth.

The arrival of Sarapha from the skies, and the process of making sympathetic human contact with her hardly change from the earliest draft to the final script. However the subsequent account of her life with Latham undergoes a series of fundamental changes. In the earliest drafts, Sarapha arrives with no language with which to communicate, but a phenomenal intellect enables her to learn Spanish, English and guitar-playing in no time at all:

In the course of time Sarapha very soon adapted herself to the household menage. She liked Nagia, and of course, worshipped Professor Latham, who discovered that she had a quick and absorbing mind. She would sit in the Professor's study, pouring over grammar books. [...]

To please the Professor, she tried to behave like a human being. She even went so far as to want an operation and have her wings taken off. Of course the Professor would not hear of such a thing and reprimanded her for it.

There were, however, moments of digression, when Sarapha's bird-like temperament would predominate, when at meal times, she would scatter food in all directions. This happened when Nagia, forgetting Sarapha's abhorrence of eggs, would innocently put an omelette on the dinner table.

Now she dined with the Professor regularly, In her playful moods she would whimsically imitate him, pretending to get confused as to which knife or fork was for cutting. If they had fish, she would bone it with her fingers for him, then take him by the fringe of his hair and thrust it down his throat, as a bird would feed its young.

---

* Draft screenplay, undated. Chaplin Archive, Chm00263.

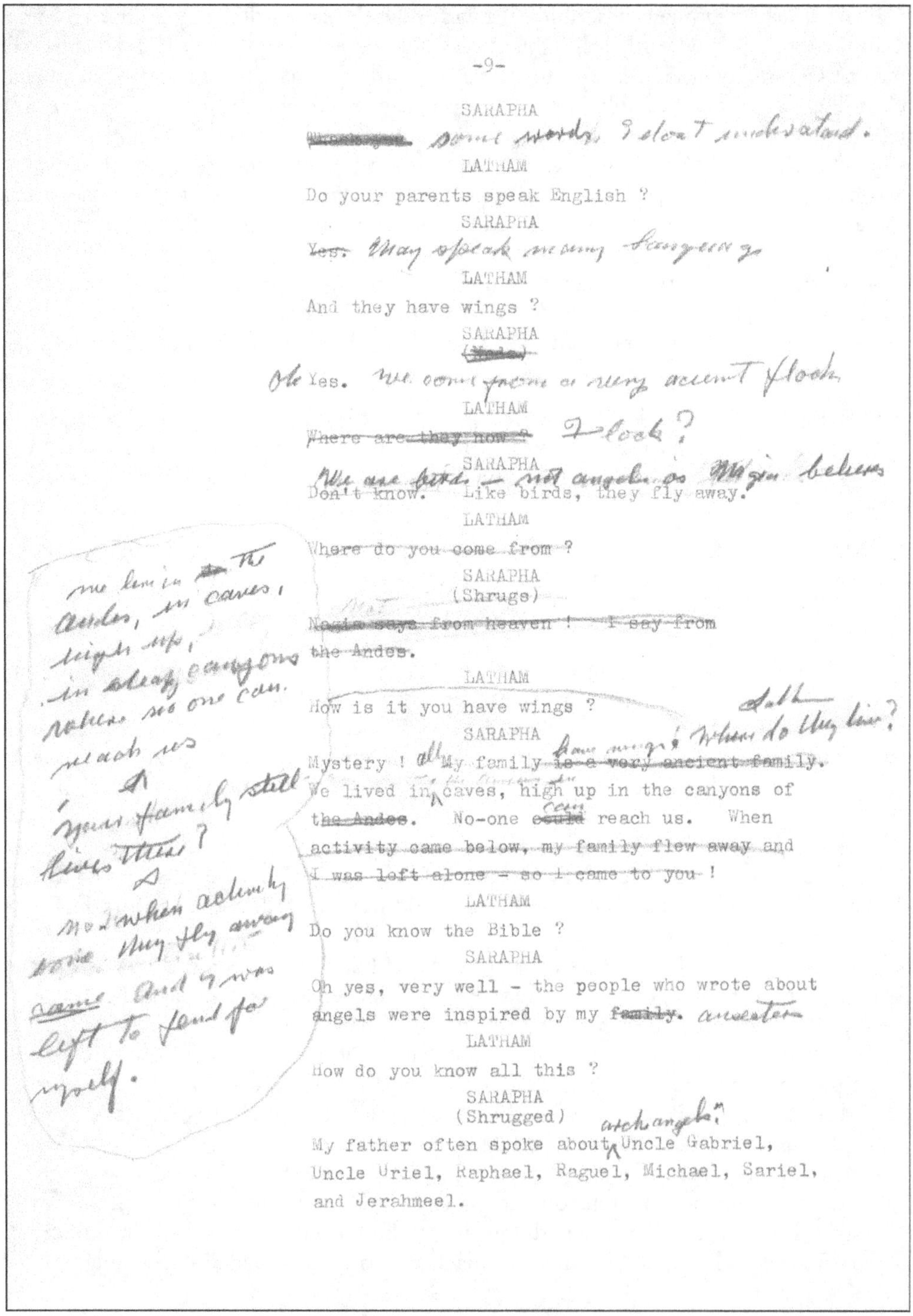

-9-

SARAPHA

some words I don't understand.

LATHAM

Do your parents speak English ?

SARAPHA

~~Yes.~~ They speak many languages

LATHAM

And they have wings ?

SARAPHA

~~(Nods)~~

Oh Yes. We come from a very ancient flock

LATHAM

~~Where are they now ?~~ Flock?

SARAPHA

We are birds – not angels as you believe

~~Don't know.~~ Like birds, they fly away.

LATHAM

~~Where do you come from ?~~

SARAPHA

(Shrugs)

~~Nagia says from heaven ! I say from the Andes.~~

LATHAM

How is it you have wings ?

SARAPHA

Mystery ! all My family ~~is a very ancient family.~~ have wings! Where do they live?

We lived in caves, high up in the canyons of ~~the Andes~~. No-one ~~could~~ can reach us. When ~~activity came below, my family flew away and I was left alone – so I came to you !~~

We live in the Andes, in caves, high up, in steep canyons where no one can reach us

Your family still lives there?

No, when activity came they fly away And I was left to fend for myself.

LATHAM

Do you know the Bible ?

SARAPHA

Oh yes, very well – the people who wrote about angels were inspired by my ~~family.~~ ancestors

LATHAM

How do you know all this ?

SARAPHA

(Shrugged)

My father often spoke about archangels Uncle Gabriel, Uncle Uriel, Raphael, Raguel, Michael, Sariel, and Jerahmeel.

Draft screenplay page of *The Freak.*

The improbability and necessary time-lapsing of this process was eventually avoided by making Sarapha the (phenomenal) child of English missionaries, rather than a specimen from a native mountain tribe of winged humanoids. This also made it easier for Chaplin to pursue the love intrigue between Latham and Sarapha, which in the early conceptions of the story had an overwhelming interest for him. In the early treatments the way is left clear by making Latham a bachelor. Margaret, back in London, is, at this stage, his sister. As to the newly arrived Sarapha:

> She was beautiful! No matter what biological or scientific interest the Professor might have in her, he could not ignore her beauty—she was most appealing. She had a terrific attraction for him and she knew it, and encouraged it.

Meanwhile,

> Sarapha was in love with Professor Latham. Yes, in love—with all the ardour and romance of her sixteen years. Her bird instinct for reproduction was natural and expedient. She even knocked on his bedroom door one night with the excuse that she could not sleep
> "It's the moon," said Sarapha looking at him reproachfully.
> "There, there, you must go back to bed and try to sleep," he said kindly.

In later drafts, the reference to "the ardour and romance of her sixteen years" is modified to read "her seventeen years," either from discretion or to keep up with Victoria Chaplin's birthday on May 19, 1968.

Sarapha's bedroom visit and Latham's discreet dismissal of her advances remain in the finished script, but in the early treatments, the temptation was evidently mutual:

> Latham was confined to his bed with a cold. Perhaps from torment of resisting Sarapha's amorati [sic] for her beauty obsessed him. Often in the night he was tempted to turn the handle of her bedroom door, but the restraining hand of his ecclesiastical background prevented him.

In another draft:

> He considered that he was not snobbish, nor did he conform to ordinary standards of behavior—But with Sarapha he must have scruples.
> What's more he intended to take her to London on a world lecture tour. Yet how could he introduce her to the world as his protégé? It would create no end of ugly gossip. Yet if he left her to her fate, heaven knows what would become of her. At all costs, he must protect this electrifying, pretty young thing with wings from the savagery of a modern civilized world.

In the script, Latham and Sarapha are left alone when Nagia, Latham's Indian servant, goes to Valparaiso, to care for her sick father. Sarapha's nursing of Latham when he is confined to bed with a cold, already suggests a fairly intimate relationship, which here results at best in some allusion.

Above and right: Sarapha and Latham. Storyboard by Gerald Larn.

In one of the earlier versions, Latham's confinement to bed and Sarapha's care for him has an interesting elaboration:

> Professor Latham was confined to his bed with a cold. He was suffering from his old complaint — lumbago. Nagia, his Indian housekeeper would massage his back when his condition was severe. And as the severity increased, Nagia was compelled to massage his back every day for the next week.
>
> Sarapha was worried and very jealous. One morning, as Nagia was about to enter the Professor's bedroom. Sarapha blocked the doorway and made threatening faces at Nagia. Then when Nagia had fled to the kitchen, Sarapha entered the Professor's bedroom and sweetly explained that Nagia wasn't well and was also stricken with a cold, and that she, Sarapha, would take her place! In her absorbing determination, she had forgotten the massage oil... "Oh!" she said, "I won't be a moment." Then she left the room hurriedly and went to the kitchen. She crept threateningly towards Nagia whispering, "The massage cream?"
>
> Nagia, terrified, gave it to her, then Sarapha, lady-like, entered the Professor's bedroom.

Nevertheless a fragment of dialogue, in manuscript only, shows Sarapha having doubts:

> "What's the use," said Sarapha. "You love and beget children.
> "What's the use of falling in love? We'd get married and have children — and
>   supposing they had wings?"
> "You talk so ruthlessly"
> "How can you say that?"
> "Say what?"
> "Would have wings."

In some versions of the treatment, Dr Piestroz's anxiety about the temptation to which Latham might be exposed is certainly more motivated and greater than in the final script:

> Latham: The worst of it is I'm in love with her
> Piestroz: I hope nothing intimate has happened between you and that creature...
>   Yet...
> Latham: Oh no!
> Piestroz: You must never allow that image to steal into your fantasy, although I can
>   well understand her ornithopter attractions (thoughtfully) and I must say the
>   creature is quite pretty.

("Ornithopter" — generally used to describe aircraft operated by mechanical flapping wings — is a strange choice of word.) In a single version of the narrative treatment, Chaplin involved Dr and Mrs Piestroz in a bizarre incident:

> "In fact the doctor here could marry us." The doctor almost choked on his coffee. "Well — yes," he said with a reservation. "I'd be only too pleased to conduct the ceremony, but it may create a lot of opposition. The church might endorse the idea

Preparatory notes and sketches by Chaplin for *The Freak*.

X2 This feeling tormented her and barred her from entering another world.

-6-

control this animalism".   The moment he said 'animalism' he
wished he could have retracted it.

"I'm sorry", said Sarapha quietly.   "It will never
happen again".

Days that followed, Sarapha would wander alone to the far
end of the plateau.   She grew thoughtful about her relationship
with the professor.   She loved him in spite of the fact that he
was without wings.   This worried her a little; how could she
reconcile this physical impedimenta ?   How could they enjoy life
together and share the pleasure of fleetness, and fly above the
mountain tops, skim the ocean and fly up and land on rocks.   He
was a man confined to legs that drag one after the other; that
depended on automation to get him somewhere.   It was a terrible
sacrifice she ~~thought~~.   She had never been in love before.
It was a strange feeling.   She wanted to be with him, close to
him always.   Love, she thought, must be an antidote for loneli-
ness.   ~~but it was natural for her to be alone, and she always~~
~~wanted to be near him.~~   He was the only protection she had in
the world.

~~He had told her that he was engaged to be married, but~~
~~that didn't bother her.~~   "You can have all the wives you want as
long as you still love me", she said innocently.

"But that is impossible if I have a wife", said Latham.
"What does that matter", she replied, "I'm no swan".

She often thought of pregnancy, and thrilled at the idea
of it.   But in the ornithological sense, she did not want an egg !
~~But~~ she wanted Latham's child, even if it had no wings.

The ironic fact was that ~~the more the professor tried to~~
~~train her to be human,~~ the more was her tendency to remain a bird.
This feeling tormented her and barred her from entering another world,
In spite of her love for him, she became estranged.   She wanted
to fly, to lift her feet off the ground and soar to the sky and
breathe mountain air.   She had not flown since the night they
found her on the roof.   Now she needed practice.   She stood a
moment and flapped her wings, closing her eyes and breasting the
wind; then ran - but she could not get off the ground.   She ran
again, and after several attempts, stumbled and fell.

The professor had witnessed the scene from the library
window and ran to her aid.   Tenderly he brought her to her feet.
She was weeping.   He did not question her - he understood.
"I'll never fly again", she said tearfully.   The professor made
no comment but walked with her to the house in poignant silence,

Draft screenplay of *The Freak* with Chaplin's manuscript notes.

because it would probably look upon Miss Sarapha as an angel. There is, of course, the theistic attitude to which the Church might object — that of a deity marrying a common mortal."

The ceremony was very touching. Sarapha's wings trembled all through the service and the Doctor's wife, true to form, fainted immediately the service started.

Although this specific idea seems to have been instantly and perhaps sensibly abandoned, it does already posit the film's running comedy gag of the number of ordinary mortals who faint away at first sight of Sarapha — the young nun, Father Donovin, Dr Everman as well as Dr and Mrs Piestroz, who are serial swooners, taking turns at passing out.

Despite initial hesitations, however, in the treatments the affair seems to be consummated. When they find themselves watching a sunset, Latham says to Sarapha, "Red sky at night is the sailor's delight."

Sarapha looked at him with mild surprise. It was unlike him to be glib at such a beautiful moment. She smiled weakly and for comment placed her small hand in his. It was small and rough from work. They stood in silence, drinking in the mystic beauty of the scene. A turquoise streak appeared and breathed the harbinger of evening twilight. Suddenly he became conscious of her hand and she instinctively knew it and squeezed his. He stopped and kissed her, tenderly at first, then passionately — that was the beginning of their tenderness, their love and abandonment. *

A much more dramatic and erotic treatment of the moment of consummation was considered during the script stage, but it exists only as a single-page draft, and was never incorporated into the script:

Moonlight streaks across the floor. The effect is eerie. The door opens gently to the ancient music of the love song.

SARAPHA ENTERS and walks across the floor... She is imbued with the magic of the moonlight. She strips off her clothes and stands in silhouette before the window looking out at sea. Then LATHAM appears in pyjamas, standing at the door. He is overwhelmed by Sarapha's beauty. She turns and reaches out her arms to him. He goes forward and embraces her as the MUSIC SWELLS.

In all subsequent versions of the treatment and in the script, Sarapha's hopes of permanent love with Latham are shattered when she opens a letter she finds in his study, addressed to Margaret Latham. In early treatments, Margaret is his sister, but quite early she is identified as his wife. In the ultimate treatment he writes:

Dear Margaret, I believe I wrote to you some months ago about the remarkable advent of finding an angel or bird, or whatever it is, on the roof of my house — an incredible creature with a quick absorbing brain, beyond anything human. Well it is in love with me! This sounds ridiculous and somewhat scandalous — especially if I am to bring it to London on a lecture tour.

---

* Draft screenplay, undated. Chaplin Archive, Ch0048.

Sarapha's distress at being referred to as "it" is understandable:

> She could read no further, she was hurt. She suddenly grew up. The ironic fact was that Sarapha was deep in love with Professor Latham. But subconsciously she knew that their alliance was impossible; that being what she was—their relationship was hopeless. The more he had educated her, the more conscious she was of her human passion and inadequacy—she was a freak! This humility [sic? humiliation] she could not impose on Latham. But she would have to go on in spite of everything. She could not give him up yet. She loved him too much.
>
> Sarapha's sadness deepened. She consoled herself, however, with the bitter thought that whatever happened, Latham could never enjoy the pleasures of fleetness, flying above clouds and skimming the sea. He was confined to legs that dragged one after the other—and that depended on automation to get him somewhere.
>
> In spite of herself, her ornithological urge began to grow. She wanted to fly again, she wanted the power again to lift her feet off the ground and soar to the sky and breathe fresh mountain air, to fly away from sadness.[*]

It is at this point that, watched by Latham, she discovers that she has lost the ability to fly. "I wonder if I will ever fly again," she said sadly.

The arrival of the Indian caravan seeking healing for a young girl, and the coincident visit of Dr and Mrs Piestroz were carried over to the script with little change except that in some treatments, Latham is still explaining Sarapha's origin as a member of an ancient winged community:

> "Yes, I am coming to that," said the Professor earnestly. "They are a very ancient race. The legend goes beyond biblical time. They were supposed to come from the island of Atlantis. Thus their race inspired the concept of the angel."[†]

The arrival of Jackson and Ryman's helicopter and the kidnap of Sarapha are consistently plotted very much as in the final script, except that in some treatments there is a second woman conspirator posing as an invalid on board the aircraft, and a lively introduction of Jackson (who in earlier versions is called Juleson, and has a wife, who is a conspirator *in absentia*).

> Mr Joyce Jackson had taken a business course at an American university, and had a large advertising business which was very successful. His confidant was Ryman, his pilot.
>
> Jackson was lucky. Everything he touched turned to money. His success was in phallic advertising: a woman's red lips enlarged to cover the whole page of a magazine; several lipsticks in bright colours, standing up on end—a woman's arms enlarged and bent so as to look like the cheek of a woman's buttocks; the round smooth shoulders of two girls, so arranged as to look like woman's breasts. His

---

[*] Draft screenplay, undated. Chaplin Archive, Ch00052.
[†] Handwritten notes, undated. Chaplin Archive, Ch00047a.

advertising business brought him over two million dollars per year. Nevertheless, he could not bear to miss the opportunity of a new enterprise.

In another version of the treatment, Chaplin gives a physical description of the two miscreants:

> One was dressed in a grey checkered suit, and the other in a dark grey one. Both were young, not over thirty. The man in the dark grey suit wore a thin, dark moustache. His eyes were perhaps too close to his head, and there was something about the protuberance of the brow that reminded her of the head of a tiger. He could have been attractive but for his thin lips. The other, in the checkered suit was clean shaven and had an innocuous weak face which looked as though it was about to break into a smile.

Already on the journey Jackson, in conversation with Ryman, is plotting his many strategies to exploit Sarapha to maximum commercial effect.

From Sarapha's escape from Jackson's plane, the later treatments generally anticipate the eventual final script: her flight to London, descent into the church with the never-explained transition from the church to Westminster Cathedral, her Sunday in the Opera House and her search for Margaret's house, including her encounter with the bewildered drunk (Chaplin's own anticipated signature walk-on). The only difference of detail is that Margaret's address—as memorized by Sarapha from Latham's letter—is 25 South Molton Street; but in what seems the latest version of the treatment this is changed in pencil to 25 Brook Street (in the script this becomes 27 Brook Street).

At the same Brook Street address, in a beautiful Georgian-style house, for over thirty years lived George Frideric Handel, whom Chaplin quotes almost subliminally in the script of *The Freak*. Before Sarapha appears in front of the crowd of worshippers, they intone a few verses of a song set to music precisely by the German composer.*

Chaplin had been born and raised in London and since his move to Switzerland had resumed frequenting the English capital rather assiduously. It is therefore reasonable to assume that the choice to locate Margaret Latham's home on one of these two (adjacent) streets, in the heart of Mayfair and a few steps away from Grosvenor Square, may not have been entirely accidental. Chaplin wrote in *A Comedian Sees the World*: "With its elegant dwellings arranged in a circle and its solemn Greek columns like austere sentinels, Grosvenor Square represents for me the elegance of the Victorian age and all its most illustrious figures." From 1960 the entire west side of Grosvenor Square was occupied by the American Embassy building in front of which all the major political and civil protests took place between 1967 and 1972.†

---

* This is the traditional English carol "While Shepherds Watched Their Flocks," attributed to the Irish poet Nahum Tate. Perhaps fearing that it would seem too didactic, Chaplin omitted the lines that directly mention the angel Seraphim: "Thus spake the Seraph and forthwith/Appeared a shining throng/Of angels praising God on high/Who thus addressed their song [...] Thus spoke the Seraph and immediately/appeared a shining throng/of angels praising God on high/ready to address their song to him."

† Mayfair is one of London's most elegant and exclusive neighbourhoods, located in a quadrangle bounded by Park Lane to the west, Piccadilly Street to the south, Regent Street to the east and Oxford Street to the north. This area developed between the 17th and 18th centuries. Its name dates back to 1686, when the May Fair, which took place every fifteen years, was held for the first time at The Haymarket

The residential district of Mayfair in London on a late-1960s map.
Margaret's home is at 27 Brook Street.

Margaret's characterisation also develops at various points:

> Margaret was beautiful, besides having an excellent mind, she was young and
> sophisticated, and extremely rich. Her father had vast metal interests throughout
> the world. Since his death she had inherited his fortune, her mother having died
> when she was three. Since her marriage to Professor Latham, she had settled in
> England. She was still friendly with the Professor. Her country house was the
> nada [sic] of all the art world. Here, she entertained her friends. She liked Sarapha
> because she aroused her pity.

The Margaret of the final script was somewhat less glamorous than this promises.
"She was still friendly with the Professor" suggests that they are separated, but this is not
made clear. Indeed, the marital status of the Lathams seemed a continual enigma to Chaplin.
Throughout the scripts, the crucial letter which Sarapha finds in Latham's study, varies in

---

and moved to Fair Field in the Bow district in 1764. The Royal Family owns properties in this district
identified as "Crown Estate," and Queen Elizabeth II herself was born in Mayfair and spent part of her
childhood there. In the past, famous figures such as the Duke of Wellington, Horatio Nelson, Benjamin
Disraeli, Handel and Florence Nightingale lived here. Jimi Hendrix lived in the same building as Handel
between the late 1960s and most of the 1970s. A museum dedicated to the two musicians is located at
23 Brook Street.

identifying Latham, as Margaret's devoted husband, or her still-cordial ex-husband. Several times it is actually altered in manuscript. Not until the very last versions of the script, when Chaplin had found his perfect *deus ex machina* in the person of Margaret's horrible new husband, Sir Rex Horton, is the question of the Lathams' marital status firmly resolved.

Although there would be some development of the dialogue, the scenes of Sarapha's first meeting with Margaret, the incursion of Jackson and Ryman, and Sarapha's obedience to their demand that she join them in their suite in the Savoy Hotel are very much as in the final scripts, although at this stage the threat of the immigration and quarantine authorities are a more central concern, giving Jackson the leverage he needs. The meeting with Gidson, the evangelist, is already worked out in detail in the later treatments, although the script omits one gag from the treatments. In the script Jackson's negotiations with Dr Gidson are accompanied by the noise of Sarapha loudly chewing cornflakes. In the treatments however, Sarapha forcibly shares her cornflakes with Gidson, causing him to choke. Also abandoned is a subsequent scene where Margaret comes to have dinner with Sarapha in her room at the Savoy, and searches to discover a "dictaphone" hidden under the sofa.

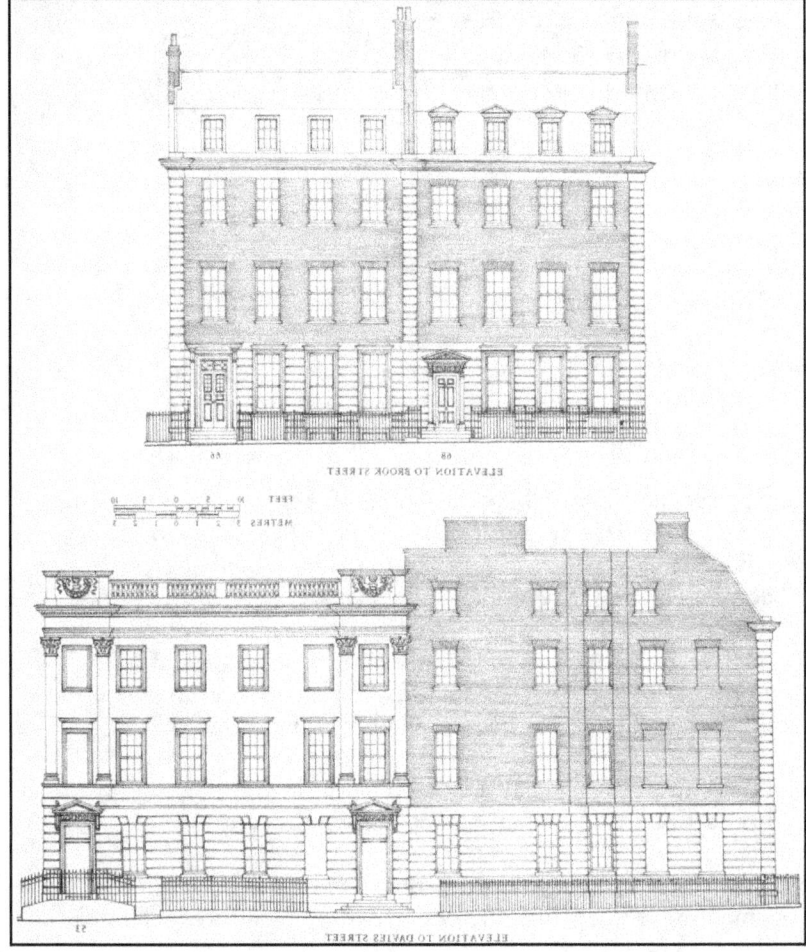

Plan of the buildings on Brook Street, Institute of Historical Research, University of London.

Possible location for the Pentagon family's villa in Trent.

In the treatments, the Earl's Court evangelist meeting is described briefly, but in the same terms as in the finished script. However, Sarapha's speech at this preliminary stage of writing is longer and more substantial:

> After the silence, Sarapha spoke: "I don't know who I am. We are all angels of God. I live as all people live, enjoying this beautiful earth: 'God so loved the world that he gave his only begotten son that who so ever believeth in him should not perish.'" She paused again. "So don't let us make any more human sacrifices…" She shook her head before uttering the next sentence. "But sometimes I feel he touches me as he does tonight!… I believe God is in everything. I see him in the vastness. In a dead seagull. God seems more present in the dead than in the living. God is everywhere— in every one. The sick can cure themselves, because God is within them."

When Sarapha escapes to Margaret's country mansion at Trent, the latest versions of the treatment engage them in a conversation that only partially appears in the script:

> Margaret had a biting wit, some thought it cruel. But it was a defence against her sentimental nature which she loathed. She was odd and abrupt, and was too intel-

ligent to have many friends. Nevertheless, she was kindly disposed to Sarapha: "I like you," she said. "There is an affinity between us. I have had too much freedom in my life. My mother died when I was three, my father when I was seventeen. I was married at eighteen and divorced at nineteen—so you see I have had too much freedom, and you haven't had enough—we are diametrically akin."

"Why did you divorce Professor Latham? Do you still love him?"

"Yes."

"Then why get divorced?"

"Because we're both idiots," said Margaret.

Sarapha looked at Margaret and wondered if she could confide in her—Could she tell her how madly in love she was with the Professor? Could she tell her that she was with child by him? No! She could not tell anyone,

Margaret made some Bovril and they talked "You must tell me about yourself," said Margaret.

Sarapha shrugged "I'm half bird and half woman—a freak!"

Margaret smiled! "Just a mixed up kid, eh? You certainly have an inferiority complex!"

"Have you ever been in love?" [asked Margaret]

"I really don't know. I have felt excited and passionate about someone, but—"

"That isn't love, that's growing pains, but you can foul up your life with that."

"I'm beginning to wonder what love is," said Sarapha ruefully.

"A human distraction, my dear. When I'm bored, I fall in love and forget myself. Then when I'm not bored—I usually fall out of love!"

Sarapha had seen few people and those she had seen saddened and bewildered her. But Margaret was a new experience, she had won her confidence.

This confirms Chaplin's continuing consideration of a full and consummated love affair between Latham and Sarapha. The more startling notion in this version of the treatment however, is that Sarapha is pregnant with Latham's child. At this stage Chaplin seems to have toyed with another idea involving Sarapha's pregnancy, though he swiftly abandoned it. The mentions of this scene are few and apparently incomplete as they have survived. At the Pentagons' ball, Sarapha meets Margaret's debauched brother, Clifford.

Clifford, Margaret's brother, was asleep in an anteroom, recovering from a champagne binge. He was an alcoholic, and a habitué of sanatoriums, taking cures and now started drinking again.

When he came to, he discovered he had been sleeping on a chair with his feet up on another one, and Sarapha looking at him. He blinked his eyes, and thought he had… Clifford gazed at her steadily without making any reaction, then turned as though he had seen nothing; winced several times and shook his head as though ridding himself of the hallucination.

Sarapha left the anteroom.

He is startled to see Sarapha, but appears subsequently to have seduced her and caused her pregnancy.

Even the most extended treatments end with the Pentagon fancy dress ball. In early drafts the ball is given by Margaret herself, in her mansion, with the Pentagons as colourful guests. The latest treatments are very close to the final script. They reveal however that some quite elaborate ideas were abandoned, but leave sometimes hardly comprehensible vestiges. An example is the incident of Countess Lebendoff's diamond ear-ring, which Sarapha finds in the corridor leading to the pink room and "innocently fastens into her left ear." Margaret fortunately spots it there, and manages to get it back to its owner without anyone else being the wiser. In the finished script the incident appears as a curious digression. It is in fact the residue of a developed exploration of Sarapha's authentically avian magpie characteristics. In the drafts the finding of the ear-ring is not accidental: she takes it from where the Countess has laid it down in the powder room—and swallowed it. She has already explained her problem on first meeting Margaret:

> In her boudoir Margaret started to take off her rings and her necklace. Sarapha watched her, and a strange look came into her face. Her eyes became glassy as she stared transfixed, at Margaret's jewelry.
> "What's the matter?" asked Margaret.
> "They sparkle," said Sarapha, trance-like.
> "My dear you alarm me—for a moment I thought you were ill."
> Sarapha shook her head: "It's the magpie in me. Every time I see something sparkle—I must take it."
> Margaret looked at her with alarm—but with humour:"Well, I'm glad you told me," she said, putting her necklace and rings into her private house safe and locking it.

When Margaret presents Sarapha to Lady Pentagon at the Pentagon Ball, "Sarapha could not take her eyes off Lady Pentagon's 30 carat blue-white diamond. She gazed at it, trance-like," until Margaret became uneasy and sent her off to dance with Lord Pentagon.

A feature of the treatments, which is absent from the final scripts, is Chaplin's notion of the Sarapha affair taking on national and international consequence. At one point, the revivalist meeting was to have been followed by a scene of an emergency debate in the British parliament:

> "Gentlemen, the question is whether to debate or defer the matter until we can establish a 'corpus delicti.' If this creature is defined as an animal, or a bird, then this house must act at once and have it quarantined—especially as there is a prevalence of hoof and mouth disease in the country. I cannot sufficiently impress on this house the seriousness of this plague. Each day, this country is losing thousands and thousands of pounds and we are shooting hundreds of our best cattle. On the other hand, if this House decides that this creature is a human being with wings—then we must act differently.
> "There has been a considerable nuisance in regards to this matter. This creature has aroused a degree of public hysteria, and is upsetting the tranquility of our country by suggesting universal peace—the abolition of all air defences—which it has certainly been doing since the house has prorogued the matter. We must act quickly and define what this creature really is. In the meantime, it should be

confined until we determine its status—Not to a prison, that would be inhumane and cruel. But if the creature is free of any contagious disease—then to the zoo. Caged of course, separated from other animals and under the government's clinical care until the matter is definitively determined as to whether this creature is a freak, a bird, an animal, or an angel. Of course the latter supposition is absurd!"

"Why?" asked an opposition back-bencher.

The Minister was nonplussed—"Well," he said, "An Angel!"

"Well, it's in the Bible."

The Minister made a disparaging gesture: "That's merely a figure of speech!"

"Then we are not to take the Bible seriously or to believe it?"

"We are not questioning the validity of the Bible" said the Minister. "We are questioning the fact that this freak is an angel! However, whether she is an angel or not, she is violating our immigration laws by entering this country illegally."

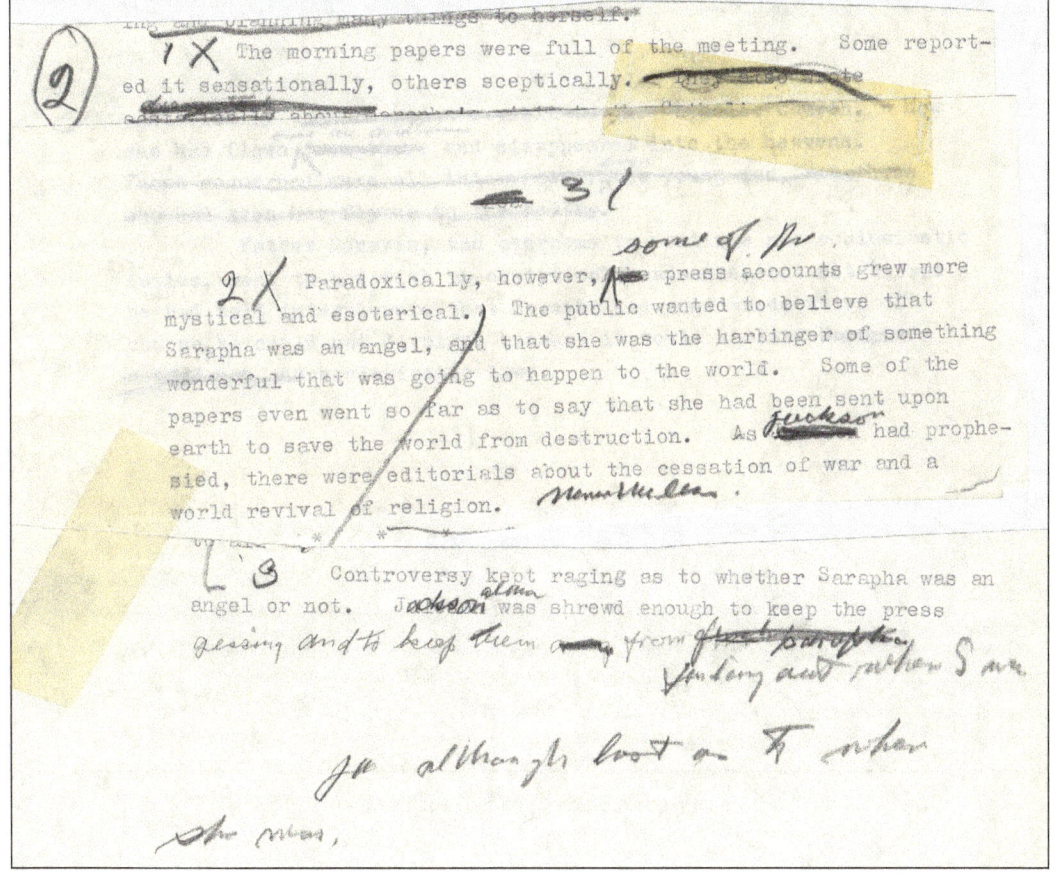

Preparatory notes for *The Freak*.

*   *   *   *   *   *   *

The effect of Sarapha's appearances had created worldwide ~~revolution,~~ and ~~in many instances chaos.~~ In ~~America,~~
there were ~~many~~ strikes, ~~novel~~ parades, and street battles, ~~and~~
~~disobedience corps parading~~ ~~Crowds gathered in huge demonstrations~~ ~~We shall~~

It was impossible to combat this universal ~~opposition.~~
Peace was immediately declared; ~~the~~ cheering crowds lined the
streets as the Marines marched down Fifth Avenue to the roar of
happy thousands who welcomed them. ~~Negroes were embracing~~
~~white men and vice versa.~~

*   *   *   *   *   *   *

At the **height of** this Professor Latham returned
to London. He was still on good terms with his wife who ~~greeted~~
~~him and~~ accepted him in a kindly, objective manner. ~~He had~~
~~been away for two years.~~ And now they dined quietly at 25 South
Molton Street. Margaret's behaviour was matured and sophisticated. She confessed that she ~~had had two lovers since he had~~
~~left Iany.~~ It was a strange meeting, ~~and the atmosphere was~~
rather sad. She talked of Sarapha and how she had taken the
world by storm. She told many anecdotes about her and her love
of jewelry.

Latham sat silent and listened.

She picked up a newspaper with black headlines and read :
'The angel has brought peace to the world. Even the Chinese have
been stupified by the altruistic action of the Americans. They
have moved their troops out of Pakistan - Red Danny is no longer
red, but has dyed his hair black ! ~~Mr. Jackson, under whose~~
~~management Sarapha has been, is with the 'angel' on her tour~~
~~through Scotland.~~ Since her tour in Scotland, Buckingham Palace

Preparatory notes on Sarapha and the events of 1968.

Protests at the United States Embassy in Grosvenor Square, London, March 1968.

In another proposition about Sarapha's global impact, we can see the effect upon Chaplin of the dramatic world events of 1968 — the very moment when he was still working on his treatment. Chaplin, as we know, was always absorbed with what was going on in the world, and this precise moment in history saw a worldwide escalation of social conflicts, predominantly characterized by popular rebellions against military and bureaucratic elites, who responded with an escalation of political repression. This was the moment of the Black Panther Party and heightened civil rights movements, international opposition to the Vietnam War, protests in Eastern European socialist countries against Communist abuses of human rights, symbolised by the Prague Spring, the May protests and strikes in France.

In an extraordinary fashion, Chaplin sought to identify the impact of Sarapha with world events of 1968:

> The effect of Sarapha's appearances had created world-wide sensation. In all parts of the world [*changed in manuscript from* "In America…"] there were strikes, parades, and street battles, student corps paraded and held meetings in Trafalgar Square… It was impossible to combat this universal appeal. Peace was immediately declared; in the States cheering crowds in New York lined the streets as the Marines marched down Fifth Avenue to the roar of happy thousands who welcomed them.
>
> At the height of this happy festival, Professor Latham returned to London. He was still on good terms with his wife who accepted him in a kindly objective manner… Margaret's behavior was matured and sophisticated. She confessed that she did not love him. It was a strange meeting.

> She picked up a newspaper with black headlines and read, "The Angel has brought peace to the world. Even the Chinese have been stupefied by the altruistic action of the Americans. They have moved their troops out of Pakistan—Red Danny is no longer red, but has dyed his hair black!"

A variant of this passage adds:

> Their leader was Sarapha. She had ignited in them a spiritual revolt, had inspired them to demand new reforms. Slum clearances were carried out, and new cities were being built to facilitate modern traffic. It was impossible to combat this universal innovation. Peace was immediately declared amongst warring nations.

No hint of this '68 utopian fantasy was to survive in the final script.

The casual mention here of Latham touches on a problem that besets the script to the very end: the disappearance of the male protagonist less than a third of the way through the story. After Sarapha is kidnapped by Jackson, Latham is effectively abandoned in Chile without a word of farewell. In the final script, he reappears at the last minute, in a way that is not entirely clear (did a letter from Margaret call him back to London?) but very timely, to save Sarapha from murder charges and prove his humanity.

Probably aware that this could also have had its repercussions when it came to casting (the actors he had in mind, Richard Chamberlain, James Fox or Robert Vaughn, would certainly have been puzzled by a role absent from the screen for more than half of the film) Chaplin tried to reintegrate Latham into the story by anticipating his return to London, but did not persevere in the attempt.

In several early treatments there are proposals, eventually abandoned, to have him arrive at the South Molton Street address referenced in the letter intercepted by Sarapha, just in advance of the evangelical meeting. The most developed proposal for this is from a very early treatment, in which Jackson is still named Juleson, and in which the address is referred to as the home of Latham's "future mother-in-law."

In order to keep Sarapha out of sight before the great evangelist meeting, Juleson has entrusted her to the care of his sister, in Richmond:

> However, he allowed her to be photographed standing by the river or sitting alone in the garden. She never quite understood the importance of these snapshots, and how many thousands of curiosity seekers were milling round the house, and this made Sarapha very nervous.
>
> Juleson kept the magazines away from her with the advertisements showing her at breakfast with cereal packages placed conspicuously on the table, for which he received a substantial sum. Juleson never for one moment thought that Sarapha would change the way of life or be considered a divine celestial. To use the vernacular, he intended to make dough while the press were hot.
>
> He also hid the newspapers for they were veering towards controversy. The tide was slowly turning.
>
> Letters by the thousand came from all parts of England and the rest of the world. So many that it was impossible to answer them. Sarapha, in order to amuse herself ,would sort out the interesting ones. She was careful to watch for a Chilean

postmark, which Juleson and his secretary were also careful to watch for. One, however, escaped him. Sarapha saw it, and recognised the small positive handwriting so characteristic of Latham's hand writing.

Her heart thumped when she saw it. Quickly she hid it under other letters, then when she was alone—read it.

Yes—it was from—Professor Latham! He had arrived in London and was living in South Molton Street, in a house belonging to his future mother-in-law. He would, however, be at the meeting. He was concerned about her, her health, and state of mind. If he could be of any assistance, she must let him know.

Sarapha would see him as soon as possible, but of course she could not divulge this to Juleson. She would have to visit him at night when the household was asleep. She looked at several maps of London to find out where South Molton Street was.

That night, unbeknown to anybody, she crept to the window and quietly opened it. She wore a cape and heavy-lined pants to keep her warm, nothing heavier, otherwise it might impede her flying.

It was midnight as she stood on the window-sill ready to take off. She vaguely knew the direction. She would fly north-west as Richmond was located approximately south. She knew the location was near Bond Street. Happily it was Sunday and the theatre crowds had gone home early. Bond Street was completely deserted as she flew over it.

Aerial view of London, 1969.

Sarapha in London. Storyboard by Gerald Larn.

South Molton Street was difficult to find, especially from the air. She flew in low in order to try and read the name of the streets. At one quiet corner she decided to fly down and look to see where she was.

She alighted perfectly but had trouble reading the names of the street. As she was peering, a drunk staggered round the corner.

He stopped abruptly and blinked. Sarapha, forgetting who she was, turned to him and innocently enquired, "Could you tell me where South Molton Street is?"

She saw that the man was struck dumb, his eyes bulging: "Oh, don't bother!" she said impatiently, then took off again and flew into the night. Over Bond Street, she looked down and noticed the man was still standing where she had left him.

She flew over small streets toward Marble Arch. It must be in this direction, she thought. She hovered a moment to make sure that nobody saw her. Then, using her bird instinct, she landed in a small street—And there it was! South Molton Street.

She was about to ring the bell of number 25 South Molton Street, but realised that everyone would be asleep. She flew up to the bedroom windows to hold on to the window sill and gently flapping her wings to see.

One window was open. Without hesitation, she jumped in. Professor Latham, sat up in bed with a start, then realized who it was.

"Sarapha!" He rubbed his eyes then looked again.

"I must be dreaming," he said

"Well, I never thought I would ever see you again!" He looked at her pants. "Good heaven! What are you wearing?"

"To protect me from your English climate," she said, smilingly.

"Wait a moment." He put on a dressing gown. "I want to have a good look at you.

She looked pale and very tired and utterly lost.

"My poor Sarapha," he said, taking her in his arms tenderly. She began to weep.

"There, there," he interposed.

"I feel so lonely."

Frustratingly, no more of this scene seems to have survived. It is very evident that—with Jackson still as Juleson—this is one of the earliest drafts.

In later versions of the treatments, Chaplin proposes to bring Latham back at the time of the Pentagon ball:

Lady Pentagon was talking to Margaret: "My dear, I'm sure that XVIIIth century gentleman with the mask is your ex-husband." At that moment the gentleman in question approached: "Lady Pentagon, do please introduce me to my wife!"

"John" [sic], said Margaret. "When did you arrive in London?"

"This morning" replied Latham. "And on finding Lady Pentagon's invitation, I hustled and managed to get this outfit."

"Take off that wretched mask," said Margaret.

Without comment he took it off.

He was always handsome, but his expression had matured, and he was even handsomer than ever. A pang of regret and thrill at seeing him again came over her—she needed a moment of adjustment: "Have you finished your book?."

"Yes," he said simply. "I understand our friend has created quite a lot of excitement."

Margaret laughed uneasily: Yes. Shall we dance?"

Latham bowed.

They dance—and the orchestra plays the same music as on the night when Latham and Margaret had first met. Margaret reveals that Sarapha is here—she felt that she would be safer than in hiding.

Meanwhile Sarapha has caused a stir at the buffet by throwing ham and eggs ordered by another guest to the floor. She then goes into the ballroom:

Margaret and Latham saw her. Sarapha recognised him, and with a little shriek, she ran into his arms, then buried her face in his neck—then suddenly turned away and ran out of the ballroom. He followed her...

She finds herself everywhere confronted by Jackson or the police:

Her mind was now deranged. She began to scream like a seagull. She ran back into the ballroom and began to fly. She flew around and above the chandeliers. The guests stood aghast. As she darted down, they scattered.

On the evidence of the surviving typescripts, it was at this point in his writing that Chaplin moved on from his progressive narrative treatments to full script form. As script, the treatments provided approximately 85 per cent of the final script.

It was possibly at this point, in July 1969, that Chaplin asked Miss Ford to prepare a synopsis to submit for the purpose of securing copyright. In fact the application was rejected, as the synopsis was deemed inadequately short. It does however serve to reveal that at this stage Chaplin was still far from his eventual concept of the structure and dramatic drive of the climax of the film. The synopsis briefly but accurately summarises the story from the Chile opening to Sarapha's escape from Jackson and her sheltering by Margaret, and already has the ending of Sarapha's attempted but fatal flight to Chile; but the story-line between appeared at the least inadequate:

She is sheltered by Latham's ex-wife, Margaret, who has become very fond of her. However, she has been seen several times and the newspapers print stories about her, leading Jackson to demand her return. Afraid of quarantine and immigration she goes back and takes part in a giant Revival-meeting with the famous Dr Gidson. It ends with her being frightened into flying away again, to Margaret. Jackson follows her trail and has her captured and put into quarantine. Margaret and Latham, who have arrived in London, establish her human condition by finding her birth registrations and she is released. But after her experiences she only wants to return to Chile. She attempts to fly there, and her body is found floating in the Atlantic Ocean

It was evident that Chaplin was still in need of a heightened dramatic climax which would place Sarapha in acute peril; a consequent dénouement, which would lead to the already decided ultimate fate of his Wonderful Visitor — or Freak.

His decision was that this exquisite aerial creature would be submitted to a gross and common sexual assault, and that in self-defence she would kill the perpetrator.

The first plan for this scene was to use the already resident villain, Jackson. After escaping from the Pentagon Ball, Sarapha chooses for no very clear reason, to go to the Savoy Hotel.

DISSOLVE TO LONG SHOT.

Riverside exterior of Savoy Hotel.

Sarapha flies in and hops on to the top of the tree. Her expression is haunted as she looks up at the open window of the sixth floor. With fear and anxiety she looks around, then flies up to it.

CUT TO INTERIOR OF SIXTH FLOOR SUITE.

Sarapha appears and cautiously ENTERS through the open window. She looks round the room, then thinking someone is coming, she quickly tries the door and discovers that the lock is broken. She places a chair under the handle of the door, then collapses on the bed. Very soon she is asleep, but is awakened by someone gently tapping on her bedroom door. Quickly she sits up and sees the door handle turning and the door being gently pushed in, but the chair stops it.

SARAPHA
(*scared*)
Yes? Who is it?

There is a pause.

VOICE OF JACKSON
(*whispers*)
Is that you, Sarapha?

Sarapha pauses before answering.

SARAPHA
Yes?

VOICE OF JACKSON
(*whispering*)
It's me, Jackson!

SARAPHA
What do you want?

VOICE OF JACKSON
I have good news from the Immigration Department. They have
dropped your case! Open the door!

Sarapha hesitates then decides to open it.

Jackson has been drinking. He looms up in the doorway and looks at her in a peculiar, evil fashion.

JACKSON
Hello, stranger

SARAPHA
(*fiercely*)
What do you want?

JACKSON
Just a little chit-chat—that's all.

He goes forward towards her. She backs away from him and snarls. But he continues
going towards her.

JACKSON
I know you hate me!

```
                              14, Vincent Square,

                              London, S.W.1.

                          Tel:  01-828.2747.



Mr. Jay Kanter,
Winkast Film Productions, Ltd.,
3, Tilney Street,
LONDON, W.1.                      8th December, 1969.



Dear Jay,

      Enclosed is Charlie's script - Just for your eyes.

      I took the script from him in haste.   There are
several discrepancies regarding time, settings, etc.,
but Charlie is aware of these and has already fixed
them.

      But, more important, when reading the script just
keep in mind he is working on the following sequences:

      1. The opening of the film.

      2. The arrival of Jackson at Margaret's
         house and why she goes to the Savoy
         so easily.

      3. He is building up the discussion for the
         big rally and the preparations for it.

      4. Also, within the rally itself, he is
         building up the entrances of Gidson and
         Sarapha.

      5. Also, he is motivating why the crowds
         begin chanting 'No more wars ... No
         more wars'.

Call me after you have read it.

                   Many thanks,

                       Best,



                   JERRY EPSTEIN.
```

Letter from Jerry Epstein to Jay Kanter (Winkast Film Productions).
Chaplin is rewriting some passages, 8 December 1969.

He extends his hand and tries to grab her wrist but she backs away and snarls at him.

SARAPHA
Get away from me—Or I'll scream.

JACKSON
Why can't we be friends

SARAPHA
I've warned you—If you come near me I'll—

But he still advances. She is about to scream, but he puts his hand over her mouth and she bites it. He pushes her back on the bed, his hand bleeding profusely. In the struggle that follows, he grabs her by the throat and begins to strangle her. With her free hand she manages to reach the dressing-table, on which is a pair of scissors, and stabs him in the back and chest. Then, seeing what she has done, she opens the window and flies away.

FADE INTO MARGARET'S SITTING-ROOM.

Margaret is listening tearfully to the radio.

VOICE OF LAWYER
(*from radio*)
Mr. Jackson, impresario and publicist, was found stabbed to death in his room at the Savoy Hotel. Jackson is reported to have kidnapped the reputed angel, whose recent appearance at the Royal Albert Hall [sic] created a sensation. Since this discovery, the angel has been missing. She is wanted by the police for questioning.

BUTLER ENTERS.

BUTLER
 Professor Latham, Madam.

Latham ENTERS immediately and embraces MARGARET who sobs on his shoulder.

Chaplin clearly recognized the improbability of Sarapha, having fled from the Pentagon ball expressly to escape Jackson, making her way to his suite at the Savoy. Consequently he next devised an alternative scene in which Jackson invades Margaret's country house to carry out his assault.

CUT TO NIGHT TIME. MARGARET'S COUNTRY HOUSE.

CUT TO SARAPHA.

She appears and ENTERS a window. She looks about and finds herself in a large hall with a grand staircase. Quickly she trips up the stairs, half flying, half hopping. She is obviously nervous and afraid. At last she reaches her room, but for some reason, she cannot lock the door. With a look of frantic despair, she gives up trying to lock the door. As she starts undressing, a slight tap at the door brings her to a sudden standstill. She turns quickly and sees the handle of the door turning. Before she realises it, the door opens and Jackson appears. He has been drinking although he doesn't show it.

CLOSE UP JACKSON.

> JACKSON
> Good evening. I had the devil of a time following you. Fortunately, when you escaped from this house, you dropped your key! So it's quite hopeless trying to escape. The police know where you are every minute of the day. And so do I!

SARAPHA is silent. She just stares at him with a look of hate.

SARAPHA backs away from him.

> JACKSON
> (*continuing*)
> Why do you think I've gone to all this expense, putting you up at the best hotels? I've got all the money I want! (*an evil look comes over his face*) It's you I want! I guess I must be crazy, but you're beautiful. I don't care if you're a bird, a freak, or whatever you are—(*he catches her by the wrist*) The desire for you has burnt into my brain!

> SARAPHA
> (*looking hypnotically at him*)
> Get away from me!

> JACKSON
> (*still holding on to her wrist*)
> You're exciting! Wonderful!

> SARAPHA
> (*she breaks away from him*)
> If you come near me I'll... (*Jackson still advances*) Get away from me—or I'll scream! I've warned you—If you come near me I'll...

But he still advances. She is about to scream, but he puts his hand over her mouth and she bites it. He pushes her back on the bed, his hand bleeding profusely. In the struggle that follows, he grabs her by the throat and begins to strangle her. With her free hand, she manages to reach the dressing-table, on which is a pair of scissors, and stabs him in the back and chest. Then, seeing what she has done, she opens the window and flies away.

This version of the death of Jackson has a unique and interesting account of Latham's return to London. He appears fortuitously as Margaret is tearfully discussing the event with the police, her lawyer and the press. Latham takes over and provides a virtual press conference.

BUTLER ENTERS.

> BUTLER
> Professor Latham, Madame

MARGARET gets up tearfully to acknowledge the announcement.

LATHAM ENTERS.

MARGARET goes forward and falls weeping in his arms. In this scene, one feels that there is a reconciliation.

> LATHAM
> If there is anything I can do… I can be a witness

> REPORTER
> I understand, Professor Latham, that you have just returned from South America.

> LATHAM
> Yes, I went to Chile to write a book.

> REPORTER
> You didn't take Madam Latham with you?

> LATHAM
> No.

> REPORTER
> Isn't that where you discovered Sarapha?

> LATHAM
> Yes. I discovered her wounded on the roof of my house. She had been attacked by eagles. Then Jackson kidnapped her.

Victoria as Sarapha. Illustration by Gerald Larn.

REPORTER
If this creature is captured, will you be a principal witness for the
defence?

LATHAM
I certainly will.

REPORTER
There were rumours that Madam Latham was getting a divorce.

LATHAM
They seem to know more about this than I do!

REPORTER
Then you're not getting a divorce?

LATHAM
Certainly not. (*he looks at Margaret*)

REPORTER
And you arrived from South America last night?

LATHAM
Yes. And the moment I landed in England I heard this unfortunate
news.

Clearly Chaplin was not content. Jackson had certainly served his term of villainy since his first nefarious appearance in Chile. He was at once a too obvious choice for the climactic crime, and at the same time might be thought to have proved too cool and calculating in his wrong-doings and marketing of sexuality to collapse suddenly into drooling lechery.

Yet it seemed only when he came to the final version of the script, ready to go into production in September 1969, that Chaplin discovered his *deus ex machina* in Sir Rex Horton. This hypothesis is supported by the fact that in the storyboards John Rose created in June and July of the same year, the attacker is still Jackson. The first sighting of Sir Rex is a typed note headed *Suggestions for Story*:

After Sarapha is installed in Margaret's country house, Margaret receives a telegram informing her that Rex, her new husband, is returning from India where he has been playing polo.

Rex is a drunkard who married Margaret for her money.

He is a jealous, belligerent man.

He makes his wife unhappy with his neurotic jealousy.

He is, of course, jealous of Edward, who corresponds with Margaret from Chile.

Since his return, Margaret is drinking heavily.

It is obvious that Rex encourages her.

There is a pathetic and funny scene where Margaret, in a stupor, is put to bed by Sarapha.

One night, Sarapha is wakened by a terrible row going on downstairs in the drawing room.

The row becomes so violent that Rex threatens to hit Margaret.

Sarapha joins in the fray and attacks Rex, biting and scratching etc.

After this unhappy sojourn in his home, Rex decides to go shooting in Africa.

In the meantime, while Rex is in Africa, the rest of the story takes place. Lord Pentagon's party, etc.

At this stage Sir Rex is perceived only as a colourfully awful supporting character, to account for Margaret's injudicious abandonment of Latham. Chaplin seems however quite quickly to have had the inspiration of having him, in the final version of the script, replace Jackson as the sexual aggressor, killed by Sarapha in self-defence. Sir Rex was perfect: he was already part of the household, so *in situ* for the assault; while his unregretted decease facilitated the reunion of Latham and Margaret and their collaboration in saving Sarapha and establishing her true origins and identity.

The second version of the script involving Jackson as the assaulter gives the longest and most emotive speech to the Counsel for the Defence:

Ladies and Gentlemen of the Jury, you have heard all the facts of the case—that Professor Latham was there, and witnessed the kidnapping. How she was lured into a helicopter and escaped when she arrived in London. In spite of the fact that there are extenuating circumstances, nothing is analogous in this tragedy. Witnesses have testified that she is a freak, half woman and half bird. But I say she is essentially a human being, hounded and alone. She has been kidnapped, caged, and incarcerated. Are not these things enough to beset her with terror and unbearable agony? What has happened was in self-defence which is quite evident. I was going to say in defence of her honour—but the word "honour" is trivial compared with the tragedy of her life. With these words, I leave her fate in your hands.

A final unsolved mystery is an unexplained and inexplicable scene which in several versions of the completed—but not final—script precedes Sarapha's descent on the church (or, as described here, convent), on her first arrival in London.*

DISSOLVE TO SARAPHA FLYING HIGH ABOVE LONDON.

DISSOLVE TO A POOR CONVENT IN HACKNEY, LONDON.

DISSOLVE TO A VERY PLAIN ROOM IN CONVENT.

A Mother Superior is seated at a desk. There is a knock at the door.

>   MOTHER SUPERIOR
>   Come in.

A middle-aged nun, MARIA, enters, and MOTHER SUPERIOR points to a chair.

>   MOTHER SUPERIOR
>   How is she to-day?

>   MARIA
>   (*looking troubled*)
>   Better, thank you, Mother. (*shakes her head and thinks to herself*) But
>   I'm afraid we'll have trouble with her.

>   MOTHER SUPERIOR
>   (*stops writing*)
>   I thought you said she was better.

>   MARIA
>   Yes, in health, but she is losing her mind.

>   MOTHER SUPERIOR
>   (*thinks for a minute*)
>   We must be patient. The mind is very frail.

---

* This scene appears in two of the bound screenplays, Chm00275 and Ch00051.

Victoria as Sarapha. Illustration by Gerald Larn.

MARIA
(*troubled*)
She still has visions.

MOTHER SUPERIOR
Well, that is normal. (*gets up from desk and looks at shabby street*)
So long as she's not obstreperous.

MARIA
Oh no. She's quite gentle.

MOTHER SUPERIOR
Is she still in her room?

MARIA
Yes, Mother.

MOTHER SUPERIOR
Then we'll visit her. (*they both EXIT*)

CUT TO SMALL ROOM. A young nun, her face lifted as though she sees a vision, is startled when she hears a knock at the door. Two nuns ENTER.

    MOTHER SUPERIOR
    My dear, you look much better.

    MARGARET
    Yes, thank you Mother. I believe I'll be able to go to Mass this morning.

    MOTHER SUPERIOR
    Do you think you ought to?

    MARGARET
    Oh yes. It will be good for me.

DISSOLVE TO SEMI-LONG SHOT.

SARAPHA alights on the roof of the church.

Nothing in the preliminary treatments or the final script give us any preparation or explanation for this scene. The name Margaret can hardly be a coincidental choice, since this was from the start the name given to Latham's sister, fiancée, wife or divorced wife, according to the momentary needs of relationships. At no point is there any suggestion of any religious bent or affiliation or of psychological problems. Yet this strange scene persists in several—if not most—versions of the script, still an impenetrable mystery.

Oona and Charles Chaplin at the Manoir de Ban, ca. 1960.

Victoria Chaplin wears the wings while rehearsing on the lawn of the Manoir de Ban under her father's supervision, August 1974. Photograph by Jean-Baptiste Thierrée.

5

A Story Finally Told
A Conversation with Victoria Chaplin and Gerald Larn

In 2016, after the Chaplin Office acquired a substantial amount of unpublished material belonging to Jerry Epstein, we decided to share some of our recent discoveries with Victoria Chaplin. Since then, Victoria has always responded with great generosity to all our questions and curiosities. Some of her stories have raised further questions and suggested new directions for research. Her memories of the long working sessions at Shepperton Studios, for example, encouraged us to contact Gerard Larn, the artist commissioned to illustrate the flight sequences and create the drawings on which the construction of the wings would be based. His sketches, marked with the initials G.L., are still preserved in the Chaplin archives.

The two conversations that follow, conducted by Cecilia Cenciarelli together wtih David Robinson and Kate Guyonvarch, are the result of meetings with Victoria in Paris (September 2016) and with Gerard Larn in London (January 2017). Victoria was also present at this meeting with Larn. The two had not seen each other for almost fifty years.

Victoria Chaplin: My first memory of *The Freak* predates the late 1960s; it goes back to my childhood. I have this memory of a restaurant. We were having dinner, and my father told us the story as if he already knew it… this woman who is found on the roof and no one knows anything about her, no one knows who she is or what she is. It was quite a long fairy tale. He told us many fairy tales. Some of them were very scary. [*laughs*]

There was one about a dog that was left to look after some children one evening. The parents said to him, "Take care of the children while we're away." When they came home, they found the dog with his muzzle covered in blood and put him down, only to realise later that the dog had defended the children from a wolf that wanted to eat them. He told us these terrifying stories that he must have heard as a child in England, where they have a long tradition of Gothic-inspired fairy tales. So in my memory, *The Freak* is part of these stories. It was a kind of fairy tale. Then I don't remember anything else except that suddenly I'm older, and I find myself interpreting that story.

Cecilia Cenciarelli: Had you ever acted before that?

VC: No, not really. In *The Countess*, Josephine, Geraldine and I had tiny parts… that was my only real acting experience. When I was fourteen or fifteen, however, I was quite good at dancing, and my father must have noticed that I moved well. My parents thought I had a chance of getting into the Royal Academy of Dramatic Art and that it would be a good idea to take private lessons before applying. But I think my father always took it for granted that I could act, and often said to me, "Here's my actress!"

Victoria and Jerry Epstein, ca. 1969.

David Robinson: It is said that he believed you had inherited the "gift of comedy."

VC: Well, yes… that's possible. But before *The Freak*, he had another project in mind, a mythological story. I remember that during that period, my sisters and I spent a lot of time on the swing and sang constantly: "Que sera, sera, whatever will be, will beeee…" Dad really liked hearing us sing, so we went through the whole history of mythology singing. He was a strict father, but he always tried to entertain us — always. There was another project too, about the history of Hollywood, which my mother loved. But then Dad threw himself heart and soul into this "story of the winged woman." I think it was in the summer of 1967.

CC: He told you right away that he had thought of you for the lead role. How did he tell you?

VC: From the moment he started working on *The Freak*, this story was always in the air, even when he wasn't working, but he never came to me to tell me that I would be playing the part. I remember that he revealed the story to me little by little, and then I realised that it was the same fairy tale we had heard for the first time in that restaurant many years earlier. He didn't go into detail about the character's intentions, but maybe at dinner, or after we had finished eating, he would ask me to repeat a few lines, to show him some expressions or a dance step. Other times, he would act out a few passages for me. For example, I remember when he mimed the girl in the cage, ready to fly away. He was able to render a scene convincingly and clearly with a few precise words and very measured gestures. It was truly incredible. Other times he would talk to me about his point of view on the story or on a particular scene. He wanted me to feel privileged to have been given this part.

DR: So at a certain point it becomes clear that this film is going to be made. Did he tell you who Sarapha was?

VC: Dad hadn't yet decided whether she was a woman, a bird, a monster, or an angel. He talked about her as an extremely human being who, however, when frightened, turned into this kind of science fiction creature. Sometimes he seemed to suggest that, in the end, it wasn't so important to know who she was. I believe Sarapha is different, an outsider who ultimately falls victim to her diversity. It's a wonderful story, so contemporary. Sarapha is a character with great dramatic potential. I don't know how much I realised that at the time; I was so young, but I'm sure my father knew it very well.

CC: So it was clear to you that it was going to be a drama?

VC: Yes and no, because, for example, I remember my father playing the role of the maid in the scenes where she faints. It was pure comedy! And then there was a very strong satirical element, about religious fanaticism and the innate need of human beings to believe in something transcendental, not to mention the fierce criticism of the thirst for money and the excessive power of advertising and the mass media. *The Freak* is also a visionary story. Honestly, I don't remember ever thinking in terms of genre; for us, it was simply a "Charlie Chaplin film." And then there was the music. Dad had composed some music for the final scene, Sarapha's last flight over the ocean, and I remember this old Chilean song. We had a cassette tape where he hummed this tune and accompanied himself on the piano. I remember it very well; it was a blue cassette tape. It must have ended up in the countryside somewhere. I wonder if Geraldine remembers it. He composed it on the piano, and I think it was reused for something else later on.

DR: If I remember correctly, Chaplin worked on it with Eric James, and some of that material was adapted and reused for the soundtrack of the re-release of *The Kid*.

Kate Guyonvarch: There's also a song, published by Bourne, and someone else wrote the lyrics. It's in the documentary *The Gentleman Tramp*.

DR: Do you remember if your mother was involved in the project from the beginning?

VC: I remember that they often talked about the film and that my father read her the script late at night, and she gave him her opinion. Even though it was clear to all of us that dad had this story on his mind from morning to night, I don't remember any big announcements about it being his next film. I sincerely believe that after *A Countess from Hong Kong*, he was scared. It's hard to imagine, isn't it?—after living such a full life, making all those films, being so successful, suddenly feeling so insecure. It must have been very difficult for him. And then that broken ankle… I'm sure it must have undermined his confidence quite a bit, for someone like him, with his physicality. He complained about not being able to play tennis, but I think it was more complex than that. Maybe that's also why he wanted to make a film with us; not just with the idea of launching us, but perhaps because he wanted to work in a more protected environment, with non-leading actors.

Oona and Geraldine on the lawn of the Manoir, 1960s.

Every now and then he would grumble: "Don't go out to discos—remember that we have to make this film together!" Can you imagine an angel with a disco hangover? [*laughs*] "Get that disco look out of your eyes," he would say. When *Countess* was released, he was against the idea of us attending parties organised to promote the film. He believed we were still too young and inexperienced, and even a little naive.

CC: The Chaplin archive contains an impressive number of notes on a wide variety of stories and subjects, as well as pages full of philosophical reflections. It seems like among other things, he thought a great deal about the role of religion in Western society. Earlier, you mentioned religious fanaticism…

VC: Yes, my father had a keen interest not only in religion but also in all its ramifications. I remember him often mentioning Billy Graham, and although he never explained to me how the mystical element had anything to do with the story, I heard him say several times that *The Freak* was also a film about religion and Billy Graham. We used to watch these huge crowds of believers gathering in the United States on television—a phenomenon completely absent in Europe, where there was a distinct feeling that religion was dead and buried. It was rather disturbing to watch those gatherings, but there was also something hypnotic about them.

CC: Did your family often watch television and comment on the news? Did your father discuss politics with you?

Charles and Oona, ca. 1960. Photo by Roger Wood Studio.

VC: For many years, we didn't even have a television at home. Every now and then we would go and watch TV at our neighbours' house, a farming family who lived across the street. They were very kind to us. [*laughs*] Then in 1963, when Kennedy was assassinated, we bought a television, I would say that very same day, because my father wanted to see with his own eyes what had happened. He had always been very interested in politics. Every Sunday he would go down to the village to buy *The New York Times* and then discuss politics with my mother or his friends. Jerry was very concerned about the Israeli-Palestinian conflict. And then there was May 1968, De Gaulle, and the invasion of Czechoslovakia, which at first left him stunned and confused. He was interested in everything, he was interested in the world. He always wanted to understand.

DR: *A King in New York* is an extremely political film, especially the character of Michael, who is incredibly sad.

VC: I remember one evening many years ago; it was 1972 because *The Kid* had been released again in cinemas. We were having dinner in London and at that time I had my political convictions. I was very politically active. And my mother said something like, "*The Kid* is not a political film," and I said, "Of course it is, it's an extremely political film, everything is political!" My father started laughing, and in the end they began to tease me a little, calling me a revolutionary. I almost had tears in my eyes when he turned to me and said, "It's a film about the struggle for life, for survival. So of course it's a political film."

Charles Chaplin with his daughters Victoria and Josephine, and Jean-Baptiste Thiérrée, early 1970s.

CC: Did you watch many films together?

VC: His screening room was off-limits; only my mother had access to it. At home, they watched holiday videos and little else, but I remember we often went to the cinema when we were in London, to that theatre near the Hilton. I think it was the Curzon Mayfair… We would make sandwiches and go to the cinema; it was something we loved doing. Dad took us to see *Persona*, which he loved unconditionally. One film he didn't like at all was *The Sound of Music*. [*laughs*] I think he left the cinema before the end of the film. *2001: A Space Odyssey* also made a deep impression on him, but I wasn't with them that time. And then we watched all these films with flying scenes, flying actors and so on, like *Barbarella*, but he didn't like that either, if I remember correctly.

DR: When did you leave Manoir-de-Ban?

VC: Shortly before Christmas 1969. I was 16. I was attending a boarding school in Oxford-shire and Jerry would come and pick me up on my days off to take me to London to try out the wings, which went on for several months. When I came home, my father would talk to me a lot about *The Freak*. Every now and then he would study me and ask me to try out certain movements or facial expressions. Sometimes, when I came home, he would say, "Today we're rehearsing!" and he would read me the script or tell me about the story.

And there was also my sister Josephine, who was going to play the scientist's wife. I think Josie was a little jealous that I had the lead role. [*laughs*] We rehearsed in the library, and I particularly remember the scene where the two meet, when I appear at her window. He would show us the part and then ask us to imitate him and make us repeat the same scene over and over again, or he would say to me, "Now I'm going to the living room and I want to hear you read from there." It was awful reading our lines out loud because we lost control of our voices and our acting. It seemed very difficult to us. He wanted to see if we were capable or if we had musicality. I don't think he was ever particularly satisfied!

CC: Did your father intimidate you a little?

VC: Well, yes, quite a lot. We were very excited, and proud in a way, but definitely intimidated too. He was opposed to any kind of forced interpretation, and I think he particularly loved our freshness and spontaneity, the same spontaneity he loved in children. We were shy by nature, but at the same time we felt that we could do it, that with his guidance we would succeed. We were happy to go along with him and wanted to make a good impression on him.

DR: And then what happened?

Jerry Epstein at the Manoir de Ban, 1965.

VC: I remember it was December [1969], and we were decorating the Christmas tree. They had met with the executives of United Artists and Jerry received a terrible letter. I remember very well the expression on my mother's face becoming increasingly sad. Then they started talking about the special effects again, saying they were too complex, and considering other systems with mirrors and models. They asked this famous English actress, Margaret Johnson, to give me private lessons to prepare me for the Royal Academy of Dramatic Art entrance exam. She had also taught Michael before me and at one point she gave me Shakespeare to read. It seemed so far removed from my life… I was just a teenager and couldn't see any connection with my aspirations. That was when I started receiving letters from Jean-Baptiste, this charming young man full of ideas, who wanted to start a revolutionary circus. Anyway, it was 1969, I was very young, I was living in Switzerland, and I was bored to death, [*laughs*] so I replied that I thought it was a fantastic idea, that I loved the circus too, as did my whole family, and that he could definitely count on me! We continued to write to each other until we finally met. We fell in love immediately.

CC: You know that many people attributed your father's decision to leave *The Freak* to this?

VC: Yes, yes, of course, I know. After all, it's my father who says so in *My Life in Pictures*, that he would have loved to make the film with me but that I ran away with a clown. [*laughs*] And actually, I really wanted to do it too, and my mother and Jerry knew that because I kept saying so. And even when Jean-Baptiste—who was a big fan of my father's—and I talked about our plans, we both knew that if the film went ahead, that would be my priority. But my mother, understandably, hesitated and didn't trust him. She and dad asked Miss Ford to gather information about Jean-Baptiste, and I was really grateful to her because she knew they were worried and would have loved her to come back and tell them he was a fraud. But no, she told my parents that he was a brilliant young man, that he only had four years' experience in theatre but that he was a very interesting guy. She gave every indication of being very honest.

At that point, I told my mother, "If the film doesn't happen, I'm going ahead with my plans with Jean-Baptiste," and she said, "I'll stop him from making the film because it would kill him. After *Countess*, embarking on such a complicated production, financing the film… can you imagine the stress? It would be lethal for him. No, it won't happen." I don't know how many times I must have repeated to my mother and Jerry that if things changed, if they managed to resolve the flight issue, the financial issues, if her concerns were dispelled—in short, anything—I would return immediately.

CC: Did you discuss this with your father?

VC: No, not with him, not directly. Obviously, I adored my father, but he intimidated me a lot. So I slipped away quietly, like a real coward. I wrote to him often from France, though, because at that same time Michael had gone to London and we hadn't heard from him; he never called or wrote. My parents were upset, so I tried to write as often as possible, telling them how we were going to revolutionise the circus and all our crazy ideas. It was a very exciting time for me; so many things were happening. But I want to repeat: I always said I would come back at any time to do *The Freak*.

I've thought about it many times… Maybe my mother never told him. She was visibly worried about him, so she was very protective. I don't rule out that she never told him that it was she who made the decision. The years passed and in 1971 my mother came to visit me in the south of France for the birth of Aurélia, and when I returned to Switzerland with the baby for the first time, my father was enchanted. He loved children very much.

CC: Did he ever consider shooting the film without you, with another actress?

VC: At one point, the name Christiane [Fugger von Bebenhausen] came up. She was a friend of my sister Annie's; half Indian and half German, with beautiful skin and light green eyes. I remember her coming to our house for Sunday lunch. She was lovely. She later married a French actor, Jean Yanne, and I heard that she sadly died young, about ten years ago.

DR: So you and Jean-Baptiste used to visit your father and mother regularly with the children?

VC: Yes. I remember once when Geraldine and Carlos [Saura] came to pick me up at the airport, and I got the impression that the project was back on track. Dad talked about it with the press and Geraldine also mentioned it to a journalist. Josie and I had tried again during one of my visits. I don't think it was ever a question of money, and of course there were all my mother's concerns. But I think the real obstacle was this sense of insecurity that had grown in him after *A Countess of Hong Kong*. That was it more than anything else… and age, of course. But Jerry kept saying he was open to discussing the project with him, and no one could really say to him, "This film isn't going to happen." His health deteriorated in 1973, but creating was his life, so the film remained in his thoughts until his death. I don't think he ever completely abandoned the idea of making *The Freak*.

DR: There is this wonderful home movie of you wearing wings in the garden of the Manoir. When was that filmed? Was it Jean-Baptiste who filmed it?

VC: Yes, I watched it again recently. It must have been in 1974, at the end of the summer, because James was born at the beginning of May and you can see him for a moment; he's very small. We were all there. We took the wings out of the cellar and I put them on. I wore them for him, because he loved to digest and try things out, and he asked me to hiss, like animals do when they're scared, and to run and fall on the lawn. I remember him whispering all the instructions to me. Michael and Patricia were there too. And Jerry, who has always been so loyal to him — a lovely person. Jean-Baptiste had a camera and so did my mother, and I think they both filmed for a few minutes. In the film, you can clearly see dad directing the action, framing the image with his thumb and forefinger. Framing me, I mean. Then we sat down to read the script, and even then he kept correcting our intonation and pronunciation. By then we knew full well that the film would never be made, but that day we were completely immersed in that story.

Above, right and over: stills from a home movie with Victoria Chaplin,
on the lawn of the Manoir, August 1974.

In 1964, at the age of 32, Gerard Larn began working at Shepperton Studios, in the largest and most active special effects department in the United Kingdom. His role as a matte artist consisted of painting on large glass plates using paints or pastels, which were then integrated into the shots or affixed to the film.

Larn remained at the disposal of the department head, Ted Samuels, until the studios changed ownership. During those years, Larn's work was used in numerous films, including *Dr Who and the Daleks* (Gordon Flemyng, 1965); *Doctor Zhivago* (David Lean, 1965); *Casino Royale* (John Huston et al., 1967); *The Taming of the Shrew* (Franco Zeffirelli, 1967); *Macbeth* (Roman Polanski, 1971) and *Alice's Adventures in Wonderland* (William Sterling, 1972).

CC: Do you remember how the project started and who first told you about it?

Gerard Larn: I remember it very well. Jerry [Epstein] came to Shepperton in 1969. Ted Samuels, my boss, who was head of the Special Effects Department at the time, called me and introduced him to me, and we had a meeting afterwards, where Jerry gave us a rough idea of what they wanted from us. He told us that Charlie was working on a screenplay that would launch his daughter Victoria's film career, and that the story, set in a remote region of the Andes, was about a young girl who was born with wings. Our department had been chosen specifically to create the special effects on which the film was based. Two or three weeks later, we received an invitation to meet him at the Savoy Hotel, in the suite where he stayed whenever he came to London. The studio provided us with a Rolls Royce and driver. It was me, Samuels, and our cameraman Peter Harman. It was a truly extraordinary experience for all of us.

DR: You worked at Shepperton for several years. It was a golden age for the studios.

GL: Many important films of the time were shot and edited at Shepperton. You often found yourself dealing with art directors who lacked a strong artistic sense, or working with set designers who weren't particularly interested in set design. An interesting part of my job has always been to satisfy the aspirations and requests of the director, but this often meant having to overcome the obstacles put in place by the art director or set designer. There were only two people in this field for whom I always had great respect: John Box, who worked with David Lean, and production manager Terry Marsh.

CC: You worked with Lean on *Doctor Zhivago*. That must have been a truly unique experience.

GL: It certainly was, but the work was essentially post-production. I think it was the only time in my life I worked with the original negative. Bryan Evans and I worked on half a dozen sequences. I remember we added snow to some desolate landscapes, and we worked on the long shot with the sledge moving towards the house and generally on snowy landscapes and winter skies. But with *The Freak* it was different, something really unique, because we started from scratch on a project conceived by a brilliant man. It also happened at a time when business at Shepperton was slowing down, so we were delighted to be able to devote ourselves to a project of this stature.

DR: Did the work on *The Freak* involve closer contact with the director than usual?

GL: Definitely yes. In this case, it was necessary for the more technical aspects to work perfectly, and the drawings obviously had to fit the nature of the film. My job was to provide sketches, drafts and storyboards for some of the sequences.

CC: Did you ever read the final script?

GL: Actually, no, and I'd really like to read it! We worked on individual parts of the film. I remember Sydney Chaplin sitting next to me, telling me about passages from the story. I still have my notes… For a long time, that was the only material to work with. At first, I had wings that you [Victoria] would have had to wear and use, and that's when I spent a lot of time with Jerry, thoroughly analysing the story to determine exactly what physical performances the character would require. I also had to produce drawings illustrating the possible use of matte paintings, split screens, and other optical techniques for some of the film's flight sequences. At the time, Charlie watched many films with special effects or that contained flying scenes. I remember, for example, that he did not like *Barbarella* at all!

CC: You were always present at meetings with Chaplin. Were they long meetings?

Victoria Chaplin and Gerald Larn in London, 27 January 2017. Photograph by Cecilia Cenciarelli.

GL: Yes, I was always present at those meetings, but no, they weren't long. They were fairly short meetings, but extremely precise. Charlie was very clear and detailed about what he wanted and what he expected from us. After the meetings at the Savoy, we would return to the studios and take stock of what had been said in order to clearly define the objectives to be achieved and proceed from there.

CC: Was there ever a moment, after one of these meetings with Charlie, where you or Ted Samuels thought, "This is impossible"?

GL: No. We talked about it. We thought it would be a difficult project, but not impossible. The good thing was that we always got feedback from Charlie. He saw the designs and we always knew if we were working in the right direction. Among other things, at that time we had some internal problems in our department. Ted Samuels was getting on in years and unfortunately was very ill. He was an engineer, so he didn't really deal with the visual aspect of special effects. He and his team made wonderful models and things like that, and since he was the boss and didn't like to receive criticism for the work done by his department, he kept saying to me, "Gerald, nothing artistic please, nothing artistic!" That's why many of the drawings I gave to Jerry and also to Charlie were rather… "stiff." But the dimensions were always correct.

KG: Did Chaplin show you or describe to you the movements that Victoria would have to make with her wings?

GL: Yes, he described everything to me. At first, what he and Jerry hadn't realised was that it wouldn't be enough to just apply wings just for flying. Victoria needed wings when she was sitting down, when she was walking around, and then folded wings. Then there would be moments of transition between talking to someone at a table and deciding to fly away, so what would we do for the transition between when the wings are static on her back and the wings she can fly with? There's got to be something in between to make it work. It wasn't always easy to understand, especially for Jerry, that at least three pairs of wings were needed: static, flying, and transitional. Victoria, do you remember when you used to come to the studio? You came with Jerry once a week, maybe for two or three months. I spent a lot of time taking all your measurements, like a tailor, and taking photographs.

VC: Yes, I remember. I remember well being measured and photographed all the time. [*laughs*]

CC: In the Chaplin archives there is a photo of Victoria, with her back to the camera, wearing a miniskirt, in pure Swinging London style.

GL: Yes, well, Victoria initially wore some very cute miniskirts, but then she started coming in jeans. And that's why she's wearing jeans in all the photographs. Everything had to be done with the utmost precision. All those measurements, the distance between your elbow and your shoulder, had become my bible! We had a very brilliant colleague, Bill Jarret, an engineer I worked with from the beginning. The movement of the wings had to be produced by your arms, so we had to be absolutely sure that all the operating mechanisms, especially where they were hinged and where they closed, were exactly where you were supposed to hold them. All these details—what kind of engineering and mechanical device would be needed for everything to work properly—had to be discussed. I kept a few drawings and some notes, a few storyboards. Everything else was sent to Vevey, to Charlie.

KG: How amazing that you kept everything. Did you keep everything on every project you worked on, or just this?

GL: I've got quite a lot, yes, but this was material that was completely particularly unique because we were starting from the ground up on a fantastic project with Charlie Chaplin!

CC: Do you remember a certain John Rose?

KG: The Chaplin archives contain a number of his drawings and storyboards.

GL: No, I've never heard of him. I don't know of anyone else who did drawings for this film.

KG: A doll was also produced. Did you design it? It was used for long-distance shots. A clockwork specialist was involved.

Victoria Chaplin rehearsing for Gerald Larn at Shepperton Studios.

GL: No, I had nothing to do with that I'm afraid.

VC: Dad really liked having something tangible to hold in his hand, to take home and continue thinking about the project, to do some tests.

CC: Jerry took a lot of notes. There are lots of lists of telephone numbers, names and contacts. For example, this one, from March 1969: Eugene Flying Ballet, Wally Wivers, Maurice Carter Art Director.

GL: Really? Wally was the head of my department for years. I had no idea he was involved in the project and I didn't know he was going to be the film's set designer. This is all new to me.

CC: "Kirby's Flying Ballet Company" is also mentioned. They were responsible for the special flying effects in *Peter Pan* at the beginning of the 20th century, right, David?

DR: Yes, that's right. George Kirby founded the company at the end of the 19th century, and they invented all kinds of flight systems, harnesses and equipment for shows and pantomimes, ballets and operas throughout the United Kingdom and the United States.

Victoria Chaplin as Sarapha. Drawing by Gerald Larn.

GL: And that's exactly what we used. I have a photo of you, Victoria, wearing a very interesting corset to which Kirby's ropes had to be attached. In the test footage that was shot, I remember you flying horizontally. I don't remember if there's any footage of you flying vertically.

VC: Now that we're talking about it, the memories are coming back. I was in a horizontal position…

GL: Yes, that's right. You were in the air, in a horizontal position, held by the harnesses designed by Kirby. The point is that all the special effects scenes, especially the close-ups, would have to have a black background so that all the extra things, like the environments she was moving in—for example, in the scenes flying over the rooftops of London—could be recreated correctly, and this could only happen if the footage with Victoria had a black background behind her. Bill and I decided that the front edge of the wings would be made of fibreglass, and we also created a wing with swan feathers, but it was complicated because swans in this country are sacred. They are the property of the Queen!

KG: You know that these wings survived, don't you?

GL: No! Really?

KG: Yes! They are on display in Vevey, at the Manoir de Ban, now home to Chaplin's World, the Chaplin museum.

Above, right and over: Sarapha, wing tests. Drawings by Gerald Larn.

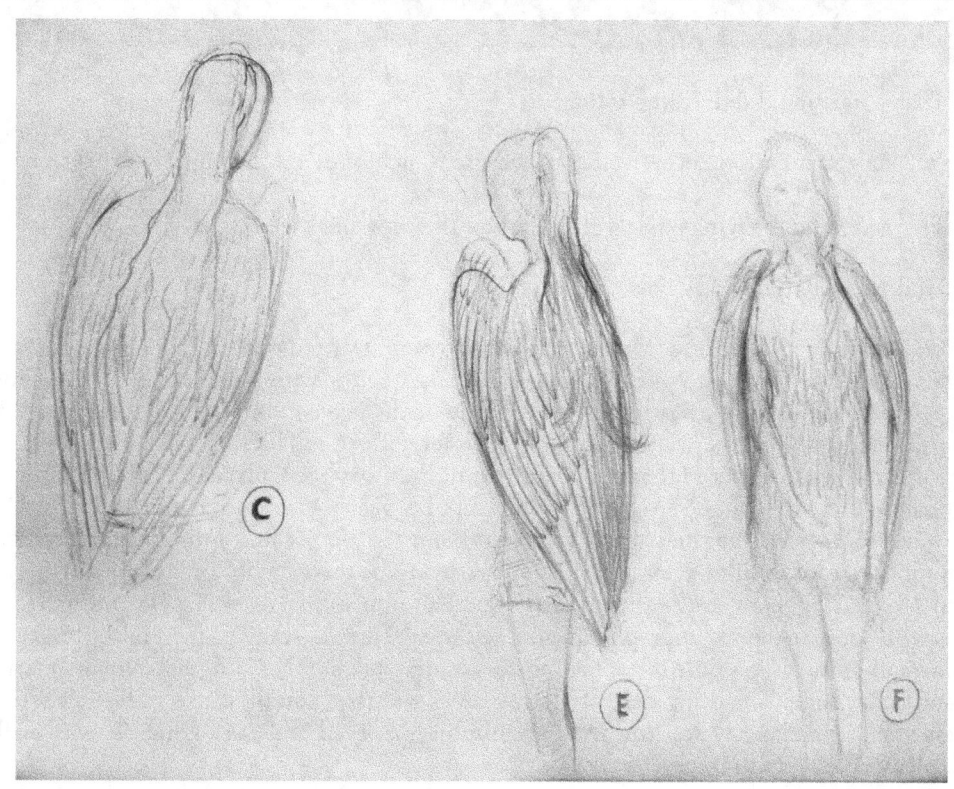

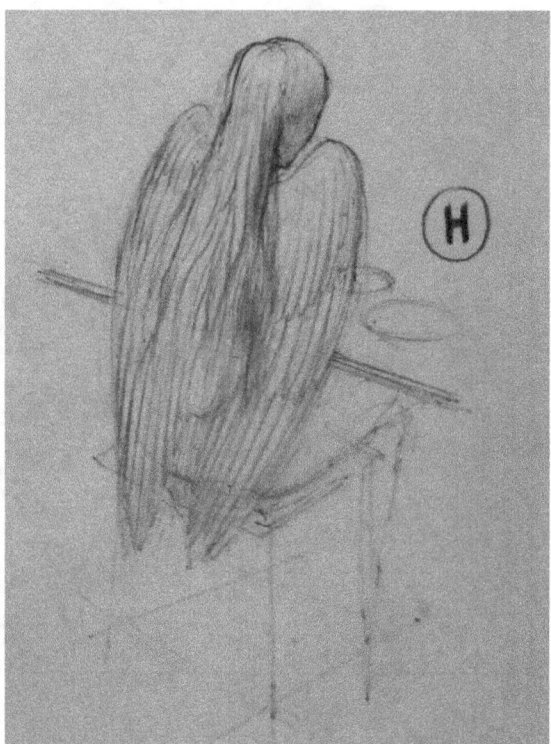

GL: That's amazing, I didn't know that!

DR: Earlier you mentioned three pairs of wings. Which ones are the ones that survived?

GL: They must be the wings for flying. They're the only ones we made.

CC: And was Charlie happy with the wings?

GL: Oh yes, he was delighted. We met at the Savoy eight or ten times in all, but he also came to Shepperton. He was also very happy with some scenes with Victoria that were shot as tests. We were all eagerly awaiting the next phase of the project, but we still knew very little about the story. I remember one time, we were in Jerry Epstein's kitchen in Vincent Square [in London], and we discovered that the beginning of the story took place in Chile. What would Sarapha look like in Chile? She certainly wouldn't be wearing jeans or a miniskirt, so when it came time to imagine the sketches, it was a problem for me because I didn't know what she was supposed to wear. But again, I wasn't supposed to be too artistic, and that's why Sarapha ended up wearing jeans in the sketches. It's such an interesting story. Tragic and incredible. When you look at the photographs of yourself at seventeen—they're incredibly full of life. It was really a turning point for someone so young, and then nothing happened. It was an extraordinary time. The thing that struck me most was that you didn't seem like an aspiring actress at all, if I may say so. You were so humble, reserved and easy-going. It was really a huge pleasure to be with you.

DR: And little did you know that Victoria would continue to create and play wonderful and extraordinary creatures for decades to come…

VC: [*laughs*] It's wonderful that someone is telling this story. I really feel like I'm learning a lot. What strikes me is how much my father wanted to make the film. In 1975, he still wanted to do it.

CC: Was there ever a moment when you were told that the film was going into production or, later, that the project had been cancelled?

GL: No. All information came through Jerry Epstein, who also came to see us on his own. And when he stopped coming, we didn't hear anything more. We didn't even know why we weren't hearing anything more about the film.

CC: On January 20, 1970, Jerry wrote several letters to all the parties involved to announce that the project had been cancelled. One of these is addressed to Ted Samuels.

GL: I never received that information. But Ted wasn't well at the time, so I'm not surprised. It was certainly a disappointment, but we understood that the film wasn't going to happen and moved on to other projects. It was only later, through Jerry's book, that I understood what had really happened, and that your mother thought it would be too much for him. But let me tell you, *The Freak* was a wonderful subject, and that was an unforgettable time for us. Today the story is finally being told.

One of Victoria Chaplin's first rehearsals at Shepperton Studios, before the wings were built.

6

Ready to Go

Over five hundred pages testify to Jerry Epstein's presence in Chaplin's professional and personal life over the course of twenty-five years. From these papers, in particular from the correspondence between Jerry and Oona (who was always more inclined than her husband to correspond), a profound affective relationship emerges: friend, confidant, factotum, mediator between the parents' apprehensions and the children's little rebellions, Epstein was clearly "one of the family." In a letter addressed to Oona soon after Chaplin's death, Epstein writes: "I am not exaggerating when I say that Charlie illuminated my life, gave me meaning and substance [...] Nothing and no one will ever be able to match the fun, the energy, the trepidation I felt working with him. But perhaps the happiest moments and memories of my life are those with you two, together."

It is no wonder, then, that Epstein jumped into the making of *The Freak* headlong, working day and night even before his role as producer or the nature of his compensation had been formalised.

Epstein took part in the project from its genesis in 1967, immediately taking care of the most problematic aspects, i.e. the flight scenes and special effects.

Jerry's great meticulousness in documenting all stages of his work, from the script revisions to the visits to the studios (from Shepperton Studios to Ardmore Studios in Dublin, an option that would allow them to shoot on location, using Ireland's majestic cliffs for scenes set on the Chilean coast), his accuracy in writing down meeting notes and noting down the names and addresses of every interlocutor—potential producer, distributor, artist, craftsman— allowed us not only to date the final script for the first time, but also to follow the short but intense production life of *The Freak*.

Between September and October 1969, pre-production work was further accelerated: on September 16, assisted by accountant Arno Rudolph, Epstein finalised a first detailed version of the budget; on the 22nd, he drew up a complete list of sets and scenes (indoors and outdoors) with precise reference to the sequences indicated in the script. After two weeks, the budget items were slimmed down in order to keep the costs within one million dollars; the budget was finally further revised between the end of October and the beginning of November. The detailed working plan included a detailed and numbered rundown of scenes, their classification according to studio, setting, special effects or any planned process (studios provided staff and rates according to the services required); it also provided a detailed list of special effects and location shots. Some locations were left out, including Westminster Cathedral, which would have involved various difficulties and huge costs, given the frequency of religious services (a change that we in fact find in the final script where the cathedral becomes a "Church of London"). Certainly some issues remained unresolved, Chaplin and Epstein probably expected to be able to polish the script on the set or in the editing room, as was usually the case.

"We are ready to go!" wrote Jerry, in late October, in a note to Charlie.

In the following pages, a selection of production papers are reproduced, in particular: receipts for materials (photographic paper) purchased from the Shepperton Studios special effects department; budget pages of September 16; revised budget dated October 3; and a breakdown of scenes and locations.

Receipts for the purchase of materials for the design of the wings, 1969.

'T H E   F R E A K'

PRELIMINARY BUDGET   16th September '69.

NO.	SET TITLE.	CONSTRUCTION.	PROPS.
1. {	INT. LATHAM'S HOUSE - GUEST BEDROOM *(Revamp)*	*£ 400* £ 1,800	*£ 20* 450 *240*
2. {	INT. LATHAM'S HOUSE - SITTING ROOM, LIBRARY, PASSAGE AND KITCHEN	*£ 6,500* £ 7,500	£ 1,750 *£ 850*
3. {	INT. LATHAM'S HOUSE - LATHAM'S BEDROOM ..	*£ 900* £ 2,000	£ 500 *300*
4. 4A	EXT. LATHAM'S HOUSE - ROOF AND STAIRS UP *(many clouds)* .. " Door ..	£ 1,250	£ 50
5.	EXT. SECTION OF CLIFF EDGE	£ 500	£ 150
6.	INT. HELICOPTER CABIN	£ 850	£ 300
7.	INT. SET PLANE CABIN AND COCKPIT SECTION	£ 1,500	£ 850
8.	EXT. ROOF OF CHURCH TOWER ..	*£ 800* £ 1,800	£ 50
9.	EXT. CHURCH ENTRANCE AND SECTION OF STREET ..	*£ 2,500* £ 4,500	£ 400 *300*
10.	INT. CHURCH AND CHAPEL OFF ..	*£ 5,000* £14,500	£ 1,800 *1,600*
11.	INT. CHURCH BELFRY ..	*2,200* £ 3,200	£ 400
12.	EXT. ROOF TO COVENT GARDEN MARKET	£ 2,500	£ 150
13.	INT. PASSAGEWAY AND DRESSING ROOMS, OPERA HOUSE ..	*£ 1,800* £ 2,250	£ 500 *400*
14.	EXT. DOORS TO OPERA HOUSE	£ 1,200	£ 300
15.	INT. SUITE OF ROOMS AT SAVOY HOTEL	*£ 5,500* £ 6,500	£ 1,000 *850*
16.	EXT. DRESSING ROOM WINDOW, OPERA HOUSE	£ 500	£ 150
17.	EXT. LONDON STREET (DRUNK SEQUENCE) } IF PINEWOOD USING EXISTING LOT SET	£ 5,000	£ 1,800
18.	EXT. BROOK STREET, LONDON		
19.	INT./EXT. LATHAM'S TOWN HOUSE - BEDROOM AND BOUDOIR *5,000*	£ 6,000	£ 1,600 *1,400*
20.	**INT. LATHAM'S TOWN HOUSE - STAIRS AND HALLWAY *(Revamp)* .. *£ 300*	£ 4,500	£ 1,000 *£ 450*
21.	EXT. TREE AND WINDOWS AT SAVOY HOTEL	£ 2,500	£ 800
22.	EXT. SECTION OF EMBANKMENT GARDEN AND SEAT ..	£ 500	£ 200

*air fares —
£1,000 per
week over

Rushes £20 - £100 print
crew

Wardrobe
17/0.6

CCrew OVER 4×£45 /180 —
Sound org 4×45 180 —
Electrical 4×45 180 —
Constn (There finds crew

2000 Hansets*

Above and over: the first detailed budget, September 16, 1969.

'T H E   F R E A K'

PRELIMINARY BUDGET - Cont'd.   16th September, '69.

NO.	SET TITLE.	CONSTRUCTION.	PROPS.
23.	INT. EARLS COURT - SPEAKERS ROSTRUM AND CHOIR (MATTE)	£ 5,500	£ 1,200
24.	INT. EARLS COURT - SECTIONS OF AUDIENCE	£ 1,500	£ 800
24A			
25.	EXT. ROOF OF MARBLE ARCH	£ 600	£ 50
26.	INT. MARGARET'S LIMOUSINE — _Trathry Matte_ ..	£ 200	£ 50
27.	INT. LATHAM'S COUNTRY HOUSE - HALL AND STAIRS .. £ 7,500	£ 8,500	£ 2,000
28.	INT. LATHAM'S COUNTRY HOUSE — BEDROOM 1,750	£ 2,000	£ 1,500 900
29.	INT. SECTION OF SEATS HOUSE OF COMMONS £ 500 ..	£ 1,800	£ 450 250
30.	INT. LATHAM'S COUNTRY HOUSE - SITTING ROOM £ 800	£ 3,500	£ 1,500 850
31.	EXT. ROOF OF LORD PENTAGON'S COUNTRY HOUSE ..	£ 800	£ 150
32.	INT. LORD PENTAGON'S HOUSE - GRAND STAIRWAY AND HALL 7,500	£ 9,500	£ 2,500 2,000
33.	INT. BALLROOM, PASSAGE TO PINK AND ANTE ROOMS .. 8,000	£12,000	£ 2,800 1,800
34.	EXT. ROOF OF HOUSE OPPOSITE TOWN HALL	£ 600	£ 100
34A		£ 750	150
35.	INT. LECTURE ROOM IN TOWN HALL	£ 2,500	£ 500
36.	INT. REX HORTON'S BEDROOM. (REVAMP LATHAM'S BEDROOM)	£ 500	£ 700
37.	INT. POLICE CELL	£ 400	£ 50
38.	INT. POLICE COURTROOM. (REVAMP LECTURE ROOM) ..	£ 750	£ 250
39.	**INT. LATHAM'S TOWN HOUSE - SITTING ROOM .. .. £ 1,000	£ 2,700	£ 1,000 850
40.	INT. QUARANTINE DEPARTMENT OFFICE AND CAGES ..	£ 1,200	£ 200 500
41.	**EXT. ROOF OF MARGARET'S TOWN HOUSE	£ 500	£ 50
42.	EXT. SECTION OF ROOF TOWN HALL	£ 850	£ 50
43.	TANK AND BOAT FOR RECOVERY OF BODY 650	£ 500	£ 150
44.	INSERTS AND ODD SHOTS	£ 1,000	£ 500
45.	SECTION OF ROOF WINDOW EARLS COURT	£ 850	£ 100
46.	EXT./INT. OF COMMITTEE ROOM TOWN HALL	£ 1,800	£ 300
47.	ART DIRECTOR MODELS	£ 300	£ 100
48.	TEST SETS	£ 450	£ 250
		£ 1200	£ 450

49 INT. Earls Court, Drawing Room, Corridor —

                     TOTAL STUDIO SETS   £132,250   £ 31,550

** Starred sets could be omitted.

                                             95,550   25,050
                                          + 7,000   30,
                                          102,550

' T H E   F R E A K '

<u>PRELIMINARY BUDGET</u> - cont'd.   16th September '69.

PRELIMINARY   COST   TO   OPERATE   EFFECTS   STAGE

BASED ON SHOOTING REQUIREMENT OF 21¼ DAYS.

Experimental work and test shooting for flying	£15,000
Manufacture of three sets of flying wings ..	£ 3,000
Manufacture of five sets of plastic fighting wings ..	£ 4,000
Manufacture of two sets of folded wings	£ 800
Repair and maintenance of wings ..	£ 2,500
Build and paper curved screen for blue light mattes ..	£ 6,000
Mounting projector on crane and hire of same ..	£ 2,000
Lamping and associated gear for projectors	£ 1,500
Rostrums and other construction work	£ 8,000
Hire and operating of Kirby wires for girl	£ 2,500
Special lamp hire	£ 600
Special effects crew and gear for storm effects, etc. ..	£ 2,800
Scenic work and special backing	£ 2,000
Half scale automated figures and wire flying rig	£ 2,000
Operating crew for projectors of blue light	£ 1,500
Stage rent on basis of large stage 6 weeks	£15,000
Processing cost for travelling matte shots @ 1,000 ft. ..	£ 7,500

£69,200

✓ ○ } S.E stage   X – cancelled
✓ → regular set

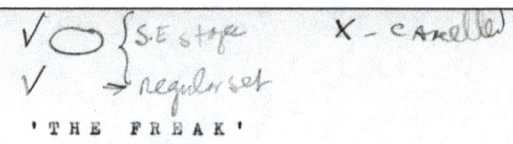

'THE FREAK'

PRELIMINARY BUDGET - cont'd.   16th September, 1969.

SPECIAL EFFECTS REQUIRED.

*Starred Scenes shot in Built Sets (Others can be shot on SPECIAL EFFECTS STAGE).

SCRIPT SCENES.		POSSIBLE METHOD & REQUIREMENT.	SHOOTING DAYS.
✓ Sc. 7.	EAGLES ATTACKING SARAPHA.	Travelling Matte Plate of sea and cliffs. Two prop eagles on wires. ~~Wire rig for girl.~~ ~~Storm effects.~~	½
✓ Sc. 8.	ROOF OF LATHAM'S HOUSE.	Painted backing possible. Glass projected clouds. Storm effects.	¼
✓ Sc. 24.	EDGE OF CLIFF.	Travelling Matte Blue Plate of sea and cliffs. Wire rig for girl. Wind effects.	¼
✓ Sc. 25A	SARAPHA FLYING.	Travelling Matte Blue Sky and sea. Wire rig for girl.	½
✓ Sc. 25B	ANOTHER ANGLE.	As above.	¼
✓ Sc. 25C	ANOTHER ANGLE	As above.	¼
✓ Sc.118.	SARAPHA ESCAPES FROM PLANE.	Travelling Matte Blue. Plate of London Airport. Built section of aircraft. Wire rig for girl.	¼
✓ Sc.119.	SARAPHA HIGH OVER LONDON.	Travelling Matte Blue Plate of London below. Wire rig for girl.	¼
✓ Sc.119A	C.U. SARAPHA AGAINST SKY.	Night sky backing. Wire rig for girl. Wind effects.	¼
✓ Sc.120.	EYELINE OF LONDON.	Photo effect shot.	
X Sc.121.	SARAPHA GLIDING DOWN.	Travelling Matte shot. Photo plate of London. Wire rig for girl. Wind effects.	¼
✓ Sc.122.	SARAPHA OVER CHURCH.	Travelling Matte Blue Plate from model. Wire rig for girl. Wind effects.	¼
X Sc.123.	SHE ALIGHTS ON CHURCH.	Painted night backing. Built section of church. Wire rig for girl. Wind effects.	¼
X Sc.124.	SHE LOOKS ABOUT HER	As above.	¼

'THE FREAK'

PRELIMINARY BUDGET

(REVISED FIGURES)   October 3rd, 1969.

NO.	SET TITLE.	CONSTRUCTION.	PROPS.
1.	INT. LATHAM'S HOUSE - GUEST BEDROOM (Revamp)	400	250
2.	INT. LATHAM'S HOUSE - SITTING ROOM, LIBRARY, PASSAGE & KITCHEN.	6,500 5500	850
3.	INT. LATHAM'S HOUSE - LATHAM'S BEDROOM	900	300
4.	EXT. LATHAM'S HOUSE - ROOF AND STAIRS UP 3000	1,250 1100	50
4a.	EXT. LATHAM'S HOUSE - DOOR		
5.	EXT. SECTION OF CLIFF EDGE £100	500	150 (?)
6.	INT. HELICOPTER CABIN	850	300
7.	INT. SET PLANE CABIN AND COCKPIT SECTION 1050 (?)	1,500 (?)	850 (?)
8.	EXT ROOF OF CHURCH TOWER	800 1000	50
9.	EXT CHURCH ENTRANCE AND SECTION OF STREET	2,500	300
10.	INT. CHURCH AND CHAPEL OFF.	2000 3,000 (?)	1,000
11.	INT. CHURCH BELFRY	2,200 -	400
12.	EXT. ROOF TO COVENT GARDEN MARKET 1,000 1,000	2,500	150
13.	INT. PASSAGEWAY AND DRESSING ROOMS, OPERA HOUSE	1,800	400
14.	EXT. DOORS TO OPERA HOUSE	1,200 (0000)	300
15.	INT. SUITE OF ROOMS AT SAVOY HOTEL 2,500	5,500	850
16.	EXT. DRESSING ROOM WINDOW, OPERA HOUSE	500	150
17.	EXT.LONDON STREET (DRUNK SEQUENCE)) IF PINEWOOD	2,500 (if EXT)	
18.	EXT. BROOK STREET, LONDON) USING EXISTING LOT SET /12,000		1,800
19.	INT/EXT. LATHAM'S TOWN HOUSE - BEDROOM & BOUDOIR 3,000	5,000	1,400
20.	**INT. LATHAM'S TOWN HOUSE - STAIRS & HALLWAY (Revamp)	500	400
21.	EXT. THREE AND WINDOWS AT SAVOY HOTEL 2,500 £1000		800
22.	EXT. SECTION OF EMBANKMENT GARDEN AND SEAT	500 £500	200

£8,000

Budget revision, October 3, 1969.

Bruno p174.

```
                    "THE FREAK"              22nd September, 1969

                    Breakdown
```

L O C A T I O N S

LOCATIONS	SCENE NOS	ARTISTES	SCENES	PAGES	SCHEDULE
EXT. CHILIAN COAST AND ADOBE *L*	125	2 DOUBLES LANDROVER	3	½	
EXT. ROOF OF ADOBE *ST*	8	LATHAM NAGIA SARAPHA	1	1	
EXT. ADOBE, CLIFFS AND SEA AND TOP OF PLATEAU AND FIELD NEAR BY *L*	23-25 37 39 41 42 43 46 78 79 85 87-91 103N 104N	LATHAM SARAPHA INDIANS CRIPPLED GIRL RYMAN JACKSON SECRETARY HELICOPTER RYMANS PLACE (PARAGUAY)	19	7¼	
EXT. WESTMINSTER CATHEDRAL TOWER AND ENTRANCE *L*	122-126N 131N 132N	SARAPHA POLICEMAN	7	½	
EXT. MARKET GLASS ROOF - COVENT GARDEN *ST*	168-170 173	SARAPHA	4	¼	
EXT. STAGE DOOR - COVENT GARDEN THEATRE *L*	174-177	SARAPHA CHARWOMAN	4	½	
EXT. STREET CORNER - LONDON *ST*	199-202 204	SARAPHA DRUNK	5	½	
EXT. BROOK STREET *ST*	206-213N 222 224 357	SARAPHA JACKSON RYMAN	11	1½	

Above the left: scene and location breakdown, September 22, 1969.

LOCATIONS	SCENE NOS	ARTISTES	SCENES	PAGES	SCHEDULE
SET EXT. ROOF HOTEL AND EMBANKMENT GARDENS	225-227N *10*	SARAPHA TRAMP	3	½	*1*
SET EXT. AUDITORIUM AND SKYLIGHT – EARLS COURT	249N 253-273N *40* *250* *250* *5000*	SARAPHA JACKSON RYMAN GIDSON 25 INVALIDS 500 CROWD	22	4½	*2*
SET EXT. MARBLE ARCH	277-280N *5* 281N *5* *75*	SARAPHA MARGARET CROWD LIMOUSINE	5	½	*½*
LOCAL EXT. LORD PENTAGONS HOUSE AND ROOF *300 301 302a 303 304 305 328 329* *N*	299-305N *10* 326-329N *500* *10*	SARAPHA WATCHMAN PARTY GUESTS POLICE POLICE DOGS	11 6	1½ 1	*1*
SET ROOF 299 300 302 326 327		*5 SARAPHA*	5	½	*½*
EXT. TOWN HALL AND OPPOSITE BUILDINGS *SET*	330-333N *6*	SARAPHA	4	¾	*½*
LOCATION. EXT. OCEAN AND FISHING TRAWLER *LOT*	*26* 358N 360- 362 *362*	SARAPHA CAPTAIN CREW	4	½	*½ ½*
LOMA LOT	*362a*	*5 SARAPHA*			*½*
LOCAL EXT. HOUSE AT TRENT *297*	286N 287N 340 *90*	SARAPHA MARGARET DRIVER *RYMAN JACKSON MAN*	3	½	*1*

5715

<u>I N T E R I O R S</u>

<u>INTERIORS</u>	<u>SCENE NOS</u>		<u>ARTISTES</u>	<u>SCENES</u>	<u>PAGES</u>	<u>SCHEDULE</u>
✓ INT. ADOBE HOUSE (LATHAMS) CHILI	3 4 6 7 9 11–20 25–32 35 36 38 40 44 45 47–60 61 65 62–64 66–77 70 83 81 82 86 295	40 15 10 20 40 60	LATHAM DR PIESTROZ MRS PIESTROZ NAGIA SARAPHA 6 INDIANS CRIPPLED GIRL	54	17½	8
✓ INT. LARGE HELICOPTER (P)	92–102	40	SARAPHA RYMAN JACKSON BIG WOMAN	11	4	2
✓ INT. RYMANS PRIVATE PLANE (P)	105N 107–114 117 118	40	SARAPHA RYMAN JACKSON BIG WOMAN	11	2½	½
INT. LONDON AIRPORT CONTROL ROOM (P)	116		2 CONTROLLERS	1	¼	½
✓ INT. WESTMINSTER CATHEDRAL	128–130 133–137 139–166 189 190	45 750	SARAPHA FATHER DONOVAN MOTHER SUPERIOR YOUNG MAN PRAYING WOMAN SCREAMING GIRL YOUNG NUN 50 WORSHIPPERS	37	6	3
✓ INT. DRESSING ROOM (P) PASSAGE AND STAIRS *OPERA HOUSE*	178–188 192–197	20	SARAPHA CHARWOMAN	16	3½	2
✓ INT. JACKSONS SUITE SAVOY HOTEL	191 228–247 248a	45 10 10	SARAPHA RYMAN JACKSON DR GIDSON BIG WOMAN	12	9¾	3
✓ INT. MARGARETS BEDROOM BROOK STREET	214–221N 223 248	50 90	SARAPHA MARGARET RYMAN JACKSON	11	11¼	5

INTERIORS	SCENES	ARTISTES	SCENE NOS	PAGES	SCHEDULE
INT. DRESSING ROOM – EARLS COURT	250N–252N 256N	SARAPHA RYMAN JACKSON DR GIDSON	4	1½	1
INT. MARGARETS LIMOUSINE (BP)	281N–285N	SARAPHA MARGARET DRIVER	5	⅜	½
INT. SITTING ROOM, HALL AND STAIRCASE – TRENT	288N 289N 292, 293, 294. 296.	SARAPHA MARGARET BUTLER RYMAN JACKSON SIR REX	8	3½	1½
INT. SARAPHA'S BEDROOM – TRENT	290 342 344–346 348	SARAPHA MARGARET SIR REX POLICE INSPECTOR DETECTIVE POLICEMAN	6	4¼	2
INT. HOUSE OF COMMONS	291	MP MEMBERS	1	½	½
INT. GRAND STAIRCASE BALLROOM AND ANTE ROOM – PENTAGONS	306–316 323 324 325	SARAPHA MARGARET LADY PENTAGON LORD PENTAGON BUTLER ORCHESTRA RYMAN JACKSON 200 GUESTS	14	3¼	2
INT. PINK ROOM & PASSAGE	317–323	SARAPHA MARGARET LADY PENTAGON COUNTESS	7	1½	1
INT. CHAMBER PASSAGEWAY AND STAIRS – TOWN HALL	334–336N	SARAPHA MAN	3	½	½

Handwritten annotations: 20, 10, 60, 40, 2, 5, 105, 40, 250, 10, 2000, 20, 10

INTERIORS	SCENE NOS	ARTISTES	SCENES	PAGES	SCHEDULE
✓ INT. VILLAGE LECTURE HALL	337N 339N	SARAPHA DR EVERMAN 50 AUDIENCE	3	½	½
✓ INT. BLUE GUEST ROOM – TRENT	343N	SIR REX BUTLER	1	½	½
✓ INT. POLICE CELL	349	SARAPHA MARGARET LATHAM CONSTABLE	1	½	½
INT. JACKSONS APARTMENT	347	RYMAN JACKSON	1	1	½
✓ INT. MAGISTRATES COURT	350	SARAPHA MARGARET LATHAM MAGISTRATE CLERKS POLICE	1	1	1
✓ INT. SITTING ROOM BROCK STREET	354 356 364	SARAPHA MARGARET LATHAM BUTLER	3	2½	1½
✓ INT. OFFICES, CAGES QUARANTINE DEPT.	355	SARAPHA MARGARET LATHAM OFFICER PHOTOGRAPHERS REPORTERS	1	1½	1

PLATES   24 92 102 106N 118N 119N 120N
                123N 167 168 198 203 285

INSERTS   10 21 22 27 33 34 106N 115N
                138 171 172 193 195 363

TRAVELLING MATTE 24 118 119 121 123 167 198
                203 274 275 277 298 359N

Afterword
The Last Chaplin
Gian Luca Farinelli

> I'm not an angel. I'm a freak,
> half bird and half woman. Is that all right with you?
>
> Sarapha in *The Freak*

In 1969 Chaplin was eighty years old. During the production of *A Countess from Hong Kong* he had suffered a serious fracture that made him realise that Charlot—that divinity without physical limits, that acrobat of impossible gestures, capable of transcending human boundaries—had left him forever. His new film germinated precisely in this phase: its protagonist would be a bird-woman. Now that life imposed new limits on him, Chaplin wanted, with this final film, to cross the boundaries of space, of gender, and even those between human being and animal.

I like to imagine that one of the inspirations for this new film came from a hugely successful work of six years earlier, which terrified audiences around the world: *The Birds*, starring Tippi Hedren, discovered and then discarded by another Englishman, Alfred Hitchcock, who was also born in London, ten years after Chaplin, in 1899. Perhaps it is only a coincidence, but Chaplin would be the only one to offer Hedren—unlike all of Hollywood—an important role, alongside Marlon Brando and Sophia Loren in *A Countess from Hong Kong*.

The Freak would never be made, but this book allows us to dream it, through the many discoveries, the invaluable interviews, the drawings, the final version of the screenplay. It would have been a film that, like all of Chaplin's works, beneath a simple surface is in fact extremely complex. Let me take, for example, one of the most famous endings in the history of cinema, that of *City Lights*. At first sight, chance seems to resolve the story of the two protagonists positively: in the final sequence they meet and, touching hands, recognise one another. A magnificent and moving happy ending! But is it really a positive ending? Can the Tramp and the Flower Girl love each other, even if reality is so far from their dreams?

Chaplin is the master of simplicity, but in truth, time and again, he draws us—without our noticing—into the extreme complexity of life.

For this reason *The Freak* is a wholly Chaplinesque work. With the advent of the feature film, his works became increasingly lucid and sincere meditations on himself, on the present state of humanity, and on our future. *The Freak* is a fantasy conceived by an ageing master, but it is also a film firmly rooted in 1969, just as Truffaut's *The Wild Child* or Hopper's *Easy*

Rider are. A simple film to make, without stars, and yet it was never made, even though its author had been the goose that laid the golden eggs for the global film industry.

A simple film, but impossible; timeless, yet embedded in the late 1960s, the moment when Hollywood began to turn the page, and the success of an independent production like *Easy Rider* marked the beginning of a new era. *The Freak*, too, from a production standpoint, was born outside traditional parameters. It was a film with a "small budget," independent, almost familial, with Chaplin's young daughter Victoria in the leading role.

The Birds can help us understand what Chaplin probably had in mind. Like *The Freak*, it is a profoundly nineteenth-century story and, in order to become cinema, required a major effort in special effects. But *The Freak* is not a science-fiction film, and we must not think of today's special effects: we must imagine the "human" effects of the 1960s. This too is a curious detail. The director who had made the least use of special effects (risking countless times to break his neck) envisioned for his final work a film whose most important and captivating moments would lie in the liberating flights of Sarapha, the protagonist.

But who is Sarapha? A unique being. She has lost her parents, has no siblings, and only at the end of the story is her identity certified by an English court, granting her the possibility of obtaining an identity document. But this is of no interest to her, for in London, in Great Britain, she has always felt unhappy. The only Englishman who, upon seeing her, did not faint or show fear, was a tramp.

And yet Sarapha is a beautiful being, though her beauty will bring her no joy. Quite the opposite, in fact. She is an ancient being, hailing from a primordial region of the world: Patagonia, traversed in the nineteenth century by another subject of the English crown, the anthropologist Charles Darwin, who encountered the Fuegians, a people who would become extinct over the course of the twentieth century. It is with them, we learn at the beginning of *The Freak*, that Sarapha was taken in after the death of her parents.

Shall we draw a simple parallel? Sarapha is Chaplin. He is English, but cannot live in England. He is an ancient figure, as is Charlot, who represents one of humanity's most ancient achievements—comedy—and who, like the bird-woman, is unique, unrepeatable.

But if the parallel between Sarapha and Chaplin/Charlot has its obvious reasons, Sarapha is a woman. Indeed, her extraordinary femininity is one of the driving forces of the story. Latham takes her in because he is immediately attracted to her; Sarapha will be forced to kill Rex to avoid being raped. All of Chaplin's cinema is a masculine universe in which the woman points the man toward possible redemption, but also, in many films, represents an unattainable dimension. In *The Freak*, Chaplin intended to center the story on a female protagonist—one of the rare films in his career to do so—and she was portrayed as the story's morally sympathetic character. It was to be his homage to women, to his great leading ladies—Mabel, Edna, Paulette, Claire—to his companion Oona, to his beloved daughters, to Victoria, to whom the father seems to want to pass the torch. But above all, now that he has freed himself of the body, now that imagination can run completely free, the tramp, the outsider, the last of them all, can take the form of a freak, a bird-woman. He, who—wearing the costume of Calvero—had already died in 1952, on stage in *Limelight*, could now let his very soul die, in the waters of the Atlantic.

It has been written that *A Countess from Hong Kong* was the staging of falsity, the representation in comic form of a world where all points of reference had been lost. Latham declares at the beginning of *The Freak*: "What a mystery life is!" But the society the film seems to want to portray knows mystery no longer; it is a world where the sacred has disappeared, populated only by unscrupulous financiers, wretched preachers ravenous for money, and vast manipulated crowds, a world in which, if a cripple stands up from his wheelchair, you can be sure he will receive a fee for his performance.

Chaplin's poetic and consoling humanism was far away; *The Freak* would have been very close in spirit to Federico Fellini's last film, *The Voice of the Moon*: a hopeless look at the future of the world. And if Fellini, in his penultimate scene, has advertising proclaimed to the Moon, Chaplin would have closed his work with the line spoken by Latham after learning of Sarapha's death: "Hers was an impossible life—now her problems are over."

Chaplin died on Christmas night in 1977. Some months later, his body was stolen by two refugees, a Bulgarian and a Pole, who were eventually captured by the Swiss police. *The Freak* would not become his last film, but it would be the last work on which he laboured. The photographs and home movies documenting its preparation tell us of an important moment of family happiness, even as life for everyone was changing. It would never become a film, but perhaps it is something even more important: the artistic testament of Charles S. Chaplin.

Chronology
1953—1977

5 January: The Chaplin family moves to Switzerland, to the Manoir de Ban, Corsier-sur-Vevey. Since the end of September 1952 they had been in exile in Europe, where they had traveled for the London premiere of *Limelight*. While sailing to London, they were informed that the U.S. authorities had revoked Charles Chaplin's right to re-enter the country for alleged anti-American activities.

March: Holiday on the French Riviera.

6 March: *Limelight* receives the award for Best Film from the Association of Foreign Critics in the United States.

10 April: Chaplin surrenders his permit to re-enter the United States.

Summer: He begins working on the screenplay for *A King in New York*.

23 August: Eugene Anthony Chaplin is born.

18 September: The Chaplin Studios in Hollywood are sold.

10 February: Oona Chaplin renounces her American citizenship.

2 May: The production of *A King in New York* is announced.

27 May: Chaplin receives the World Peace Council Prize.

Work on *A King in New York*.

1 March: Chaplin sells his remaining shares in United Artists.

1956

Chaplin composes the music for **A King in New York.**
24 April: Meets Khrushchev and Bulganin at Claridge's in London.
25 May: Becomes an honorary member of ACTT (Association of Cinematograph, Television and Allied Technicians).
May–July: Filming of *A King in New York* in London.
August—October: Editing, sound recording, and dubbing of *A King in New York* in Paris.

1957

Work continues on *A King in New York*.
23 May: Jane Cecil Chaplin is born.
24 June: Chaplin goes to Paris to record the music for *A King in New York*.
12 September: Premiere of *A King in New York* at the Leicester Square Theatre in London.
24 September: The American press is barred from the Paris premiere of *A King in New York*.
30 September: Wheeler Dryden, Chaplin's half-brother, dies.

1958

13 January: Edna Purviance, the leading lady of Chaplin's early films until 1923, dies. Chaplin had never lost contact with her.
21 February: Chaplin's name is excluded from the Hollywood Walk of Fame in Los Angeles.
November: Chaplin works on *The Chaplin Revue*, an anthology reissue of *A Dog's Life* (1918), *Shoulder Arms* (1918), and *The Pilgrim* (1923).

1959

Chaplin composes the music for *A Dog's Life*, *Shoulder Arms*, and *The Pilgrim*. He begins writing his memoirs, a task that will occupy him for the next five years.
16 April: He turns seventy.
24 September: *The Chaplin Revue* is released.
3 December: Annette Emily Chaplin is born.

1960

July: Holiday in Ireland.
20 December: Mack Sennett dies. With him and his Keystone Cops, in 1914, Chaplin began his adventure in cinema.

1961

July: Trip to the Far East (Japan, Hong Kong, Bali, Indonesia, Singapore).

1962

April: Holidays in Switzerland, Ireland, London, Paris, and Venice.
27 June: Chaplin receives an honorary degree from the University of Oxford.
6 July: He receives an honorary degree from the University of Durham.
8 July: Christopher James Chaplin is born.

1963

June: The Roy Export Company wins its case against Atlas Films for the unauthorized distribution of *The Gold Rush*.

1964

Chaplin begins writing the screenplay for *A Countess from Hong Kong*.
He considers writing a slapstick comedy for his son Sydney Chaplin.
June: Attends the gala at the Paris Opera in honor of Maria Callas.
September: *My Autobiography* is published by the London publishing house Bodley Head.

1965

16 April: His brother Sydney Chaplin dies in Nice.
2 June: Chaplin receives the Erasmus Prize, together with Ingmar Bergman.
1 November: Press conference in London to announce the start of production on *A Countess from Hong Kong*.

1966

25 January–11 May: Filming of *A Countess from Hong Kong* at Pinewood Studios in London.

11 October: Chaplin breaks his ankle in London.

1967

2 January: World premiere of *A Countess from Hong Kong* at the Carlton Theatre in London. The critical reception of the film is largely negative.

12 January: French premiere of *A Countess from Hong Kong* at the Opéra Garnier in Paris.

18 June: Roland Totheroh, director of photography on all of Chaplin's films from 1915 to 1947, dies.

August: He writes a treatment about the birth of Hollywood. He also contemplates the idea of a film on Roman mythology.

The Freak

September: Chaplin begins work on a project about a bird-woman.

25 September: Universal Pictures confirms to Jerry Epstein the delivery of 150 meters of color aerial footage.

October: With Eric James, Chaplin works on composing a soundtrack for the reissue of *The Circus*.

1968

Chaplin works on various treatments and the screenplay for the film about the bird-woman.

20 March: Chaplin's son Charles Chaplin Jr. dies.

21 March, 29 March: Discusses the new project with Jean Renoir and with Trudi Pacter of the *Daily Mail*.

July: Holiday in Porto Ercole.

26 July: The article "Charlie Chaplin Hale at Near 80" appears. It is reported that Chaplin will make a new film after seven years, with his daughter Victoria in the cast, the theme of the film being today's youth.

September: For the first time in the draft screenplays the name of the protagonist appears: Saraph, later Sarapha.

November: Chaplin thinks the new film will go into production within six or seven months.

Christmas: Jerry Epstein is in Vevey with the Chaplins, and on 27 December he is asked to read the screenplay aloud to Charlie, Oona, Victoria, and the French actress Nöelle Adam, wife of Sydney Chaplin.

1969

Chaplin continues working on the screenplay. Jerry Epstein, who will produce the film, organizes the work to begin shooting in September–October.

30 March: Epstein looks for companies to produce the wings and for experts in flight simulations. He contacts Ted Samuels, head of the special effects department at Shepperton Studios in London; Wally Wivers (previously a collaborator with Chaplin on *A King in New York*, later special effects supervisor on *Dr. Strangelove*, *Battle of Britain*, *2001: A Space Odyssey*, *Superman*); Leonard Rudkin (production manager on more than twenty-five films since the late 1940s, including *Dr. No* and *Goldfinger*). Epstein also contacts various London special effects firms, including the Eugene Flying Ballet Co. and the Kirby Flying Wire Company. A memo includes the names of Gerald Larn and John Rose.

31 March: Epstein and Chaplin meet with the heads of the special effects department at Shepperton to discuss issues relating to the filming of the flying scenes, the backdrops, the use of split-screen, and the preparation of the wings.

April: The special effects team at Shepperton Studios, directed by Ted Samuels, begins work on the construction of the wings. In May the work intensifies and the team is

April: The press begins reporting on Chaplin as a potential nominee for the Nobel Prize in Literature .

16 April: Chaplin turns eighty.

expanded. By June, ten technicians are working on building the wings and devising the flying scenes.

11 April: First meeting between Chaplin and Adrian Worker, manager of Shepperton, to examine the wings. Chaplin says he is satisfied with the work. First estimate for the wings: £2,000.

14 April: Shepperton Studios requests a meeting to discuss the budget and studio booking; they report that the production of the wings is progressing well.

30 April: Additional flight experts are sought for the wing project.

May: The screenplay is in an advanced stage. Oona helps her husband with drafting and revising the text. For the first time the title that will become definitive appears: *The Freak*. The first estimates arrive from Shepperton Studios and Associated British Production Ltd. Work continues at Shepperton on the construction of the wings, involving J. Grant, Gerald Larn, and Ted Samuels. Tests are carried out on 16mm.

15 May: Contacts with Shepperton regarding studio availability for September.

29 May: Jerry Epstein contacts several studios—MGM Boreham Wood, Pinewood, ABPC Boreham Wood—asking about the availability of three large soundstages (one dedicated to special effects) for filming scheduled to begin between September and October, with a total expected duration of sixteen weeks.

31 May: Shepperton sends an updated expense estimate.

2 June: John Rose is hired from 30 May to 10 June to prepare drawings and storyboards, for a total fee of £240.

3 June: *The Los Angeles Times* publishes an article by Joyce Haber titled "Chaplin to direct movie in London": the new project is called *The Freak*, the producer is Jerry Epstein, and the cast includes Victoria, Sydney, and Josephine Chaplin.

5 June: Shepperton Studios proposes postponing the shoot.

18 June: Epstein continues to contact different studios for filming, including Elstree Studios and Ardmore International Film Studios in Dublin.

1–10 July: Epstein reaches out to potential producers and distributors. Italians Cristaldi, Lombardo, and Cigoni decline the offer to distribute *The Freak*. Under the heading of casting, the names Richard Chamberlain, Robert Vaughn, and James Fox appear. Epstein contacts film studios in Denmark and Sweden and visits Pinewood Studios for rear-projection tests.

11–13 July: Epstein books a London cinema (M.C.A.) for three days, where Chaplin and his family watch several films with flying scenes: *Mary Poppins*, *Water Birds*, *Barbarella*, *The Absent-Minded Professor*, *Isadora*, *Sweet Charity*.

15 July: Epstein meets in London with Lew Wasserman of Universal.

17 July: Work is undertaken to register copyright for *The Freak*.

21–25 July: The distributor British Lion expresses interest in optioning *The Freak*; Epstein contacts Humphries Laboratories to request an estimate.

7 August: Epstein writes to Nathan Cohen (Anglo Amalgamated Film Distributors) apologizing for the delay in sending the budget. The Shepperton Studios manager informs Epstein that the wings are much heavier than expected.

8 August: Epstein drafts six pages of notes on filming and flying techniques with precise references to the pages of the screenplay.

10 September: Adrian Worker tells Epstein that the construction of the wings is of unprecedented complexity and that an aeronautical engineer has been hired to oversee the operation of the 120 mechanical parts that compose them. There is discussion of the difficulty of sourcing feathers in Great Britain; companies in France and South Africa are considered.

16 September: Epstein finalizes a first detailed version of the budget.

22 September: A complete list of sets and scenes (interiors and exteriors) is drawn up, with precise references to the sequences indicated in the script.

29–30 September: Meeting at Shepperton Studios between Jerry Epstein, Leonard Rudkin, and Maurice Carter to discuss Victoria's wardrobe, hair, and makeup; possible use of a helicopter for the flying scenes; costs of filming around Westminster and proposed alternative locations; costs of a Japanese model-making company; use of a large tank for the final ocean scene; use of a safety net for all scenes in which Victoria is suspended from wires more than seven meters high. Carter considers the possibility of obtaining from America a brand-new camera capable of filming inside a model.

3–9 October: Epstein and accountant Arno Rudolf work on revising the 16 September budget, trimming it. Michael Chaplin appears among the budget lines (£30 a week). The plan calls for: 15 days of exterior shooting (7 in London), 20 weeks of pre-production, 4 weeks for flight simulations, 28 weeks of production, 8 music recording sessions, 4 editing sessions.

10 October: Distribution of the film in France is considered.

14–15 October: Further revision of the budget. Epstein tries to contain the costs of filming and special effects.

4 November: Epstein and Rudkin review the budget revised by Arno Rudolf. The possibility of shooting *The Freak* at Ardmore Studios—offering a 20% saving compared with other studios—seems at this point the most likely option.

17 November: Epstein sends the screenplay to Davis Chasman of United Artists, noting, however, that Chaplin is rewriting and refining certain passages, including the film's opening, Jackson's arrival at Margaret's house, and the attitude of the crowd during the evangelical rally; he is also further developing the preacher's character and better defining his entrance, as well as Sarapha's appearance before the crowd. Epstein also notes that Chaplin is composing the music for *The Freak* and that filming is about to begin, most likely at Pinewood Studios.

7 December: *The New York Times* publishes an article by Vincent Canby titled "If you haven't laughed lately," reporting that *The Freak* will star the eighteen-year-old Victoria.

8 December: Lee Davies of Ardmore Studios expresses regret at the news that Chaplin will not be shooting his film in Ireland.

Christmas: Oona Chaplin informs Epstein that production on *The Freak* must be suspended and the project abandoned. Chaplin himself is never told of the decision.

1970

Mo Rothman acquires the rights to distribute Chaplin's films, starting with those from the First National period.

20–22 January: Epstein writes to Nathan Cohen (Anglo Amalgamated Film Distributors) and to Denis Holland (Rank Organisation, Pinewood Studios) announcing that production of *The Freak* has been abandoned for reasons exclusively personal.

23 April: Letter from Graham Greene mentioning that Chaplin is working on the film.

1971

Chaplin composes the music for *The Kid* and *The Idle Class*.

12 May: Receives the rank of Commander of the Legion of Honour at the Cannes Film Festival.

July: Holiday in Scotland and Ireland.

August: Holiday in Eastbourne.

31 October: Receives the Grand Vermeil Medal of the City of Paris.

1972

Chaplin composes the music for *Pay Day*.
8 February: Goes to London for the reissue of *Modern Times*.

22 February: Shepperton Studios requests to use the wings in preparation for William Sterling's new adaptation of Lewis Carroll's novel. The matte painter is, once again, Gerald Larn.

24 February: Chaplin goes to Milan to be invested as an honorary citizen of the city.
25 February: A gala performance in his honour is held at La Scala Theatre in Milan.
March: Chaplin's name is added to the Hollywood Walk of Fame in Los Angeles.

12 March: *The Los Angeles Times* Calendar publishes William Wolf's article "Ready or not, Fans, Here He Comes": Chaplin speaks about *The Freak*.

April: Charlie and Oona Chaplin return to the United States for the first time in almost twenty years.
3 April: Attends a gala at Philharmonic Hall, Lincoln Center, New York.
6 April: Receives the Handel Medallion in New York.
10 April: Receives a Special Academy Award in Hollywood.

June: In *Show* magazine, in the article "Chaplin at 83. American rediscovered hero," Chaplin again speaks about *The Freak*.

July: Holiday in England.
3 September: Receives the Golden Lion at the Venice Film Festival, where a retrospective of his films is organized.

1973

Chaplin composes the music for *A Day's Pleasure*.
8 February: Filming begins at the Manoir de Ban for the documentary *The Gentleman Tramp*, dedicated to Chaplin.
March: Chaplin spends time in London.
25 May: Attends Noël Coward's funeral in London.
13 September: At the Cinémathèque française in Paris for the reissue of *Monsieur Verdoux*.

1974

Chaplin composes the music for *Sunnyside*.

21 May: Ivor Montagu, who had visited the Manoir de Ban in the early months of the year, writes a letter to Chaplin with some suggestions regarding the screenplay of *The Freak*.
August: Jerry Epstein, Victoria Chaplin, and her husband Jean-Baptiste Thierrée are at the Manoir. Victoria wears the wings and some tests are carried out on the lawn. Oona Chaplin films the scene.

October: *Charles Chaplin, My Life in Pictures* is published by Bodley Head.

24 October: *The Los Angeles Times* publishes the article "Little Tramp' Plans Movie on The Freak": Chaplin speaks about *The Freak*.
25 October: Chaplin confirms to *Le Figaro* his intention to make *The Freak*.

1975

Chaplin works on the music for *A Woman of Paris*.

January: *The Los Angeles Times* publishes the article "Queen knights Charlie Chaplin": Chaplin again speaks about *The Freak*.

March: Holiday in Brighton.

11 January: In the article "Sir Charlie's Return" in *Cinema and TV Today*, Chaplin speaks about *The Freak*.

March: In an interview with the *National Enquirer* ("Charlie Chaplin's Amazing Family"), Geraldine Chaplin states that her father is still working on *The Freak*.

4 March: Chaplin is knighted by Queen Elizabeth II.

1976

11 March: Chaplin is inducted into BAFTA (British Academy of Film and Television Arts Fellowship).
5 June: Becomes an honorary member of the American Academy of Arts and Letters and of the National Institute of Arts and Letters of the United States.

1977

June: The sound version of *A Woman of Paris* is screened at the Berlin International Film Festival.
15 October: Chaplin makes his final outing to attend the Knie Circus in Vevey.
25 December: Dies in his sleep at his home, the Manoir de Ban, at the age of eighty-eight.
27 December: Funeral takes place in Vevey.

www.ingramcontent.com/pod-product-compliance
Lightning Source LLC
Chambersburg PA
CBHW080817120626
46556CB00010B/3320